INSIGHT GUIDE

PARIS

APA PUBLICATIONS

Part of the Langenscheidt Publishing Group

ABOUT THIS BOOK

Editorial

Editor
Caroline Radula-Scott
Editorial Director
Brian Bell

Distribution

UK & Ireland
GeoCenter International Ltd
The Viables Centre
Harrow Way
Basingstoke, Hants RG22 4BJ
Fax: (44) 1256-817988

United States
Langenscheidt Publishers, Inc.
46–35 54th Road, Maspeth, NY 11378
Fax: (718) 784-0640

Canada
Prologue Inc.
1650 Lionel Bertrand Blvd., Boisbriand
Québec, Canada J7H 1N7
Tel: (450) 434-0306
Fax: (450) 434-2627

Worldwide
Apa Publications GmbH & Co.
Verlag KG (Singapore branch)
38 Joo Koon Road, Singapore 628990
Tel: (65) 865-1600
Fax: (65) 861-6438

Printing

Insight Print Services (Pte) Ltd
38 Joo Koon Road, Singapore 628990
Tel: (65) 865-1600
Fax: (65) 861-6438

CONTACTING THE EDITORS

Although every effort is made to provide accurate information in this publication, we live in a fast-changing world and would appreciate it if readers would call our attention to any errors or outdated information that may occur by writing to us at: **Insight Guides, P.O. Box 7910, London SE1 1WE, England. Fax: (44 20) 7403 0290. e-mail: insight@apaguide.demon.co.uk**

This guidebook combines the interests and enthusiasms of two of the world's best-known information providers: Insight Guides, whose titles have set the standard for visual travel guides since 1970, and Discovery Channel, the world's premier source of nonfiction television programming.

The editors of Insight Guides give practical advice and general understanding about a destination's history, culture, institutions and people. Discovery Channel and its Web site www.discovery.com, help millions of viewers explore their world from the comfort of their own home and also encourage them to explore it firsthand.

How to use this book

Insight Guide: Paris is carefully structured both to convey an understanding of the city and its culture and to guide readers through its sights and activities:

◆ To understand Paris today, you need to know something of its past. The **History** and **Features** sections cover the city's culture in authoritative essays written by specialists.

◆ The main **Places** section provides a full run-

EXPLORE YOUR WORLD
Discovery CHANNEL

Map Legend

Ⓜ	Metro
✈	Airport
🚌	Bus Station
Ⓟ	Parking
❶	Tourist Information
✉	Post Office
✝	Church/Ruins
☪	Mosque
✡	Synagogue
★	Place of Interest

The main places of interest in the *Places* section are coordinated by number with a full-colour map (e.g. ❶) and a symbol at the top of every right-hand page tells you where to find the map.

down of all the sites. Principal places of interest are co-ordinated by number with full-colour maps.

◆ The **Travel Tips** listings section provides practical information on travel, hotels, restaurants, shops, etc.

The contributors

This edition was edited by **Caroline Radula-Scott**, who studied in Paris in her youth. With 20 years of editing consumer magazines and books behind her, she has built on the previous edition by **Andrew Eames**.

The editors sought out writers with a firm knowledge of Paris. Bilingual writer **Jim Keeble**, who divides his time between England and France, did most of the leg-work for the *Places* section and **Marton Radkai** was responsible for the history chapters. Journalist **Susan Bell** was working in Paris for the London *Times* when she wrote the one-page features on different aspects of the capital, and former Paris resident **Lisa Gerard-Sharp**, a regular Insight contributor, had fun researching the chapter on shopping and markets.

With many travel books to her credit, **Naomi Peck** – whose father played in top jazz bands in Paris after the war – made good use of her inside knowledge in the other *Insight On...* photo-features.

Other writers included Scottish-born artist and writer **Jonathan Brown**, who wrote the feature on art and *A Paris Portrait*; French contributor **Philippe Artru**, who wrote on architecture; American residents in Paris, **Philip** and **Mary Hyman**, who produced the chapter on food; and **Grace Coston**, project editor of the first edition of *Insight Guide: Paris*.

Musician **Skip Sempé**, an American living in Paris with a passion for eating out, compiled a new restaurant list for the book. He also worked on the *Travel Tips*, which were originally compiled by Glaswegian writer and Paris resident **Hilary Macpherson**. The *Travel Tips* were edited by journalist **Sue Platt**, who also indexed the book. Proof reading was done by **John Leech**.

The guide was updated in 2000 by **Clare Peel**, in-house editor at Insight Guides, former French resident and regular on the Eurostar to the French capital.

Many of the photographs were taken by **Ping Amranand**; others are by regular Insight photographers **Bill Wassman** and **Catherine Karnow**.

INSIGHT GUIDE
Paris

CONTENTS

The Grand
Palais from
Pont
Alexandre III

Travel Tips

Insight on....

Information panels

Places

CITY ON THE SEINE

*The central hub of France, both physically and culturally, Paris was once described
by Charles V as being not a city but a world – and this image still stands*

Paris is a city of landscapes. In a natural basin, cut by the slowly meandering River Seine and edged with gentle hills, the layout of the French capital has been perfectly planned throughout the centuries, each new generation of buildings complementing, and often enhancing, the old. As a result, Paris has long been a honeypot to artists, writers, philosophers and composers. According to writer Jean Giraudoux (1882–1944), the Parisian is more than a little proud to be part of a city where "the most thinking, talking and writing in the world have been accomplished".

Situated on longitude 2° 20W and latitude 48° 50N, roughly the same latitude as Stuttgart in Germany and Vancouver in Canada, all the French channels of communication lead to Paris: highways, railways, airways and even Hertzian radio waves. It is the political, economic, historical, artistic, cultural and tourist hub of France.

The growth of Paris

The city itself covers an area close to 100 sq. km (40 sq. miles), running 13 km (8 miles) east and west, and 9 km (6 miles) north and south. On the map, 20 *arrondissements* (administrative districts) spiral out like a snail's shell, a pattern reflecting the city's historical development and successive enlargements. The site of medieval Paris corresponds roughly to the first six *arrondissements*. The Revolution of 1789 added the land that comprises the next five, while the territory covered by the last nine was acquired in the 19th century by the annexation of a dozen neighbouring villages, including La Villette, Belleville, Auteuil and Montmartre.

After leaving Burgundy 500 km (300 miles) away, the Seine enters Paris close to the Bois de Vincennes, in the southeast, and meanders

gently north and south past three small islands – Ile St-Louis, Ile de la Cité and, on its way out, Ile des Cygnes. Chains of hillocks rise up to the north of the river, including Montmartre, the city's highest point at 130 metres (425 ft), Ménilmontant, Belleville and the Buttes Chaumont, and to the south, with Montsouris, the

Mont Ste-Geneviève, the Buttes aux Cailles and Maison Blanche. Mont Valérien is the highest point on the outskirts at 160 metres (525 ft), providing an immense panoramic view of Paris from the west. The lowest, at 25 metres (85 ft) above sea level, is at Grenelle.

The city is contained by the Boulevard Périphérique, a major ring road stretching 35 km (22 miles) around it. Constructed in 1973 in an attempt to try and reduce traffic jams, the Périphérique is invariably congested itself, particularly during the rush hours, when an estimated 130,000 cars storm its 35 exits.

Forming two concentric rings wrapped tightly around Paris, the suburbs (*la banlieue*) are

---

PRECEDING PAGES: the Seine and Ile de la Cité; the view from Pont Alexandre III; the Eiffel Tower from the Palais de Chaillot; a celebrated café.
LEFT: barging through the city.
ABOVE RIGHT: dancing on the Pont des Arts.

divided up into *départements* or counties. The inner ring incorporates Hauts-de-Seine, Val-de-Marne and Seine-St-Denis, and the outer ring consists of Seine-et-Marne, Essonne, Yvelines and Val-d'Oise. These counties, together with Paris and the Greater Paris conurbation around it, constitute the Ile de France and are linked by eight major highways, five RER lines and an extensive rail network branching out in all directions from five stations in Paris.

At the beginning of the 19th century, Napoleon Bonaparte imposed a special status on the city of Paris, giving it the powers of a *département* in order to maintain a firm hold on the capital's politics and populace. It wasn't until March 1977 that Paris voted a general city council into office which, in turn, elected a mayor, Jacques Chirac. Today, each *arrondissement* also has its own council and mayor to deal with local affairs. Nationally, Paris is represented by 21 delegates and 12 senators in the two houses of Parliament – the National Assembly and the Senate.

The role of the river

"She is buffeted by the waves but sinks not," reads the Latin inscription on the city's coat-of-arms, symbolising a Paris born on the flanks of the River Seine. Lutctia was indeed founded by the Romans, on the site of a Gallic Parisii settlement on the largest island in the river, as these lines suggest, but today it is the Seine that cuts a swathe through the middle of the city.

The Seine is the capital's widest avenue; it is spanned by a total of 37 bridges, which provide some of the loveliest views of Paris. The river is also the city's calmest artery, barely ruffled by the daily flow of tourist and commercial boat traffic. In the 19th century, the banks were encumbered with wash-houses and watermills, and its waters heaved with ships hailing from every corner of France.

Even more difficult to imagine now are the 700 brightly painted Viking warships, which used the river to invade Paris from the north in the 9th century, or the thousands of bodies that floated past in 1572, victims of the St Bartholomew's Day Massacre. Today, barges and pleasure boats on their lazy way to Burgundy use the St-Martin and St-Denis canals to shorten their trip, cutting across the northeast of Paris.

RIGHT: how Paris looks from an orbiting satellite.

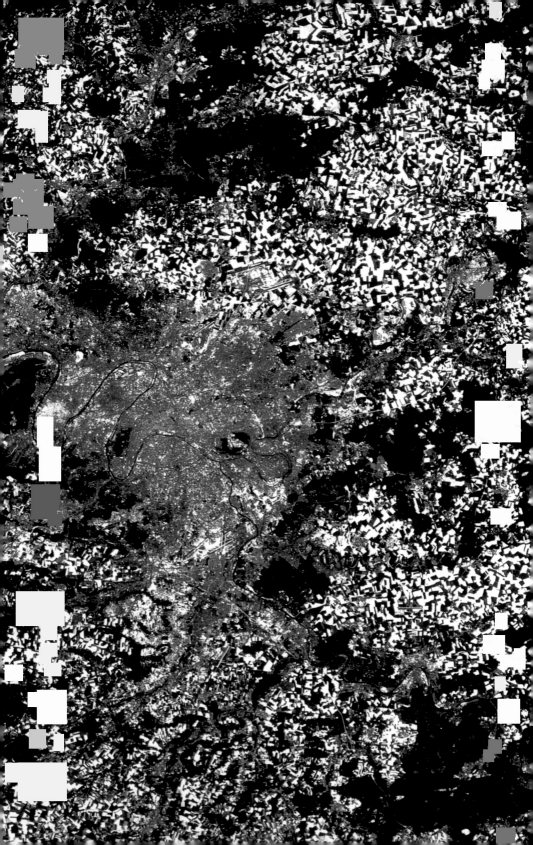

Through the heart of the city. the Seine flows for tourists, poets and lovers.

Parisian ambience

One of the most persistent images of Paris is the long avenues and boulevards graciously lined with chestnut and plane trees. Flowers and plants abound in a patchwork of 338 squares, parks and gardens, tended in the formal French tradition or following the English style so admired by Napoleon III.

Divided up by two large series of streets, one forming a long line north to south (from Boulevard de Strasbourg to Boulevard St-Michel) and the other going east to west (from the Rue de Faubourg St-Antoine to as far as La Défense), Paris is a mosaic of *quartiers* (quarters) or villages, each one having a distinctive character. Publishing houses cluster around the Odéon on the Left Bank, and Sentier is the place for garment wholesalers. Universities and colleges are in the Quartier Latin, fashion is in Faubourg St-Honoré, while the Marais is a magnet for creative types, with business around the Bourse (stock exchange), Opéra and in La Défense.

Chains of boulevards encircle the centre of the city, marking where the boundary was in medieval times. Many of the streets contain the word *faubourg*, which indicates that there was once a village or suburb in that area.

Underground Paris is a labyrinth of Métro lines, over 3,200 km (2,000 miles) of sewers, which you can visit, scores of garages and endless ancient quarries, which were converted into catacombs in the 18th century. ❐

Right: Fontaine de Stravinski on the Right Bank.

A Modern Paris

To keep up with the demands of modern life, whilst preserving the city's architectural heritage, changes have had to be made – often not without a fight. In 1969, the huge food market at Les Halles was relocated outside Paris at Rungis, the Boulevard Périphérique ring road was constructed in 1973 and, after the 1968 riots, the Sorbonne was split into 13 universities and scattered around the outskirts. The creation of La Défense as a financial centre outside the city perimeter started in 1958 with the first tower opening in 1964 – now there are 47 with more planned for the future.

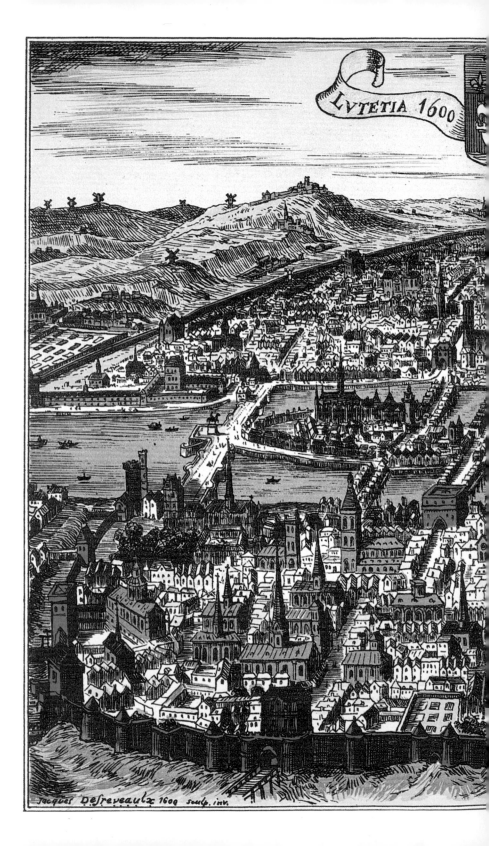

LVTETIA 1600

Jacques Defreveaulx 1600 sculp. inv.

Decisive Dates

GALLO-ROMAN ERA
c. 300 BC: Parisii tribe settle on the Ile de la Cité.
58–52 BC: Julius Caesar conquers Gaul and the Romans build Lutetia on the site left by the Parisii and on the Left Bank of the Seine.
c. AD 250: St Denis establishes the first Christian community and is eventually martyred.
360: Julian the Apostate is made Emperor of Rome while in charge of Lutetia and is believed to have changed the town's name to Paris.
451: St Geneviève saves Paris from Attila the Hun.

THE DARK AGES
486: Clovis pushes out the last Romans and, in 508, makes Paris the capital of his new Frankish kingdom.
751: The Carolingian dynasty begins, diverting power from Paris to Aachen and the abandoned city goes into decline. Emperor Charlemagne rules from 768 to 814.
885: Count Eudes (Odo) defends Paris against the Normans and becomes king of the Western Franks in 888.

THE MIDDLE AGES
Paris develops into a city of learning and political power and spreads north of the river.
987: Start of the Capetian dynasty when Hugh Capet is made king.
1108–54: Paris becomes an important trading centre.

1163: Building work starts on Notre Dame.
1180–1223: Philippe-Auguste builds the Louvre fortress and a wall around Paris.
1215: The University of Paris is founded.
1226–70: Louis IX (St Louis) makes judicial reforms and the Sorbonne University opens in 1253.
1328: The House of Valois inherits the monarchy in preference to its English cousin Edward III, triggering the Hundred Years' War.
1358: *Jacquerie* uprising of the peasants in Paris, led by clothmaker Etienne Marcel fighting for democracy.
1380: The Bastille prison is built.
1420: Paris surrenders to the English, who rule until 1436, despite Joan of Arc's efforts in 1429.

THE RENAISSANCE
At the end of the 15th century, wars with Italy expose the French to new ideas of art, wealth and luxury.
1469: First French printing works opens at Sorbonne.
1516: François I brings Leonardo da Vinci with his masterpiece, the *Mona Lisa*, to France.
1559: Henri II is killed in jousting tournament. The new Louvre palace is completed and street lamps erected.
1572: St Bartholomew's Day Massacre of Protestants.
1594: Bourbon Henri IV converts to Catholicism.
1609: The Place Royale (now known as the Place des Vosges) is built.

LE GRAND SIÈCLE
In an age of extravagance, Louis XIV the Sun King moves to Versailles and starts an opulent building programme.
1629: Louis XIII's prime minister, Cardinal Richelieu, builds the Palais Royal.
1631: Paris's first newspaper, *La Gazette*, is launched.
1635: Louis XIII founds the Académie Française.
1670: Hôtel des Invalides is built as a military hospital and retirement home for those wounded in battle.
1682: Louis XIV moves his Royal Court to Versailles.
1686: Le Procope is the first café in Paris to open.

THE AGE OF ENLIGHTENMENT
The arts flourish, science develops and intellectuals, such as Voltaire and Rousseau, exchange ideas.
1751: First volume of Diderot's *Encyclopédie* published.
1760: Louis XV builds the Panthéon, Place de la Concorde and Ecole Militaire.

THE FIRST EMPIRE
The Revolution leads to the creation of a Republic, which is soon turned into an Empire by the warring, but reforming and popular, Napoleon Bonaparte.
1789–95: The Revolution: after the storming of the Bastille and the Declaration of the Rights of Man, the

monarchy is abolished in 1792 and a Republic is born. The ensuing Terror kills more than 60,000 people.
1799: Napoleon Bonaparte, the First Consul of France, seizes power and is crowned emperor in 1804.
1800: The Banque de France is established.
1806: Construction of the Arc de Triomphe begins.
1815: Battle of Waterloo; the monarchy is restored.

THE RESTORATION
Two more revolutions hit Paris, finally unseating the monarchy once more in 1848.
1831: Victor Hugo's *Notre Dame de Paris* is published.
1842: First French railway links Paris with St-Germain.
1848: Louis-Philippe, the Citizen King, is deposed.

THE SECOND EMPIRE
With Napoleon III at the helm, Paris is transformed into an efficient, modern city.
1852–70: Baron Georges Haussmann undertakes a massive redesign of the city, building the Grands Boulevards, laying sewers and creating parks.
1855: First World Fair. The second is 12 years later.
1863: Manet's painting *Le Déjeuner sur l'Herbe* scandalises the Académie.
1870: Paris surrenders to Prussia and Napoleon flees.

THE THIRD AND FOURTH REPUBLICS
The Métro is dug and new inventions, such as the motor car, telephone and cinema, give rise to the term "la belle époque". The beginning of a new creative era.
1871: Uprising by Paris Commune with 25,000 people killed, the Tuileries palace destroyed and the Hôtel de Ville burnt down.
1888: Louis Pasteur sets up the Pasteur Institute as a hospital and research centre for infectious diseases.
1889: Eiffel Tower built for the World Fair.
1894–1906: The Dreyfus Affair.
1914–18: World War I: Paris is saved from German attack by the Battle of the Marne.
1924: The poet and literary theorist André Breton publishes his *Surrealist Manifesto*.
1934: The Depression gives rise to riots and strikes.
1937: Palais de Chaillot built.
1940: World War II: Paris is bombed and occupied by the Germans.
1944: Paris is liberated by the Allies, and General Charles de Gaulle heads a Provisional Government until 1946, when a Fourth Republic is proclaimed.
1958: The Algerian crisis topples the Fourth Republic.

PRECEDING PAGES: map of Paris in 1600.
LEFT: Louis XIV, the extravagant Sun King (1643–1715).
RIGHT: a triumphant Napoleon Bonaparte (1799–1814).

THE FIFTH REPUBLIC
General de Gaulle returns as president of the Fifth Republic, launching Paris into the Space Age.
1958–63: The construction of La Défense begins.
1962: André Malraux, Minister of Culture, establishes a renovation and restoration programme.
1968: Strikes and student riots against the university system and the Government forces de Gaulle to call an election. He wins but resigns a year later.
1969: Les Halles food market is moved to Rungis.
1973: The Périphérique ring road is built.
1977: The controversial Centre Georges-Pompidou opens. Jacques Chirac is elected mayor of Paris.
1981: Socialist François Mitterrand is elected president.

1986: Right-wing Chirac becomes prime minister in a unique "cohabitation" with a socialist president.
1989: Bicentenary celebrations of the Revolution herald the opening of the Louvre Pyramid, Grande Arche and Opéra Bastille – Mitterrand's *Grands Projets*.
1995: Chirac is elected president in May.
1997: Socialist Lionel Jospin becomes prime minister, creating a second "cohabitation".
1998: France wins the World Cup at the newly built Stade de France.
1999: Major renovation of the Louvre and the Centre Pompidou takes place in time for the millennium. The Passerelle de Solférino footbridge, which connects the Tuileries to the Musée d'Orsay, opens.
2000: The Eiffel Tower is the focal point of the millennium celebrations.

CLOVIS I.

THE EARLY YEARS

Paris has been a choice place to live for more than 2,000 years – the Parisii tribe discovered it, the Romans usurped it and the Franks invaded it

As with many of the world's great cities, the mysterious mists of antiquity veil the origins of Paris. Around 300 BC, when the Celts were chasing each other around Europe, one tribe, the Parisii, settled on an island in the Seine river (the Ile de la Cité). They were good farmers and active traders, hence the name Parisii, which is said to be derived from a Celtic word for boat. However, perhaps a more imaginative theory on the origins of the city's name claims that the tribe's founder was Paris, the emigré son of King Priam of Troy.

The ancient town of Lutetia

In 53 BC, a number of Gallic tribes failed to appear at the annual council in Ambiani (Amiens) summoned by the Romans, who were in the process of colonising Gaul. Roman Emperor Julius Caesar, sensing rebellion, quickly transferred the council into the midst of the restless Gauls, to the Parisii settlement – just an agglomeration of huts – on the Seine.

The Romans soon realised the advantage of the position, and developed the settlement for themselves, naming it Lutetia. A wooden bridge connected the island to the Left Bank, and a town grew up, replete with temples, baths, a theatre and other hallmarks of Roman civilisation. The ruins of one of the baths can be seen under the Hôtel de Cluny.

Dominating the Right Bank from its hilltop perch stood a temple to Mercury where, more than three centuries later, St Denis, a Christian agitator and the first bishop of Paris, was beheaded, giving the hill the name *Mons Martyrium* (Martyr's Mound) – Montmartre in French. According to legend, St Denis picked up his severed head and walked 6,000 steps before being buried by one of his apostles on the spot where the cathedral of St-Denis now stands.

Lying as it did exposed on a plain, Lutetia soon fell victim to frequent sackings by marauding barbarian tribes. In AD 358, Emperor Constan-

tine sent his son-in-law, Julian, to Gaul to deal with them. The young man promptly fell in love with the town and some say that it was he who renamed it Paris. He became the Roman emperor, abolishing Christianity (officially tolerated since 313) and, when not in battle, he sat in the *palais*, organising the town's accounts.

Geneviève – patron saint of Paris

Just under a century later, around 451, Attila the Hun appeared on the scene with his hordes. The Parisians prepared to flee but were stopped by the pious 19-year-old Geneviève, who assured them that the Huns would not harm the city, as long as they stayed with her and prayed. Lo and behold, the marauders passed southwest of the town and ran straight into the swords of a hastily raised army of legionnaires. Thereafter, Geneviève became the patron saint of Paris.

She was still alive when Clovis I, king of the Salian Franks and founder of the Merovingian dynasty, invaded much of Gaul, seeing off the

LEFT: Clovis I, king of the Franks, saw off the Romans.
ABOVE RIGHT: Paris's coat-of-arms.

Romans, and sweeping into Paris. He promptly made it his capital (many believe it was he who gave Paris its name) and, installing himself in the *palais*, he converted the town back to Christianity. Later a basilica was built where he and St Geneviève were buried, which eventually became the Panthéon, the last resting place for France's VIPs.

Merovingian law of succession was simple: the empire was divided among the previous ruler's offspring. As a result,

FIRST CHRISTIANS

Paris's first Christian bishop was martyred in AD 287. Christianity was tolerated from 313 to 350, when Roman Emperor Julian tried to abolish it. Clovis I converted the town back to Christianity after 485.

himself and his brother in 768 and then made himself king of the whole empire, which included a large part of Germany, three years later. He died in 814, leaving his son Louis – the first of many – in charge.

The Norman invasions of the mid-9th century brought Paris back into the limelight. After several sackings, Count Eudes (Odo) decided, in 885, to resist by building fortifications around the Ile de la Cité. The first siege of Paris lasted an entire year and

family members spent the better part of 250 years squeezing each other out. Instead of being used as an administrative centre, Paris frequently served as a favourite battleground for the murderous bickering of Clovis's descendants. Nature also conspired with floods, fires, epidemics and hurricanes.

The Carolingian dynasty

The Carolingians, who ruled from 751, felt more comfortable nearer to their homelands in the lower Rhine and moved political importance away from Paris, which was left in the charge of a count and his municipal guard. Charlemagne divided the Frankish kingdom between

almost bore fruit: the Carolingian army came to the rescue. But King Charles the Fat, instead of attacking the siege-weary aggressors, let them sail up the Seine to pillage Burgundy.

In defiance of the king, Eudes took the crown and Carolingian unity dissolved. A period of instability followed, as the French crown shifted from one dynasty to the next. The Saracens appeared in the south, Hungarians in the east, and the Vikings ran amok. All in all, it was not a happy time for France, until the ongoing power struggle led to Hugo Capet, son of Hugo the Great, a descendant of Eudes, becoming king of all France. This marked the beginning of a new, long-lasting dynasty – the Capetians.

The Middle Ages

Although the early members of the dynasty preferred crusading and hunting to governing, Paris prospered under the Capetians. New fountains were built to bring fresh drinking water to the citizens and *sergents de ville*, armed with clubs, walked a beat. Public punishment was common.

With new cloisters and churches and a cosmopolitan population, Paris very soon grew into an intellectual centre. At the start of the 12th century, monks, scholars, philosophers, poets and musicians flocked to the city to learn, argue and teach. Philosopher and theology scholar Pierre Abélard and St Bernard respectively

Philippe-Auguste built Les Halles for the guilds and improved the Seine docks. The guilds took care of levying taxes, town-crying and other municipal duties. In 1190, six guild members, so-called Grands Bourgeois (city dwellers), were chosen to act as the king's officers. The number increased to 24, meeting in regular sessions to discuss municipal business.

Later, Louis IX (1226–70), who was made a saint due to his passion for justice, created three governing chambers. These Bourgeois became an independent political force, often corrupt but, equally often, striving for democratic reforms, which had a long-lasting effect on political life.

hurled logic at each other in the open air – although the former got into hot water and was castrated, after starting a relationship with his student Héloïse, who bore him a son.

Economic life in Paris rested in the hands of merchants and craftsmen, who wisely organised themselves into guilds. The most powerful of these was the water merchants' guild, which included all river workers and gave its coat-of-arms to the city.

Far Left: Roman stonework in the Musée National de Moyen Age – Thermes de Cluny.
Left: tragic lovers Abélard and Héloïse.
Above: boatmen in front of the Pont Notre-Dame.

In 1200, the first student riot took place, which led to Philippe-Auguste (1180–1223) founding the University of Paris. Hardly a European scholar failed to visit its prestigious faculties on the Left Bank.

The first revolution

By the mid-14th century the Capetians had given way to the Valois and the devastating Hundred Years' War began. The French knights seemed powerless before the English foot soldiers. The plague made its first deadly appearance. In 1356, the English captured King John the Good at Poitiers. The citizens of Paris, tired of incompetent leadership, rebelled. Their leader, Etienne Marcel, a clothmaker and guild chairman, was the first in a long string of genial, but corrupt demagogues to emerge on Paris's political horizon. A motley crew of impoverished townspeople and peasants under Jacques Bonhomme chose the moment to begin a revolt, later known as the *Jacquerie*.

For support, Marcel unwisely chose the King of Navarre (Charles the Bad), an English ally. When the Parisians found out about the alliance, they turned on Marcel. In July 1358, as he was about to hand over Paris to the rival Navarre camp, he was assassinated by a loyalist. Three days later, John the Good's son, the Dauphin,

d'Orléans, brother of the king, who was by now mentally deranged. John had Louis murdered and, in 1409, took control of Paris.

The advance of the English

While Louis's Armagnac son, Charles, raised a new army, Paris celebrated. Into the fray stepped a butcher, Caboche, demanding fiscal and administrative reforms. All hell broke loose as John's authority slipped into the hands of Caboche and his henchmen. The ensuing Reign of Terror gave Charles and his Armagnac army a chance to re-enter and "pacify" the city. Seeing France torn apart by civil war, the English

entered the capital. The new regent, who was to become Charles V (1364–1380), hammered out a truce with the English, allowing France some time to put its house in order. Paris was relatively well treated, considering how fickle its loyalties had been: the Parliament still met but its powers were curtailed.

Behind a calm exterior, Paris was seething with anger. In 1382, during the reign of Charles VI (1380–1422), a group of citizens calling themselves the Maillotins rebelled against high taxes and were brutally repressed. Then, in 1407, the Maillotins became enmeshed in the violent struggle for power between the Burgundian John the Fearless and his cousin Louis

resumed hostilities. Siding with the Burgundians, they defeated the Armagnacs at the Battle of Agincourt in 1415.

Four years later, John the Fearless was murdered, whereupon Henry V of England married Catherine, daughter of the mad King Charles, and occupied Paris in December 1420.

The Dauphin, the legitimate French heir, had some support in the capital, but he was feeble and could not keep out the English invaders. Joan of Arc, a 17-year-old girl from Lorraine, came to his rescue in 1428 by defeating the English at Orléans and, a year later, Charles VII was crowned at Rheims. However, Paris remained in English hands until 1436, when

Charles recaptured his tattered capital, driving the English back to Calais.

By the early 16th century, Louis XII (1498–1515) was ensconced in the Italian Wars. Then François I (1515–47) began the struggle against the mighty Habsburgs in Europe and, in 1525, he was captured at Pavia. The Parisians paid his ransom and he promptly moved into the Louvre. In his wake came an army of Italian architects, painters, sculptors, goldsmiths, cabinet makers and masons,

RELIGIOUS MASSACRE

On St Bartholomew's Day, 24 August 1572, thousands of Protestants, who had come to Paris for Henri de Navarre's wedding, were slaughtered on the orders of the Catholic monarchy.

Paris, dominated by the conservative Sorbonne theologians, pushed for measures against the Protestants, known as *Huguenots*, often burning religious agitators.

Henri II's sons and heirs, François II (1559–60), Charles IX (1560–74) and Henri III (1574–89), proved inadequate in controlling France's religious factions. Nor were they helped by the intrigues of the Queen Mother, Catherine de Médicis. The country was plunged into a religious war.

who set about the task of reshaping the city's lugubrious Gothic face.

With the rebirth of the capital under François's graceful, iron hand, French culture also returned to life. Ronsard, Du Bellay and other poets of the Pléiade carried French poetry to new heights, while Clément Jannequin put the French *chanson* on the map. The advent of the printing press underpinned these activities; however, it also helped spread the new gospel of Protestantism through Catholic France.

LEFT: Henri III and Charles IX, sons of the scheming Catherine de Médicis.
ABOVE: St Bartholomew's Day Massacre in 1572.

War between the Henris

King Henri III's concessions to the Protestants infuriated the Catholics, who were led by the popular Henri de Guise and his Paris-based Holy League. In 1584, the Protestant Henri de Navarre, a Bourbon, became heir to the throne but he had to fight Henri de Guise for the right to accede to power. To this end, in 1589, Henri III had Henri de Guise assassinated. Paris threw up its barricades and the Holy League's Council of Sixteen took power and deposed Henri III, who joined forces with Navarre. His army, however, joined the Catholics. That summer, Henri III was murdered by the friar Jacques Clément, and Henri de Navarre became Henri IV.

Civil war dragged on for another five years. Paris was the stage for the Council of Sixteen's gruesome repression of real and perceived plots. In 1593, Philip II of Spain, who had entered the war on the Catholic side, pressed to usurp the French throne. Henri IV, in a brilliant piece of opportunism, chose that moment to convert to Catholicism, whereupon Paris welcomed him and overnight the war-weary nation fell in line.

Henri IV patched up France spiritually and economically. In 1598, his Edict of Nantes set up guidelines for cohabitation between the religious groups. His (Protestant) adviser, Sully, reformed the tax laws and balanced the budget.

However, in 1610 the Catholic Henri IV, like Henri III before him, was murdered, bringing the young Louis XIII to the throne.

The glorious epoch

Despite massive deficits incurred by their violent foreign policy, the Bourbons lavished huge sums on Paris, while keeping it on a short political leash. Two deserted islets behind the Ile de la Cité became the residential Ile St-Louis. New bridges crossed the Seine. Avenues cut through the dingy labyrinth. Architects built new houses, palaces and schools and restored the old ones. Parks appeared, where society could stroll in the shade and exchange ideas, gossip or tender

THE ROAD TO REVOLUTION

Louis XV was only five years old when he succeeded to the throne in 1715, giving a free hand to the Regent, Philippe d'Orléans, who left government to his ministers, while he engaged in amorous pursuits in the Palais Royal. Once of age, Louis followed suit, giving his mistress, Madame de Pompadour, the power to select ministers and generals. Meanwhile, the nation's financial situation worsened. Revolution was just around the corner.

glances. Cardinal Richelieu, who largely governed on behalf of the young Louis XIII (1610–43) while the king was growing up, founded the Académie Française.

Under the Sun King, Louis XIV (1643–1715), the spending spree reached its peak. His minister, Colbert, sanitised entire sections of the city and set up manufacturing plants to provide the French with luxury items. Louis XIV also had hospices constructed for the poor and Les Invalides was built to house war veterans.

The influx of money and the proximity of the court attracted a huge crowd to the capital. Rich wives and courtesans opened their living rooms to conversationalists. Theatres echoed with the verse of Racine and Corneille, the booing of the *cliques* and the applause of the *claques*. Everyone laughed at the writings of Molière, Boileau and La Fontaine satirising the hustling and bustling society.

But storm clouds were gathering. In 1648, Paris revolted, demanding greater political representation. The 12 provincial parliaments joined a body promoting change, as did a conspiracy of nobles under Prince Condé. The *Fronde*, as it was called, eventually collapsed, but Louis XIV later had his lavish palace, Versailles, built outside the city limits to keep his distance from the unruly Parisian mob.

The beginning of the 18th century was a period of great inequality in Paris. French high society was having a fine time in the court of the Sun King. Theatres were busy, the new café scene was lively and the city buzzed by night. But all this activity ignored the needs and wishes of the poor, who were to hit back dramatically as the century drew to a close. ❐

LEFT: Madame de Maintenon, governess to the Sun King's children, who secretly became his wife.
RIGHT: Louis XIV, the Sun King and a big spender.

LUDOVICUS ... FRANC. ET NAVAR. REX CHRISTIANISS.

LUDOVICO MAGNO

REVOLUTION AND THE REPUBLIC

As the rich grew richer and the poor had nothing, discontent exploded into revolt.

Heads rolled into the first Republic. Then along came Napoleon...

French reputation no longer rested on royal glory in the latter part of the 18th century, but on the wisdom of its intellectuals – Voltaire, Rousseau, Diderot and Quesnay. Poverty increased, and when a bad harvest in 1788 caused the price of bread to soar and the people to become restless, Queen Marie-Antoinette is supposed to have made her famous pronouncement that the hungry should eat cake.

By 1789, France's debts had reached a critical stage. The king took the desperate step of summoning the Estates General, a legislative body made up of three estates: the Clergy, Nobility and the rest of the populace, commonly known as the Third Estate, to vote for reforms to the French Constitution. Craftily, the king only allowed one vote per estate, meaning that the massive Third Estate could be out-voted two to one by the smaller Clergy and Nobility. Eventually forced out of the meeting, the Third Estate created a National Assembly in opposition to the king. On 14 July, the people of Paris stormed the Bastille prison for its weapons, proclaimed a Commune and formed a National Guard under the leadership of La Fayette, a French soldier who had recently fought in the battle for American independence.

The Revolutionary years

The explosion of 1789 swept the past away. Radicals of one hour became the conservatives of the next. Streets changed names, newborn babies were baptised Egalité, Liberté or République. The First Republic was proclaimed and, in January 1793, King Louis XVI was decapitated in public on the Place de la Concorde, followed in October by his Queen, Marie-Antoinette.

Paris was the burning centre of the French Revolution. Its temperamental and bloodthirsty mob was the force behind increasingly radical leaders. These included Mirabeau, Brissot, Danton and finally the dastardly Robespierre, egged on by Marat, whose assassination by Charlotte Corday, in July 1793, threw the Reign of Terror into top gear. Anyone suspected of stepping out of line was dragged off to the guillotine as a traitor. In July 1794, it was Robespierre's turn for the chop.

It was the young General Napoleon Bonaparte who finally drew the line under the Revolution, when he quashed a royalist uprising in 1795. Four years later, he had seized power, crowning himself Emperor of a totalitarian and military state.

Romantic Paris

The glorious Napoleonic empire ended once and for all with Paris occupied by three allied armies after the Battle of Waterloo in 1815. Bourbon Louis XVIII headed a constitutional monarchy, which placed an emphasis on law and order and *laissez-faire* economics.

The Industrial Revolution might have turned Paris into an opulent and mediocre business centre were it not for the apostles of Romanticism, led by Victor Hugo (1802–85). Inspired

---

"BURNING" BREECHES

As a Revolutionary symbol, the workers of Paris took to wearing trousers, instead of breeches (*culottes*), earning the nickname *Sans Culottes*.

POWER TO THE PEOPLE

As the citizens of Paris turned vehemently against the monarchy, the Revolutionaries instigated a number of new ideas:

- ☞ The French flag (the Tricolore) was invented, incorporating Paris's red and blue colours with the captive royal white standard.
- ☞ Worship of Reason officially took the place of Christianity and churches were destroyed or used for weapon storage.
- ☞ A Republican calendar was created with new months linked to nature.
- ☞ *La Marseillaise* (now the French national anthem) was taken up as the marching song of the Revolutionaries.

PRECEDING PAGES: Delacroix's portrayal of the Revolution. **LEFT:** detail from the Arc de Triomphe.

by the anti-establishment spirit of 1789, they waged a struggle against creaky academia and bourgeois respectability in garrets, cafés, journals and the "enemy's" own *salons*.

The revolutionary spirit also remained in the Republican forces, who reached for the Parisian mob whenever despotism reared its head. In July 1830, Charles X revoked certain electoral laws, which led to three days of bloody rioting and his abdication. His cousin, Louis-Philippe, Duke of Orléans, held power until 1848, when another revolution forced him to abdicate.

The Second Empire

When Napoleon's nephew and president of the Second Republic, Louis Napoleon, crowned himself Emperor Napoleon III in 1852, he pre-emptively arrested more than 20,000 suspected political opponents to strengthen his position.

The Second Empire was a gaudy and grandiose period in the city's history. Thousands of kilometres of new railway tracks were built to connect the city with other European capitals. Twice, in 1855 and 1867, Paris hosted the World Fair. Basking in financial ease, the city abandoned itself to the pleasures of masked balls, Offenbach operettas and *salon* conversation.

Aided by eager speculators and fat taxes, the Prefect Baron Georges Haussmann gave Paris a new face, gutting and rebuilding the centre. New water mains and a sewage system were installed to service the two million Parisians. Elegant boulevards, avenues and squares appeared: the Champs-Elysées, St-Michel, St-Germain and Etoile, to name a few. These served an aesthetic purpose, but they also facilitated swift troop deployment if trouble arose and were difficult for rioters to barricade.

Families dispossessed by the construction were forced to move to eastern Paris. This influx only added to that area's already notoriously seditious spirit.

The Commune

In 1870, Napoleon III went to war with Prussia. Parisians lined the streets to cheer the ill-equipped, ill-led and ill-fated army as it marched east. Two months later, Napoleon was beaten, the Second Empire had become the Third Republic, and the Prussians were besieging Paris. In Bordeaux, the government of Adolph Thiers waited for an uprising in heroic revolutionary style that never materialised.

On 28 January 1871, President Thiers, without consulting Paris, finally agreed to a cease-fire. A month later, the National Assembly ratified a peace treaty. The Prussians triumphantly marched through Paris avoiding the eastern districts, home of the starving, belligerent and vengeful National Guard, which felt betrayed by the French government. Sensing trouble, Thiers disarmed the National Guard and moved his government to Versailles. He barely escaped the ensuing explosion of rancour.

On 28 March 1871, a Commune was proclaimed at the Hôtel de Ville after a municipal election was boycotted by the bourgeoisie. Civil war erupted and the Hôtel de Ville was burned.

While the Communards hoisted red flags and argued over political and military strategies, Thiers was busy raising a new army. The government forces succeeded where the Prussians had failed and some 25,000 Communards were killed in the last weeks of May, the final 147 being shot in the Père-Lachaise Cemetery. With them went the revolutionary spark that had defied tyrants and kindled republics since 1789.

La Belle Epoque

With the insurrectionist working class brutally tamed, Paris became merely the stage for the squabbles, plots, demonstrations, counter-demonstrations and oral and written polemics of the Third Republic. The Republicans split into pro-clerical and anti-clerical factions. In the 1890s, after recovering from the Commune, the left gathered around the socialist Jean Jaurès. On the right was an array of diehard monarchists and nationalists with a strong vein of anti-

---

BONAPARTE'S BATTLES

The rise and fall of Napoleon Bonaparte (1769–1821) can be charted by his battles as he attempted to dominate Europe and beyond.

He won the Italian Campaigns (1796–97), capturing Northern Italy. The Battle of the Pyramids (1798) gave him Egypt, while he defeated Austria at Marengo (1800), Austria and Russia at Austerlitz (1805), Prussia at Iéna (1806) and the Austrians again at Wagram (1809).

He lost the battles of the Nile (1798) and Acre (1799), foiling his plans for the East; Trafalgar (1805) kept him from England. His disastrous Russian Campaign (1812) led to his defeats at Leipzig (1813) and, finally, at Waterloo (1815).

Semitism, as revealed by the Dreyfus Affair in the late 1890s. This scandal revolved around a Jewish army captain, Alfred Dreyfus, who was imprisoned on Devil's Island on trumped-up spying charges.

Though crackling with tension, Paris seemed more than ever ready to accept the controversial and the provocative and decided to have some fun. The Métro was dug, the Eiffel Tower built for the 1900 World Fair and the first films were shown. Between 1880 and 1940, Paris

Gay Paris

From the 1890s, the city of Paris hummed with life. Cabarets and dance clubs proliferated in Montmartre, café society flourished, the first cinema opened and motor cars galore took to the streets.

through town. In 1913, Diaghilev's *Ballets Russes* presented its superstar, Nijinsky, dancing to Stravinsky's latest composition, *The Rites of Spring*, scandalising the jam-packed auditoriums.

World War I dampened spirits as the city turned to the slaughter at hand. In September 1914, the German army came within earshot. The military governor, Gallieni, rushed reinforcements to the counter-offensive on the Marne, using anything he could lay his hands on, including the

housed more painters, sculptors, writers, poets, musicians and other creative artists per acre than any other metropolis. They chattered with philosophers, theorists, critics, brawny syndicalists, gazetteers, anarchists and socialites in smoke-filled cafés.

Almost every artistic movement flourished in Paris – Realism, Impressionism, Cubism, Surrealism, Dadaism, and so on. In the pawnshops of Montmartre, paintings by Picasso, Utrillo and Modigliani were hung up by clothes pegs. Debussy, Zola, Cocteau and his apostles strolled

Above: Bastille Day – the Revolutionaries storm the Bastille prison on 14 July 1789.

Paris taxi service. This rapid response ensured that the city was spared.

Normal life began to return after the armistice was declared in 1918. From the east came Russian emigrés, and from the west came American writers and composers. In the 1930s, Paris became a temporary haven to the refugees of fascism in Europe.

Between the wars

With one million dead, millions of others now crippled and the agricultural north destroyed by shelling, France's part in the victory over Germany in 1914 was tarnished. Conservative Republicans and left-wing coalitions, including the Communist Party (founded in 1920), tried to come to grips with the economic and social after-effects of the Great War. The extreme right, meanwhile, made some important gains.

Fascist-type organisations had started appearing in France in the late 19th century, when novelists Charles Barras and Léon Daudet founded the Royalist paper *Action Française*. In the 1920s and 1930s, such groups proliferated, fuelled by general discontent

MERCI FOR MERCY

As the Allies advanced on Paris in August 1944, the Germans were ordered by Hitler to blow up the city. Happily, the commander, General Dietrich von Choltitz, could not bring himself to do it and, after the war, was made an honorary citizen.

refused to send help to the Spanish Republicans against Franco. He also interrupted the labour reforms because of their negative effect on the economy. In 1937, in a wave of wildcat strikes, the shattered *Front Populaire* sank into the past. "Rather Hitler than Blum," the Conservatives muttered.

World War II

When war broke out against Nazi Germany in September 1939, France shored up the

and fear of Bolshevism, and inspired by the successes of Mussolini and Hitler. They focused their efforts on Paris, parading in paramilitary garb and campaigning against the internationalists, the socialists and, above all, the Jews.

On 6 February 1934, a coalition of fascist factions attempted a *coup d'état* in Paris. It failed, but the left was finally goaded into concerted action. In 1936, a front of radicals, socialists and communists, headed by the socialist Léon Blum, won the election. The so-called *Front Populaire* promised to fight fascism and improve the workers' lot.

Initial euphoria was short-lived. The struggle against fascism split the *Front* when Blum

utterly useless Maginot Line, mobilised an ill-equipped army, and waited. In Paris, statues were sandbagged and Louvre curators carefully prepared paintings for transport to safety.

On 14 June 1940, the Nazi forces of darkness marched into the City of Light, having simply gone round the Maginot Line via Belgium. There was no siege, no National Guard, no *levée en masse*, no cabbies carrying reinforcements. The 84-year-old Marshal Philippe Pétain, the withered hero of Verdun, became the head of a puppet regime in Vichy in unoccupied France.

While many Parisians welcomed the Nazis as racial cleansers, there were those who bravely resisted, joining the Free French Movement led from London by the Under Secretary for War, General Charles de Gaulle. Their defiance often cost them their lives.

On 6 June 1944, Allied forces landed in Normandy and advanced on Paris. Dietrich von Choltitz, the German commander, received orders to blow up the city, but chose to surrender instead. On 24 August 1944, Paris was liberated and, two days later, General de Gaulle paraded with his forces down the Champs-Elysées. Crowds rejoiced, while collaborators scrambled into hiding or suffered the pains of summary justice. The war still had nine months to rage on but, with Paris liberated, light had returned to the European continent at last.

De Gaulle immediately formed a provisional government, which lasted until 1946 and, with the bane of fascism at last gone, the poets and artists continued their discussions at their favoured watering holes, the Café de Flore, the Lipp and La Coupole. Political quarrelling resumed without the extreme right. Tourists returned in droves. Bebop and rock 'n' roll arrived from across the Atlantic.

But the war and its horrors cast long shadows: the stench of the Holocaust stood as indelible proof of man's capacity for evil. Post-war thought was dominated by the dark existentialism of Jean-Paul Sartre and Albert Camus. In addition, France lost two major colonial wars, the first in Indochina (1946–54) and the second in Algeria (1954–62).

May 1968 – student riots

A bloody wave of bombings swept Paris in the early 1960s, when it became clear that President de Gaulle, who had come out of retirement to head the Fifth Republic in 1958, wanted to pull out of the Algerian quagmire. De Gaulle's manner in dealing with internal matters was patriarchal and authoritarian.

His ideas, with few exceptions, were conservative. Time had eroded the legend. A generation had grown up that had not heard the comforting speeches beamed into occupied France by the BBC. It had other ideas and idols.

The 1968 agitation began uneventfully enough in March with a sit-in by students to demand changes in the antiquated university system. But instead of initiating a civil discus-

sion with the students, the *ancien régime* promptly called in the CRS, the riot police, to restore what they saw as a breakdown of order.

Push led to shove. On the night of 10 May 1968, the police stormed 60 barricades in the Quartier Latin. Unrest spread to the factories and other cities. France was soon paralysed and Paris was left in a state of siege. Petrol was rationed and cautious housewives hoarded food in anticipation of disaster. The state-run media shuffled along with heavily-monitored programming, while Parisians received the news from privateers on France's periphery or, ironically, from the BBC in London.

DE GAULLE'S ROLE IN THE WAR

General Charles de Gaulle rose to fame as the leader of the French Resistance in World War II. At the news of France's impending surrender to the Germans, he fled to England where he set up the Free French Forces, urging on BBC radio "all Frenchmen who still bear arms to continue the struggle". In 1943, he set up a Resistance Government in North Africa. After the liberation of Paris, he made his famous speech from the Hôtel de.Ville: "Paris! Paris insulted! Paris broken! Paris martyred! But Paris liberated! Liberated by itself! Liberated by its people with the help of the armies of France..."

LEFT: the liberation of Paris, August 1944.
RIGHT: quelling the student riots in May 1968.

At the end of the month, de Gaulle announced new elections and warned against impending totalitarianism. The Parisian bourgeoisie awoke. An hour later, over 500,000 de Gaulle supporters were flowing down the Champs Elysées.

The Gaullists won the election, but not for long. Disenchantment continued and the President resigned in 1969, leaving his Republic to his ardent follower Georges Pompidou.

Mitterrand and Chirac

The 1970s appeared tame but, when the Independent Republican President, Valéry Giscard d'Estaing, lost to socialist leader François Mit-

terrand in 1981, a huge crowd marched to the Bastille in celebration.

However, in 1986, the exigent Parisian character revealed itself again, during the legislative elections. Voters on the left were dismayed by what they viewed as Mitterrand's sell-out, and conservative forces, led by Paris mayor Jacques Chirac, swept in with a rightist coalition.

Chirac was a mass of contradictions. In his student days, he had been a member of the Communist youth movement, then a gung-ho lieutenant fighting with French anti-independence forces in Algeria, and, later in the early 1970s, Prime Minister for two years under President Giscard d'Estaing.

> ### LAST RIGHTS
> François Mitterrand was in control of his image to the end, even organising his funeral, which had to include the presence of both his wife and mistress at the graveside.

May 1968 had reaffirmed Paris's old rebellious spirit. Parisians still demonstrated at the drop of a hat – anti-racism, pro-gays, against altering university entrance requirements, to name but a few. The *zeitgeist* of the 1990s has found much to admire in the legacy of the *événements de Mai*.

The 1993 elections maintained the swing to the right, which was confirmed when Jacques Chirac succeeded François Mitterrand as president in 1995. Mitterrand died in January 1996. Despite all the disquiet about his personal integrity, the French mourned him as the "god" he had been nicknamed.

Indeed, despite the decline in support for his policies, his *grands projets* – from the Louvre Pyramid to the Grande Arche at La Défense and the new Bibliothèque Nationale de France-François Mitterrand at Tolbiac – he undoubtedly made an indelible mark on Paris architecture.

An uncomfortable partnership

By 1997, Chirac's popularity had sunk to an historical low, which was borne out in the June elections when socialist Lionel Jospin was made prime minister, creating a second cohabitation with the right. At the close of 1999, the coalition was in a fairly stable position, with the economy booming and unemployment low. The mayor, until the new mayoral election in 2001, is the unpopular Jean Tiberi.

The undeniable charm of Paris lies in these exquisite tensions and juxtapositions – political, artistic, social and architectural. The old lives together with the new. Beaubourg stands an equal to Notre Dame. Brash young businessmen, punks and Dior-dressed ladies share the streets used by beslippered *ménagères*. Paris, modern and sophisticated, may claim to be the heart of Western civilisation, but in its veins still flows the blood of the rustic, untamed, refractory Gaulois. ❒

LEFT: General Charles de Gaulle – war hero and president, who was finally brought down by the students.
RIGHT: La Défense, symbol of modern Paris.

THE PARISIANS

They may have a reputation for being rude and indifferent, but underneath the
cool Parisian exterior lies a warm and welcoming heart

For many of the inner city's 3 million residents and the 20 million tourists who visit each year, Paris is a grand seductress, a mistress or a lover. Hundreds of thousands of people are carrying on an illicit affair with her. Some manage a quick fling. For others, the love affair endures a lifetime.

"No other city in the world has been better loved or more celebrated," wrote American author John Steinbeck. "Scarcely has the traveller arrived than he feels himself in the grip of this city which is so much more than a city." A great part of the allure of Paris undoubtedly lies with the Parisians themselves, with their charm, their individualism and their diversity.

So who are the Parisians?

They are the old lady in her bedroom slippers, in the park feeding the pigeons, the prostitutes in the leather mini-skirts on the Rue St-Denis, the society hostess in Chanel, the yuppie stockbroker weaving home from the Bourse on his scooter, the *clochard* sleeping off a bottle of red in the Métro, the children of the Opéra ballet school affectionately known as *"les petits rats"*, the au pairs, hiding from their duties in the city's American bars, the Algerian greengrocer and the Portuguese concierge, the stately African chief from Sierre Leone and the law student from the Sorbonne . People are what lend any city its vibrancy and Paris is no exception. Stripped of its human population, Paris would be no more than a collection of buildings and monuments, architecturally beautiful maybe, but a sad, cold place nonetheless.

There is an old joke, not familiar to many Parisians but much told in bars where foreigners congregate. It goes like this. On the eighth day, God created a city in the image of paradise and named it Paris. It was a city so beautiful, so perfect, he was afraid lest the rest of the world

PRECEDING PAGES: lady and friend in the Quartier Latin; Parisian café society.

LEFT: cheerful *bonhomie* in the market.

RIGHT: traffic policeman doing a serious day's work.

became jealous. And so, to redress the balance, on the ninth day he created the Parisians.

This joke may not go down well in the capital, but you can bet that the rest of France is joining in the laughter. A national survey in the late 1990s put Parisians at the top of the list of most hated people in France (31 percent), easily top-

ping traditional targets such as civil servants (21 percent), Corsicans (23 percent) and even policemen (18 percent).

Unpopular stereotypes

Visitors *and* Parisians have their favourite stereotypical Parisian whom they love to hate. These include the haughty shop assistant, too busy adjusting her lipstick to give her customers the time of day, the swearing taxi driver, who refuses to take you because you are not heading in "his" direction and the bureaucrat who keeps you waiting for hours only to inform you that you lack a vital document, without which he is firmly unable to help you. In the past, articles have been published in the French press exhorting Parisians to good behaviour and deploring the unfriendly welcome they extended to tourists. This shows that at least today's Parisians are no longer under any illusions. In fact, only 38 percent consider themselves kind, while an enormous 92 percent admit to being under stress. Eighty-two percent also own up, undoubtedly with more than a touch of Gallic pride, to being *individualistes*, a description which anyone who has had

RED TAPE

Although the concept of bureaucracy was invented by the French, it's unforgiveable to call anyone a bureaucrat to his or her face. The polite reference is *fonctionnaire*.

more than a passing acquaintance with the city may suspect of doubling as a convenient excuse for a multitude of sins of the "me first" variety.

Yet the American author Henry Miller, who spent many years in the capital in the 1930s and was well placed to make an objective judgement of the national character, stated that he had more respect for the French "than any other nationality on the face of the earth", although they "may not be the jolliest, happiest or the easiest people to get along with".

WHO LIVES IN PARIS?

More than 12 million people live in Paris and its suburbs, making it the seventh largest city in Europe. One of the most densely populated cities in the world, there are 20,000 people per sq. km in central Paris. Immigrants make up 12 percent of the population, each group forming communities in specific neighbourhoods. The Jewish population, the largest in Europe at 200,000, lives in the Marais, the White Russians in Montparnasse, North Africans by the northern Périphérique, Oriental Asians by Porte d'Italie in the southeast and Indian Asians behind the Gare du Nord. Around 8,000 live on the streets.

Warm-hearted souls

Once one transcends the stereotype and becomes acquainted with the individual, the Parisian is no longer the intimidating, disdainful creature of legend, but actually quite human! Beneath that studied Parisian indifference beats a heart of intelligence, loyalty and warmth. Courtesy, charm and consideration, however, are not, perhaps, qualities which spring to mind while trying to navigate the busy intersection at Charles de Gaulle-Etoile, around the Arc de Triomphe, and yet they are abundantly evident in everyday life: in the friendly concern of Madame Defreitas, the concierge; the cheerful greeting of Monsieur Durand, the baker from behind his counter; and the welcoming smile of Henri, the waiter at the Café des Sports.

Despite the reputed rudeness, Paris is a city in which the majority of the population are chivalrous to a fault and in which good manners are considered essential to everyday life. While a volley of verbal abuse will barely cause the average Parisian to bat an eyelid, forgetting to say *bonjour* or *merci* is considered by many to be unforgivable.

AN AMERICAN IN PARIS

After living in Paris for several years during the 1930s, author Henry Miller praised his hosts by saying, "A Frenchman makes the best kind of friend. Though he may be difficult to get to know, once he lets you into his life he'll be your friend forever."

ments, which are packed into the city's 100 sq. km (40 sq. miles).

Virtually all Parisians live in apartments in a city where a house and garden is an almost unheard of luxury. Accommodation is not easy to come by, with families holding on to their homes for generations. There is intense competition for desirable living space, with an average of 150,000 people looking for a home at any one time. It is an oft-cited para-

Desirable residence

In the 18th century, writer Jean-Baptiste-Louis Cresset stated: "It is only in Paris that one truly lives; elsewhere one just vegetates." Given such a universal acclaim for the city, it is hardly surprising that for centuries, so many people have wanted to live there. Today, Paris is more densely populated than Tokyo, London or New York and the Parisians' high stress level can be partly put down to the fact that they live literally on top of one another, squeezed into, what are by most standards, extremely small apart-

dox that this battle for a place to live occurs in a city where 16 percent of apartments lie vacant.

Competition to live in the capital may be stiff but for the around 3 million souls fortunate enough to live in the centre, within the Périphérique, which separates the city proper from the often grim suburbs of decaying highrises and barrack-like apartment blocks, the rewards are undoubtedly very high.

While many cities in other countries seem to be disintegrating from the effects of poverty, high population density and crumbling infrastructure, Paris continues to thrive, not only as one of the world's most beautiful cities, but also as one of the best run.

LEFT: Parisians have perfected the art of cool.
ABOVE: stopping for a drink at a local bar.

Village ambience

The organisation of the capital into 20 *arrondissements* means that the city falls into easily recognised *quartiers*, or neighbourhoods, each with its own shops, markets, cafés and local eccentrics. Parisians develop lifetime attachments to their own *quartier*. Although large supermarket chains exist, residents often continue to support local merchants and to shop in specialised shops and the local markets. By always frequenting the same fishmonger or baker, or by taking their morning *café crème* at the local corner café, loyalties are quickly built up. As a consequence, each *quartier* develops a village atmosphere in which everyone is known, at least by sight and often by name. Paris works, therefore, as a series of small communities co-existing under the umbrella of a big city.

> ### TOO EXPENSIVE
> "One reason Paris has so few problems is that the type of people who make the problems can't afford to live there."
> — AN URBAN PLANNER

Lovers and lights

The city's image as the capital of romance has been built up by countless novels and films. It's

an image that holds true for visitors, but for locals the reality fails to live up to the myth: one in three Parisians lives alone and half the city's marriages end in divorce. It is hard to be sad in Paris for long, though. The capital's reputation as a good-time girl stretches back before the bright lights came to Pigalle. In the 16th century, Nostradamus, prophet of gloom, offered the comforting thought that there was one spot on earth which could be relied on to lift the

blues, reggae, African, French and international sounds. Mixed culture aside, however, there are certain recognisable types which you can keep a look out for.

BON CHIC BON GENRE

Marie-Chantals and Charles-Henris are easy to recognise. The women sport Hermès scarves decorated with dead grouse, velvet hairbands and Chanel quilted handbags; for men, Lobb shoes, Dunhill pipes and even cravats are still in vogue.

City stereotypes

The BCBG (*bon chic bon genre*), the French equivalent of the British Sloane Ranger or the American preppie, can be spotted easily in their main stamping grounds of Neuilly, Auteuil and Passy, the rich suburbs

spirits: "As long as Paris does not fall, gaiety will exist in the world," he wrote.

The listening ranks

Parisians, as a whole, form such a diverse collection of races and cultures that it is almost impossible to characterise them. On the radio there are local stations broadcasting to African, Arab and Portuguese listeners. Tune in to Radio Nova (101.5 FM), the city's most popular music station (and started by an Irishman), to hear a wonderfully eclectic jumble of jazz, rap, soul,

of the 16th and 17th *arrondissements* to the west of the city, collectively known as NAP. Also known under the acronym CPFH (*collier de perles, foulard Hermès* – pearl necklace, Hermès scarf), this type of Parisian, like their British and American counterparts, harbour a profound conservatism, adherence to all things classic and to traditional values and a marked dislike of anything new.

To see them in their natural habitat, try the VIP enclosure at Chantilly racecourse. They can also be spied sipping *chocolat africain* with pet poodle in tow at Angelina's *salon de thé* on Rue de Rivoli or, for the more *branché* (literally "plugged in") of the species, dancing the night

LEFT: trendy is not necessarily chic.
ABOVE: a proud doorman at the Hôtel de Crillon.

away at Les Bains, Paris's perpetually "in" nightclub, which is set in old swimming baths in the third *arrondissement*.

For a glimpse of a world at the opposite end of the spectrum, travel north on the RER commuter line B with *"les rappeurs"*, the descendants of African and Caribbean immigrants. With shaved heads, baseball caps set backwards at a jaunty angle and *basquettes* (trainers) by Nike or Reebok, the names of American basketball and football heroes emblazoned across their chests, the style and philosophy of *les rappeurs* are imported directly from New York. Disenchanted with a life that offers few

prospects in the grim housing estates which ring Paris, *les rappeurs* are nevertheless a gentle and graceful group compared to their more aggressive US counterparts.

In between these groups is the average Parisian – the *beaufs* (short for *beau-frère* or brother-in-law). A *beauf* is generally someone

you are associated with by obligation, rather than by choice, but agreeable and good for a laugh, nevertheless.

To discover the city's Asian community, head for Belleville in the 20th *arrondissement* or to Chinatown in the 13th, near Porte d'Italie, which is home to the majority of the capital's 38,000 Vietnamese, Cambodians, Laotians, Chinese and Japanese. Here, green tea, 100-year-old eggs and *dim sum* compete for space with the French *baguette* and *café crème*.

For a taste of North Africa, visit the area around the Marché Dejean (Métro: Barbes-Rochechouart) in the 18th *arrondissement*. Mangoes, yams and plantain spill on to the street from tiny shops.

On the streets

The city's problems seem small compared with those of most other modern capitals. The roughest parts of Paris are probably as safe as the safest parts of most American and several British cities. Traffic congestion seems to be the Parisians' most oft-cited worry. Homelessness is also an increasingly visible problem, but the tradition of romanticising the *clochards* (tramps), who sleep rough along the Seine, keeps it from coming too high up on the list of most Parisians' main concerns.

In winter, however, there is nothing romantic about life for the capital's homeless. The Government and various private organisations provide shelters with free room and board, medical care and job training. Attendance is voluntary, but the police will often round up those sleeping rough to protect them from the cold. Two newspapers, *Le Réverbère* and *Macadam*, Parisian equivalents of London's *Big Issue*, endeavour to give the capital's homeless a measure of financial independence and self-respect.

It is not all gloom and doom, however. One American resident recalls that, on her way home from the market one summer evening, she passed two good-natured *clochards*, who lived on a nearby grating. They were cooking on a small spirit stove, had just opened a bottle of wine and were listening to jazz on their battered transistor. *"Bon appétit!"* they called, raising their glasses as she passed with her groceries. For her, that really said something about Paris. ❑

A TASTE OF AFRICA

In the colourful Marché Dejean, African women in bright batik prints, babies slung papoose-style around their waists, sway gracefully among the stalls, picking out salt fish and papaya for the evening meal.

LEFT: dressed for the mosque.
RIGHT: posing in a Paris street.

THE WORLD'S GREAT FASHION HOUSES

"Haute couture" means high fashion in French, and in many other languages, too, for Paris has insisted on setting the style for what women wear

Poiret, Chanel, Dior... most of the 20th century's best-known fashion houses have been French. At the end of the Second World War, discreet salons and their *vendeuses* gave way to the bright lights of the catwalk as Dior's New Look burst on to the scene with full skirts and luxurious, fabrics.

In the 1950s, Chanel's commitment to freer, more carefree clothing paved the way to a more liberated style for women. But the revolution came in the 1960s with Yves Saint-Laurent, who designed for the new youth generation, followed by the plastic and chain-link dresses of Courrèges and Paco Rabanne. With the extravagant styles and brilliant colours of Christian Lacroix in the 1980s, Paris hit the big time again.

Since the late 1990s, young British designers have had a noticeable influence on Parisian fashion. London's *enfant terrible*, Alexander MacQueen, is now Creative Director at Givenchy, while Stella McCartney has single-handedly raised the feminine profile of the fashion house, Chloë.

Today, highly priced haute couture designs are worn by only the extremely rich, but the designs provide inspiration for new ideas and establish the all-important image for a designer, which can subsequently be applied to accessories, jewellery, perfumes and cosmetics.

△ **COLOURFUL LACROIX**
Christian Lacroix, who was born in Arles, introduced a flamboyant southern flavour to fashion in the 1980s, giving a much needed injection of *joie de vivre* to Paris.

▷ **CHRISTIAN DIOR**
Christian Dior claimed over half of all fashion exports by 1953. In the 1990s Dior appointed an Englishman, John Galliano, chief designer.

◁ **YVES SAINT-LAURENT**
Widely regarded as *the* designer of the 20th century, Yves Saint-Laurent has been celebrated for decades for h evening wear collection, including "le smoking", a tailored trouser suit which reappears, slightly reworked on a perennial basis. YSL ha an annual turnover of over $6 million, producing not on haute couture and ready-to-wear fashion, but also acces ories and classic perfumes.

▽ COCO CHANEL

Coco Chanel invented sunbathing and revolutionised women's fashion. Today, the Chanel line of boxy signature suits and quilted handbags with gold chains is designed by Karl Lagerfeld.

▽ WEIRD AND WONDERFUL

Some designers strike out into uncharted territory, such as this outfit by Issey Miyake, a Japanese who needs Paris to endorse his creations.

THE SHOWS MUST GO ON

Ernestine Carter, a legendary 1950s fashion writer, once tried to get a replacement ticket to a Balenciaga show because the original had been sent to the wrong hotel. Only when the original had been found, and torn up within earshot of the phone, was another ticket issued. Today, it is just as difficult to gain entrance to top Paris fashion shows – *haute couture* in January and July, and *prêt-à-porter* (ready-to-wear) in March and October.

Journalists, photographers, fashion buyers, actresses and pop stars jostle for tickets with the handful of women who will actually wear the original designs. The hierarchy is strict: front row seats of little gilt chairs are reserved for influential fashion editors, such as Anna Wintour of American *Vogue* (famous for wearing her dark glasses throughout the show) and Suzy Menkes of the *International Herald Tribune*, who can make or break a collection.

Behind the scenes, designers bitch about each other's collections and vie for supermodels, who may do several shows a day, ferried by limousine between the Carrousel du Louvre, the exhibition hall where most of the shows are held, and their suites at the Ritz and George V hotels. They are pinned and tucked into an array of garments and neck-breaking heels, ready to sashay down the catwalk to the popping cameras and poised pens of the awaiting press.

THE GRAND FINALE

fashion show traditionally ds with a wedding dress uch as this one designed Yves Saint-Laurent) – an m that costs buyers several ousands of dollars.

BACKSTAGE MAGIC

rope's top make-up artists d hairdressers are enlisted construct a distinctive ok" for each spring and tumn show.

THE DINING EXPERIENCE

Eating out in Paris can be a simple affair on the streets, a casual fling in a café or a more formal arrangement behind closed doors – the choice is yours

Ask a Frenchman to name a typically Parisian dish and you will usually receive a blank stare. After some coaxing, he might raise his eyebrows and hesitantly suggest *"steack frites"* (steak with French fries), before declaring that Paris is a city without any specifically regional fare. He would be wrong.

Parisian fare

One of the finest French cheeses, Brie, is produced within 50 km (30 miles) of Notre Dame, the windows of *pâtisseries* (cake shops) are crowded with Parisian specialities (*Paris Brest, L'Opéra, Saint-Honoré, Puits d'Amour, Amandines*) and the elongated French bread or *baguette,* no longer specific to the city, was perfected in Paris.

In short, Parisian foods are so frequently found throughout the country (and the world) that they are not considered "local" at all, and a list of typically Parisian bistro dishes reads like a *Who's Who* of French favourites, with such delights as *hareng pommes à l'huile* (smoked herring marinated in oil and served with warm potatoes), *tête de veau Gribiche (*calf's head with a mustardy-eggy sauce*)* or *entrecôte marchand de vin* (steak with red wine sauce), followed by *mousse au chocolat* or *île flottante* (soft meringue floating in custard).

Such a listing, however, provides only a partial picture of what awaits the gastronomically curious in the French capital. Indeed, pavement vendors, café terraces, bistros, brasseries and elegant restaurants all offer different, but equally specific, "Parisian fare".

Street food

For centuries, the streets of Paris echoed with the cries of vendors carrying baskets that contained food ranging from fresh fish to *pâtisserie.* Today, that tradition still survives in the heart of

PRECEDING PAGES: ready and waiting at a fashionable watering hole.
LEFT: fresh fish on the menu.
ABOVE RIGHT: Paris takes its time over dinner.

the Quartier Latin, along the Boulevard St-Michel, and in the Grands Boulevards around the department stores behind the Opéra. There, street vendors improvise stands during the winter and tempt passers-by with the irresistible smell of chestnuts roasting over a bed of coals. Others sell kebabs and anything with *frites* or

cook paper-thin crêpes on hot griddles, stuffing them with a choice of either a sweet or savoury filling. But for anything more substantial and varied you must go indoors, although not necessarily to a restaurant.

In a Parisian *charcuterie* you can buy ready-cooked or prepared dishes such as quiches, cheese- or mushroom-filled pastries (*rouleaux* or *feuilletés*), salads and specials such as *poulet basquais* (chicken with tomatoes and red peppers) or *brandade* (salt cod purée). A slice of pâté or ham can transform a crisp *baguette* from the *boulangerie* into a sandwich, making a delicious meal when finished off with cheese from the *fromagerie*, or a cake from the *pâtisserie*.

Café lunches

When feet are sore and the queues in the shops are long, the marble-topped tables of pavement cafés look inviting, especially at lunchtime. All cafés offer a variety of sandwiches (ham, cheese, pâté), which are notoriously short on filling and long on bread. This said, for a modest supplement, butter or *cornichons* (gherkins) can be included and Dijon mustard will be supplied free. Since the bread is generally freshly baked and the butter excellent, you can begin to overlook the paper-thin slices of ham or cheese.

Crôque Monsieur and *Crôque Madame* are two other popular on-the-run café lunches. The former, grilled ham and cheese on toast, becomes the latter with the addition of a fried egg on top, making a filling, if not particularly memorable, *casse-croûte* (snack).

Cafés also serve omelettes and *oeufs en cocotte* (baked eggs). An *omelette nature* (plain omelette), slightly runny inside and browned on the outside, with a *salade verte* (green salad) and a basket of sliced *baguette* is a typical Parisian lunch, good value and brimming with flavour.

Brasseries and bistros

One step up from the café is the brasserie. Literally translating as "brewery", brasseries serve

a wide variety of dishes, including some Alsatian specialities. They were introduced to the French capital in the late 19th century, at about the time when modern methods of brewing were being perfected. Cold draft beer was a real novelty to Parisians then, as was *choucroûte* (Alsatian sauerkraut), and both specialities quickly became as popular as the *baguette*.

In Paris, the numerous brasseries also specialise in shellfish platters – baskets

A HEARTY MEAL

In a brasserie, sample the seafood as a prelude to the *coq au vin* that attracts hungry Parisians on cold winter nights. Accompany it with a glass of Burgundy and end with a wedge of brie.

1814. The Russian military were forbidden to drink, so whenever they dived into a bar in Montmartre, they demanded their refreshments urgently – *bistrot* – to avoid being caught.

Nowadays, any restaurant with a relaxed atmosphere can call itself a bistro (seafood restaurants are often called *bistros de la mer*).

Bistro-type food is also served in a *bar à vins* (wine bar). Although some more fashionable establishments offer smoked salmon and

of oysters, clams, cockles and mussels often line the pavement outside and men in sailors' caps deftly open oysters under the admiring gaze of passers-by.

Where brasseries are generally spacious, festive and slightly "exotic", bistros are traditionally small, modest and very French, generally serving typically French fare, usually at moderate prices, although some can be as expensive as a starred restaurant.

The origin of the name "bistro" supposedly lies in the days of Allied occupation of Paris in

LEFT: dining out on a summer's day.
ABOVE: a fine array of cheeses to choose from.

foie gras (fattened goose liver), the majority serve the kind of hearty food that Parisians call their own. In most wine bars as opposed to traditional restaurants, it is possible to order one dish rather than a complete meal.

Behind the scenes

Staff who prepare food in a traditional bistro are cooks (*cuisiniers*), not chefs. Generally, a chef is more ambitious than a cook and places greater importance on innovation and technical prowess. Bistro cooks pride themselves on serving well-executed versions of traditional fare.

Chefs tend to run restaurants where the food reflects both changing fashion and/or personal taste. They labour in the hope that one day their talent will be discovered.

This trend grew rapidly to the fore in the 1980s with the rise of *nouvelle cuisine,* whose supporters applauded unorthodox combinations of taste and encouraged a break with routine. "*Les chefs*" listened to the message and, today, flourless butter sauces (*beurre blanc*) have replaced the *béchamel* of yore, *feuilletés* (thin layers of puff pastry) have supplanted the once popular *bouchées* (puff pastry

French provincial cooking

Unlike other big cities in France, Paris offers a varied and changing spectrum of foreign cuisines, as well as its own local fare, making it possible to sample not only food from the provinces, but also specialities from around the world.

The oldest and largest immigrant community in Paris is the rural French. Many a Parisian will tell you that *grandmère* came from the Auvergne, Brittany or another distant corner of France. When times were hard,

shells), fish fillets have ousted whole fish from menus and *magret de canard* (duck steak) has displaced beef.

Tartare de poisson (raw fish) is no longer scandalous, and exotic combinations or tastes (fruit with meat or fish, the use of spices such as ginger or unusual herbs like fresh coriander) no longer shock but are accepted as bold touches on the part of the chef. In short, a series of new "classics" is now being served not only in Paris but throughout France. However, those with larger appetites should remember to bear in mind that the great chefs are more interested in stimulating the taste buds than filling the belly – at a price.

they flocked to the city where the streets were supposedly paved with gold. Restaurants sprang up around the railway stations where these newcomers first alighted on Parisian soil.

The Gare Montparnasse is surrounded by bars, proudly draped with the flag of Brittany, and *crêperies bretonnes* (pancake restaurants or stalls) line the side streets leading to the station. The Gare de l'Est is flanked by Alsatian restaurants (and a famous Alsatian *charcuterie*), but not far from the Gare de Lyon and the now-vanished Bastille station, traces of an Auvergnat community can still be seen.

Today, however, the regional cuisine most popular with Parisians is that of Gascony, broadly referred to as the "Southwest". Throughout the city, speciality shops sell *foie gras* and even traditional Parisian bistros now offer *confit de canard* (preserved duck) and *magret* (duck steak), both literally unknown in Paris in the 1950s, but adopted as enthusiastically and as quickly as sauerkraut was in the late 19th century.

Couscous and phô

Of all the foreign cuisines to be found in the French capital, the two favourites are probably North African and Vietnamese. Modified to suit French taste, both offer emblematic dishes:

can be found in Bellerville, northeast of Place de la République.

Parisian fare is as cosmopolitan as the city itself. Regional produce is shipped daily to Paris and nowhere else will you find such a choice of French cheeses, wines, sausages or hams on offer. Parisians are used to this agglomeration of resources and take the exceptional variety of foods available for granted. "Their" food is the nation's finest. Going to the markets in the French capital is like taking a survey of France's agricultural wealth, while dining in Paris provides a glimpse of French cuisine at its best.

couscous (steamed semolina served with a spicy meat and vegetable stew) and *phô* (beef and noodle soup) respectively.

Although the French do not consider any cuisine a rival to their own, most thoroughly enjoy *couscous* as a welcome change, and students, in particular, are happy to find a source of inexpensive meals in the Vietnamese restaurants clustered together in the Porte d'Italie neighbourhood, situated not far south of their stamping ground in the Quartier Latin. A concentration of North African restaurants

LEFT: bistros serve good-value, traditional fare.
ABOVE: a popular bistro in Montmartre.

COSMOPOLITAN CUISINE

As immigrants have settled in specific areas of the city, so restaurants have sprung up around them. Here is a rough guide to where they are:

- ☛ Chinese/Vietnamese: between Avenue de Choisy and Avenue d'Ivry near Place d'Italie.
- ☛ Indian: on the Rue du Faubourg St-Denis between the Gare du Nord and La Chapelle.
- ☛ Middle Eastern: around Strasbourg St-Denis and Goutte d'Or, near Montmartre.
- ☛ Jewish: Rue des Rosiers in the Marais.
- ☛ Japanese: Rue Ste-Anne near the Opéra.
- ☛ North African: Belleville.

Foods for thought

Not all visitors to Paris are as enthusiastic about certain classic dishes as the French. If almost everyone knows that *escargots* are snails and *cuisses de grenouille* are frog's legs, many an innocent tourist has unwittingly ordered calf's head (*tête de veau*) or calf's kidney (*rognon de veau*) thinking they were ordering veal (*veau*), or knowingly pointed to *andouillette* believing that some pork sausage would appear, only to discover a tripe-filled creation instead.

The reader should not fear the above-named specialities – after all, 50 million French (and many a foreign visitor) relish their taste – but those with a meat-and-two-veg upbringing may well be shocked by the French penchant for animal organs or offal (*les abats*) and creatures that tend to hop or crawl.

Even certain favourite French fish are not to everyone's taste. *Anguille* (eel), a speciality in both the northern provinces and the southwest, is rarely served in Paris, although *oursins* (sea urchins) are a standard feature of most Parisian *plateaux de fruits de mer* (raw shellfish platters). *Moules* (mussels), generally cooked with a little white wine and eaten with French fries, are served in many modest brasseries and are as Parisian as *steack frites*. Most Parisians prefer

their herring smoked, filleted and left for several weeks with carrots and onions in a bowl full of peanut oil (this may sound terrible but, drained and served with a warm potato salad, it makes an appetising first course).

Some familiar foods are presented in ways that have surprised more than one conservative diner. Steaks, lamb and duck, for example, will always be served *saignant* (rare), and those who prefer their steak medium are best advised to ask for it *bien cuit* (well done). *Confit de canard* (preserved duck) is a speciality that must be tasted to be understood and generally becomes a favourite once discovered. Squeamish visitors sometimes feel faint when they learn how this

DIFFERENT TYPES OF EATERIES

There is an assortment of places in which to eat, from the cheap to the expensive:

- ☛ Cafés, open from early morning until 9pm, offer drinks (coffee, alcohol and soft drinks), snacks and light meals, outdoors or in.
- ☛ Wine bars, open all day mostly until late, serve snacks and light meals with wine.
- ☛ Brasseries offer vast menus, throughout the day until late, in a jolly atmosphere.
- ☛ Bistros, open at lunchtimes and evenings, are smaller and more intimate, offering fixed-price menus.

great southwestern delicacy is produced (ducks, after a life of being force-fed through funnels to fatten their livers into *foie gras*, are salted for several days, then simmered in their own fat for many hours).

Lastly, although French cheeses deserve their international reputation and are nowhere else as good as they are in France, wary first-time visitors sometimes reel from some of the more pungent ones. More specifically, Epoisses, Münster, Boulette d'Avènes and Vieux

French etiquette

Regardless of your budget, some basic rules apply to all French meals and respecting them will help you avoid awkward situations, making you feel more comfortable, which will in turn increase your pleasure.

Before any large meal, you will usually be offered an *apéritif*. In a French home, this can be anything from Scotch to port, but, in restaurants, a glass of champagne, white wine or a *kir* (white wine with *cassis* – a

VEGETARIAN DESERT

Vegetarian dishes do not feature much in French cuisine, but you can often order two starters instead of a main course, or phone a restaurant in advance to ask for a vegetarian meal to be prepared for you.

Lille are not recommended for those who enjoy only mild Cheddar.

With all this in mind, don't consider France a country where bizarre food items make eating out a source of anguish rather than a pleasure. More familiar dishes can be found alongside the more outlandish creations. Raw vegetable salads (*crudités*) and omelettes are as common as smoked herring and snails, roast lamb more frequently served than calf's head and mild cheeses are as plentiful as the stronger varieties.

LEFT: traditional zinc-topped bar that gave the cafés their nickname.
ABOVE: proud chefs, keeping up the style.

blackcurrant liqueur) are preferred. Don't feel obliged to order an *apéritif* if you are on your own but, if your French host offers you one, it can be taken as a (minor) insult to refuse.

French wine is, of course, the perfect accompaniment to French food. Alternatively, or additionally, you can order mineral water, sparkling or not (*gazeuse* or *plat*, respectively). Beer is drunk only with sandwiches, with very simple meals such as *steack frites*, as a thirst quencher or with Alsatian meals.

Even in very modest restaurants, a meal is composed of three courses: *entrée/hors d'oeuvres* (starter/appetizer), a *plat* (main course) and *dessert* (dessert). Americans who call their main dish an entree should beware – an *entrée* (as its name implies) is a first course in France.

Grated carrots or celeriac and boiled leeks with *vinaigrette* (french dressing) are typical *hors d'oeuvre* "salads". A *salade verte* (green salad) is often served after the main course and before cheese. Though fewer and fewer restaurants offer a green salad as a matter of course, most will be glad to prepare one and it makes a refreshing break midway through the meal.

Many Parisians prefer to end a meal with cheese, rather than something sweet, so it's extremely common for moderately priced restaurants to offer fixed-price menus that

include a starter, a main dish and cheese or dessert. Note that in France, the cheese course is served before dessert, to follow on from the savoury main course. Alternating from savoury to sweet, then back to savoury, *à l'anglaise*, is considered bizarre. When ordering cheese in a restaurant, a cheese platter will be presented. Don't hesitate to try a small slice of several cheeses (in private homes three is the polite number to try) and bear in mind that a cheese platter is almost never offered a second time.

Bread is an indispensable part of every meal. It should be on the table virtually from the time you sit down until the moment dessert is to be served. Bread is usually never eaten with but-

> ### LE BEAUJOLAIS NOUVEAU EST ICI!
>
> On the third Thursday in November, the first bottles of the year's Beaujolais grape harvest arrive in Paris and the streets are festooned with bunches of grape-like purple balloons.

ter, although some might be on the table in fancier restaurants to accommodate tourists. However, butter is served with radishes, country hams, sausages and Roquefort cheese. The French also use bread to mop up any left-over sauce on their plates – a practice considered to be bad manners in countries such as Britain.

On the menu

Good-value, fixed-price menus are common in fine restaurants and in simple eating places alike, but better restaurants tend to offer them only at lunch. If you plan on ordering the fixed menu in the evening, read it carefully to make sure that the words *déjeuner seulement* (lunch only) are not included.

Some better restaurants offer a *menu dégustation* (tasting menu) and usually everyone at the table must order it to make it worthwhile, as it involves serving numerous courses and is difficult to orchestrate when some people at the table have ordered a simple three-course meal.

Coffee is never served with milk after a meal in France, unless specifically requested. *Café crème* is considered hard to digest, whereas black coffee is a stimulant to counteract that satisfied, sleepy feeling that can wash over you after a large, rich meal. This said, delicious decaffeinated coffee (*café décaféiné, déca* for short) is available everywhere.

Lastly, a wide range of *digestifs* (after-dinner drinks) are available in even the most ordinary of cafés. They range from the roughest of rough brandies (*grappa*) to the smoothest of cognacs. Fruit brandies are particularly good. Brandies are never mixed with anything else and are always served at the end of a meal.

Voilà! You are now ready for a true dining experience. Speak clearly to your waiter, listen attentively, relax and *bon appétit!*   ❏

See Travel Tips *at the back of this book for restaurant recommendations – pages 273–77.*

LEFT: pavement dining at night.
RIGHT: enjoying a meal al fresco.

SHOPPING AROUND

"All that remained was the sense of an enormous Paris – one so enormous that it would always have enough to provide for shoppers " – EMILE ZOLA

In the capital of chic, even window-shopping is a more sensuous experience than elsewhere. The French call it *léche-vitrines*, literally "window-licking" and despite the city dwellers' *Métro-boulot-dodo* (commute, work, sleep) idiom, Parisians still find time for "*le shopping slow*".

Dripping with designer style, from monumental boulevards to manicured parks, from minimalist bedrooms to monogrammed boxer shorts (even Bohemianism is cultivated rather than simply born), Paris is the market leader in all that is tasteful, with tourist tackiness restricted to Eiffel Tower statuettes, Mona Lisa socks and rubber can-can dancers. As Coco Chanel said of her city, "Fashions come and go but style survives."

The French benchmarks are quality and authenticity: *la marque, la griffe* – the label, the stamp of authenticity and status. Certainly, snob appeal is part of the picture. As a rule, Parisians err on the side of conservatism, choosing a single classic item in preference to several less expensive options. This sense of conservative chic and innate good taste extends to the home. America invented the "total designer look", from co-ordinated bathrobes to bed linen and crockery, but France does it more stylishly.

Paris à la carte – by quarters

Luxury goods are a potent Parisian cultural symbol and are what the French do best. Such was the renown of Cartier in the 1930s that American designer Elsie de Wolfe dyed her hair blue at the age of 70 so that it matched her new aquamarine tiara.

Perfumes, belts, bags, leather goods and fashionable clothes make sensible Parisian purchases. By the same token, seek out gourmet goodies such as chocolate, truffles or *foie gras*. Equally tempting are the quirky or classical

objets d'art, from crystal and ceramics to prints and paintings. Although potential gifts are scattered throughout the *arrondissements*, there are geographical distinctions. The Right Bank, being the province of commerce and luxury, is the obvious area to shop for designer items and status symbols, while the Left Bank, with a

spirit of culture, education and the arts, has an artistic soul and pocket.

Haute couture (*see pages 54–55*) is concentrated on Rue du Faubourg St-Honoré and Avenue Montaigne off the Champs-Elysées. Art galleries and trendy boutiques tend to be in the Marais, Bastille and St-Germain quarters. If you want to window-shop, while away the day in the *passages*, the renovated arcades off the Grands Boulevards. For convenience or speed, plump for the *grands magasins* (department stores). For fun, visit the colourful markets or ethnic neighbourhoods, such as African Belleville. As the consummate shopping experience, stray no further than the St-Germain-des-Prés quarter, a

PRECEDING PAGES: the extravagant Art Nouveau interior of Galeries Lafayette.
LEFT: shopping in the fashionable Galerie Vivienne.
RIGHT: Parisian dolls waiting for a home.

gorgeous patchwork of galleries, bookshops, chic boutiques and twee *salons de thé*. Even non-shoppers will be converted, or if not, at least find a café suitable for a member of the "shopaphobic" intelligentsia.

Champs-Elysées – open all hours

This grandiose part of the Triumphal Way is coolly clinical, but a mecca for late-night shopping and a magnet for sleepless tourists. The avenue is lined by endless airline offices, car showrooms, soulless and over-priced cafés and shopping arcades. **Virgin Megastore**, at Nos 52–60 (Métro Franklin D. Roosevelt) is Richard

tury, this upmarket area also includes the *grands magasins* (major department stores) and the glitzy designer paradise of **Rue du Faubourg St-Honoré** (*see page 131*) and **Avenue Montaigne**, off the Champs-Elysées. Shoppers can be easily seduced by the superficiality of wafty designer dresses, snooty shoe shops and seductive jewellers. The list of luxury boutiques on these two streets is a roll call of the top names in couture. Aloof assistants assure a chilly reception from poorly dressed shoppers.

The city's ritziest shopping quarter is crisscrossed with *passages* – 19th-century arcades that were forerunners of the ubiquitous shop-

Branson's flagship store and offers the widest musical selection in Paris, from CDs, tapes and videos to tickets for concerts and Disneyland Paris (*see page 238*). It has a late-night opening policy (it stays open every day until midnight), a chic café and endless opportunities for people-watching. Around the corner, at 109 Rue de la Boétie, is **Prisunic**, a late-night supermarket. **Drugstore Publicis**, No. 133 (Métro Charles de Gaulle–Etoile), is the place for late-night gifts, books and newspapers, a chemist and café.

Ritzy Right Bank

Encompassed by the broad boulevards landscaped by Baron Haussmann in the 19th cen-

LES GRANDS MAGASINS

Parisian department stores, or *grands magasins*, are bastions of consumer glory with *parfumerie*, books, fashion and food halls, alongside in-store tearooms and cafés for the weary. In Boulevard Haussmann, **Galeries Lafayette**, under a beautiful Art Nouveau dome, is a good place for an overview of designer *prêt-à-porter*. Nearby, rival **Printemps** is a domed 19th-century world within a world, with a fire station and post office to boot. Opposite Pont Neuf, **La Samaritaine** is full of bargains and supports a panoramic rooftop café. On the Left Bank, in Rue de Babylone, stands the city's first department store, **Au Bon Marché**, with a fantastic food hall.

ping mall. Suffused with soft, hazy light filtering through the glass rooftops, they are ethereal, mysterious places, tinged with nostalgia. The most intriguing ones are **Galerie Vivienne** (*see page 126*) and the renovated **Passages des Panoramas** s and **Jouffroy** (*see page 129*) and **Galerie Véro-Dodat** (*see page 127*).

Paris is blessed with superb specialist shops, deserving of their pretentious "temples of gastronomy" tag. There are emporia dedicated to snails, caviar, mushrooms, cheese,

MARKS ET SPARKS

Ironically, the French have fallen for Britain's Marks & Spencer, noted for its knitwear, underwear and, for Parisians, delicacies such as sliced white bread.

Les Halles – fast and furious

At the former market heart of Paris, the district around Les Halles – the first and second *arrondissements* – is the inner hub of the Right Bank. The rag trade is based in the northeast corner, around Place du Caire, and, in the grander parts to the west, designer jewellery, reputable antiques and museum shops abound.

Forum des Halles is a labyrinthine concrete shopping centre carved into the ravaged heart of the market. Essentially

honey and preserves. For a concentration of these bastions of de luxe go to **Place de la Madeleine**, where, at No. 19, you will find **Maison de la Truffe**, the temple of truffles and more. The most famous is **Fauchon**, at No. 26, the French answer to Harrods Food Hall, offering exotic groceries, charcuterie, its own-label coffee and irresistible pâtisserie. Its rival, **Hédiard**, No. 21, was founded in 1854 as a purveyor of fine foodstuffs to the upper classes. Its obsequious staff flit about the old-fashioned setting.

FAR LEFT: Kenzo's main shop in Place des Victoires.
LEFT: Eurotrash king's shop in the Bastille district.
ABOVE: a *parfumerie* – devoted to scintillating scents.

cheap and cheerful, the scruffy complex has been invaded by fast-food outlets and shoddy clothing stores for young people. One shining exception is FNAC (Forum des Halles, Level 2), the French institution selling music, books, maps and ticket bookings. **Mora**, 13 rue Montmartre, behind the church of St-Eustache, is where professional chefs buy kitchen equipment. The adjoining St-Denis area is good for china and crystal, as well as hookers and hoods.

Eastwards in the Opéra quarter, **Place Vendôme** has been the centre of the French jewellery district since the glamour of the *Belle Epoque*. It was here that Princess Diana acquired her "friendship ring" from Dodi al-

Fayed on the day of her fatal crash. The grandest house is **Cartier**, famed for the bejewelled parrot and panthers designed for the Duchess of Windsor, and for the diamond-encrusted watches that grace the wrists of Hollywood stars. Its rival, **Chaumet** has been best-known as the Imperial jeweller ever since the house created Napoleon's coronation regalia. **Chanel** offers a more eclectic array of jewellery, based on Coco Chanel's original designs. Coco was the first designer to commercialise the mixing of gems and costume jewellery. Her designs were famously inspired by gifts from her English and Russian lovers.

The interminable **Rue de Rivoli**, running alongside the Tuileries and the Louvre, leads to the huge **La Samaritaine** department store and harbours the British bookshop **W.H. Smith**, at No. 248, as well as the **Librairie des Musées des Arts Décoratifs**, at No. 107, for a comprehensive range of books on art and architecture.

At the Louvre lies an upmarket shopping mall, **Le Carrousel du Louvre**, where you can find a wide range of gifts, from designer crystal at **Lalique** to tasteful posters and all manner of art books and gifts for children at the **Boutique du Musée**, the Louvre gift shop. Elsewhere, Eiffel Tower earrings await!

OFF THE CATWALKS, INTO THE STREETS

Ironically, the capital of haute couture is increasingly dominated by foreign designers. The Japanese have always believed in Paris and have injected a note of originality into the staid world of French design. **Comme des Garçons**, inspired by Junya Watanabe and Rei Kawakubo, provides innovative clothes. Other Japanese names include **Kenzo** and **Issey Miyake** (3 Place des Vosges). German Karl Lagerfeld has long masterminded design at **Chanel** (31 Rue Cambon).

Recently, the French fashion world has experienced the thrill or chill of a British invasion, led by John Galliano at **Dior** (32 Avenue Montaigne). Stella McCartney, daughter of ex-Beatle Paul McCartney, is revitalising Chloe (60 Rue du Faubourg St-Honoré), and Alexander MacQueen heads design at Givenchy.

However, the French are still a force to be reckoned with – **Agnès B** is a model designer of the younger school, classic yet casual and quintessentially French, and **Jean-Paul Gaultier**, the ageing *enfant terrible* of the French fashion scene, presents his endearingly outrageous designs at 30 Rue du Faubourg St-Antoine.

Fortunately, Paris has numerous discount stores, called *Dépôts-Ventes*, which offer last year's stock, unlabelled stock clothes or designer seconds at up to 50 percent off. **Studio Lolita** is one such outlet.
(*For more shop details, see* Travel Tips *on pages 281–83*.)

Back across the Rue de Rivoli in the grounds of the **Palais Royal** are arcaded shops that were purpose-built in the 18th century and today harbour specialist shops. Nearby, the **Louvre des Antiquaires**, in the Place du Palais Royal, is a large antiques hypermarket, selling everything from chandeliers to chaise-longues. Art Deco mirrors and Sèvres porcelain vie with Gobelins tapestries and Post Impressionist paintings – not a place for bargain hunters.

The Marais – a new chic

The restored area of the Marais, straddling the third and fourth *arrondissements* (Métro St-

mirrors and picture frames. **Rue Rambuteau** offers mouthwatering *charcuterie* and *pâtisserie*. Echoes of the Marais's old Jewish legacy survive in the Rue des Rosiers, with **Jo Goldenburg's**, *the* kosher deli (*see page 160*), and Middle Eastern street food such as falafel.

The adjacent **Rue Vieille du Temple** is the centre of the gay community and the retro clothes scene, with 1950s' kitsch and tasteless Abba outfits from the 1970s and period clothes from the 1920s onwards, including anything from cocktail dresses, Blues Brothers suits and hippy robes to army surplus and military wear. Nearby, **André Bissonet's** engaging musical

Paul), is popular with the new aristocracy of conceptual artists, fêted designers, media pundits and would-be philosophers. Although high rents have driven out many of the craft shops that once animated the area, the emerging new identity has its own charm. Workshops have been supplanted by minimalist shoe shops and quirky fashion boutiques. Many shops flout the law by opening on Sundays.

Rue des Francs-Bourgeois is the main shopping street, with its displays of designer lamps,

instrument shop is the place to pop in for an 18th-century piano to grace your *salon*.

Village St-Paul is an upcoming crafts centre with a villagey, arty-crafty feel located in the narrow streets and hidden courtyards. The cluster of workshops include antique shops, places for art and design, *objets d'art*, retro clothing and period furniture. Towards République are the rag-trade wholesalers and loft-like art galleries. Depending on taste, the Marais shopping spree can be interspersed with visits to genteel *salons de thé*, nicotine-stained haunts, trendy brasseries or gay bars. **Les Maronniers** is an intellectual bar for floppy-haired philosophers claiming to be "counter-culturalists".

LEFT: window-shopping in the Rue de Rivoli.
ABOVE: Parisians will go to great lengths to find the right flowers.

Bastille – offbeat and funky

This hitherto working-class neighbourhood in the 11th and 12th *arrondissements* is succumbing to creeping gentrification and designer cool. Modernistic workshops and design shops reflect the Bohemian mood created by buskers, hawkers and boisterous bars and there are several funky outlets for street fashion. There is another branch of FNAC beside the Opéra Bastille. **The Viaduc des Arts** conceals designer boutiques tucked into

> ### IT's IN THE BAG
>
> "You may decide that instead of going on holiday twice a year to Bermuda, you only go once and buy a Hermès handbag for your wife."
>
> – JEAN-LOUIS DUMAS HERMÈS

on the ground in the cheap and lively **Marché d'Aligre** (Métro Ledru Rollin), whose North African flavour gives it the air of a Moroccan bazaar (*see pages 78–79*).

Studious Left Bank

The **Quartier Latin**, centred on Boul' Mich and traditionally seen as the students' quarter, is – naturally – full of bookshops. **Shakespeare and Company**, 37 Rue de la Boucherie, is the place for new and secondhand English language books (*see page 188*). Around the

the railway arches on the north side of the street. While more fashionable than Les Halles, the quarter serves a bizarre mixture of tastes, with tatty ironmongers ill at ease alongside trendy computer stores and sushi bars. Canny shoppers focus on ceramics, sculpture and jewellery in sharp contemporary designs.

Cobbled alleyways lead off **Rue du Faubourg St-Antoine**, a district dotted with craft workshops since the 18th century. Some of the best buys are from workshops that sell direct. **Prisunic**, a supermarket at 109 Rue de la Bastille, offers late-night shopping and collections of cheap clothes, crockery, kitchen equipment and foodstuffs. The Bastille keeps its feet

corner is the rival **La Librairie Canadienne**, with a good selection of American books and a warm welcome over coffee. **La Hune**, 170 St-Germain-des-Prés, is a Left Bank bookstore popular with night owls and intellectuals.

Impoverished students head for the colourful Rue de Buci market (*see pages 78–79*), off Boulevard St-Germain, where there is a cornucopia of cheeses, fruit, chocolate and charcuterie. Further on, in **St-Germain-des-Prés**, the taste of luxury beckons at **Debauve et Gallais**, 30 Rue des St-Pères, in the guise of some of the finest chocolates in Paris.

As the home of monied opinion-formers and power-brokers, St-Germain-des-Prés contains an eclectic array of shops. Cut by Rue Jacob, the quarter is lined with art galleries, antique shops, interior design shops and **Yves Saint-Laurent** at 12 Place St-Sulpice. The liberal, welcoming mood is echoed by the elegant but unintimidating boutiques.

Village Paris – a change of scene

Tucked into the shrinking remnants of working-class Paris, these old-fashioned yet quirky quarters, with the exception of Montmartre, are struggling to survive in the face of the city's gradual gentrification and the movement of the proletariat to the insalubrious suburbs on the

are not on sale locally, *chanteuse* Edith Piaf was allegedly born on the pavement of Rue de Belleville. **Place d'Italie** to the south, represents old-fashioned, ungentrified Paris. It is home to the Chinese and Asian communities, with Laotian and Cambodian specialist foodshops and Chinese eateries.

Montmartre, to the north, has a distinctly villagey feel. Although touristy, the galleries are fun and the foodshops lining hilly **Rue Lepic** (*see pages 78–79*) are delightful.

Around the Périphérique are the *marché aux puces*, or flea markets (*see pages 78–79*), fascinating places on an early Sunday morning. ❏

outside of the Périphérique. For shoppers in search of a Paris beyond designer shop windows, the diversity of these districts easily compensates for a certain shabbiness and a slightly above-average crime rate.

Belleville, situated to the east, has a Jewish and North African flavour. Apart from the kosher butchers and bakers, there are *épiceries-buvettes* – old-fashioned shops-cum-cafés – as well as stalls laden with exotic spices, artichokes and purple figs. Although her records

LEFT: antiques and junk spill out on to the street.
ABOVE: one of the many retailers in the regal Place des Vosges, which buzzes with life at weekends.

DRESSING UP THE KIDS

Unlike leading American and British designers, who create casual clothes for children who act as children, French designers create clothes for children who act as adults. However, while unfortunate junior fashion victims may end up in tortured pinafores or frilly party frocks, not all French clothes are dressy. **Bon Point** (15 Rue Royale) is one of the smarter boutiques but more eminently practical options are offered by **Tartine et Chocolat** (66 Boulevard St-Germain) and **Petit Bâteau** (13c Rue Tronchet). **Froment-Leroyer** (7 Rue Vavin) provides a comprehensive range of classic shoes for children.

BEST MARKET BUYS

The intimacy, vibrancy and informal nature of neighbourhood markets act as a welcome antidote to the monumentality of "museum Paris"

Visitors who tire of the cool chic of haute couture Paris or the impersonality of the Grands Boulevards should plunge into the nearest market. The flavour of Paris is rarely further than a couple of Métro stops away. Foodies will be beguiled by the tantalising smells of Rue de Buci (flowers mingled with ripe tropical fruit and the aroma of roast chicken). Rue Mouffetard vies with Rue de Buci as the most picturesque market, enlivened by an accordionist who passes out sheet music to encourage sing-alongs. Idle browsers may prefer the *bouquinistes*, the quaint book stalls that line the banks of the Seine. Specialists are drawn to the markets dedicated to flowers, birds, postcards and stamps. For the rest, there are funky Left Bank markets selling secondhand designer clothes, rural markets laden with produce fresh from the farm, and exotic bazaars selling piles of scented mint and coriander.

FINE REGIONAL FOODSTUFFS

Marché d'Aligre is the most authentic and exotic experience, its stalls laden with olives, spices and nuts, like an Arab souk. However, the finest French regional foodstuffs (*produits de terroir*) are available from many Parisian markets. Visitors with a nose for the right stuff may be rewarded with chestnuts from Corrèze, *choucroute* from Alsace, or calvados and camembert from Normandy. Street snacks are readily available, from pastries such as *tarte tatin* (apple tart) to sweet or savoury *crêpes*. For eating on the hoof, market fare includes a *baguette* (French stick) filled with *charcuterie* from the Auvergne, Alsace or the Ardennes. Foodies will also seek out honey from Provence or the Morvan, dairy produce and salad leaves from the Ile de France, and fruit and goat's cheeses brought from the Loire. Bear in mind food markets are generally closed on Monday (*see* page 283).

△ **PLUMP FOR THE POT**
Close to the Louvre, the colourful Quai de la Mégisserie is lir with plants and pet shops, with geese, ducks, rabbits and ev the odd goat often destined for the cooking pot.

△ **FRESH FISH**
Glistening fish are displayed on the stalls of a *poissonier* (fishmonger's) on the Rue du Seine. Equally fine seafood, including tuna and turbot, lobster and fish-stuffed *rillettes* can be bought in Rue Lepic or in Rue Daguerre in Montparnasse.

◁ **CAST IRON MONUMENTS**
Marché St-Quentin, built in 1910, is the quaintest remaining cast-iron hall.

◁ **FRUIT AND VEGETABLES**
Rue Lepic and Rue Mouffe-tard markets are both awash with fruit and vegetables. Although technically a street of fabulous food shops, Rue Lepic feels more like a chaotic market, with its cosmopolitan air and stalls lining the slopes of Montmartre. On the Left Bank, the chicly photogenic Rue Mouffetard market winds down the hill from the elegantly domed Panthéon.

▽ **CURED MEATS**
The *boucherie-charcuterie* stalls and delicatessens on Rue Mouffetard are a feast for the eyes. On display are *boudin blanc* (white pudding), *foie gras* (fattened goose liver), duck pâté and ham from the Ardennes, Burgundy or Basque country and *boudin* (black pudding). *Andouillettes* are another delicacy made from tripe.

ALL THE FUN OF THE FLEA MARKETS

Parisian flea markets, known as *marchés aux puces*, were originally clustered around the ancient city gates, and largely remain on the outskirts. At best, they offer a melange of Louis XV armchairs, Art Deco lamps, antique wrought-iron gates and rustic Moroccan pottery. Among the curios are former Soviet combat jackets, *fripes* (secondhand clothes) and general *brocante* (junk).

The best-known flea market is by Porte de Clignancourt (Sat–Mon). Set in northern Paris, this sprawling, touristy affair is home to 1,500 dealers and specialises in new, retro or period clothes, as well as books, china, linen, reproduction furniture, jewellery, junk and some genuine antiques.

Porte de Vanves (Sat–Sun) is the haunt of amateur and professional dealers. Marché d'Aligre (Métro Ledru-Rollin) is one of the most complete markets, selling food, mirrors, cutlery and clothes.

◁ **BOOKSELLERS**
The *bouquinistes* are second-hand and antiquarian booksellers whose stalls line the Left Bank of the Seine between the Quai d'Orsay and Ile de la Cité. They sell musty, leather-bound volumes as well as records, sheet music and prints.

▷ **AFRICAN SPICE**
Marché d'Aligre is a popular market with a spicy North African flavour. Olives and spices vie with mint tea, *citron pressé* and fresh fruit and vegetables.

A PORTRAIT OF PARIS

Soak up the atmosphere of present-day Paris – take time off to wander the streets and sit in cafés, just watching the world go by

The secret of appreciating Paris is to love life. The surest way to seize the city for yourself is to put aside its quicksand of historical facts and its overwhelming grandeur. Simply wander about down shady boulevards, or along the quiet and gritty pathways in the parks, soaking up the atmosphere created by the past, listening out for those telling everyday details that make this city unique.

Indeed, the best way to start may be to stop. Watch Paris breathe – heave, rather – with an endlessly fascinating mixture of energy and relaxation, passion and disdain. Find a bench, or better still a café, and watch the world go by: tourists wandering in awe, the chic, young woman in a hurry, groups of teenagers chattering, the impatient motorist, the lovers with eyes only for each other. Against the background of traffic noise rises the chirp of birds, the chatter of conversation and the chink of glasses at the tables on the pavements.

Zelda Fitzgerald epitomises the spirit and beauty of Paris in a letter to her husband, F. Scott Fitzgerald in 1930, "Was it fun in Paris? Who did you see there and was the Madeleine pink at five o'clock and did the fountains fall with hollow delicacy into the framing of space in the Place de la Concorde, and did the blue creep out from behind the Colonades in the Rue de Rivoli through the grill of the Tuileries and was the Louvre gray and metallic in the sun and did the trees hang brooding over the cafés and were there lights at night and the click of saucers and the auto horns that play Debussy…?"

All the pavement's a stage

The fact that Parisians live right at the very heart of Paris deepens the spirit of the place. This is in sharp contrast to cities such as London, where large parts are only occupied during the day by a tide of commuters that ebbs back to suburbia in the evening. The streets of Paris are very

much alive by day and by night, and in this grand theatre every pavement is a stage.

Look out for the fashionable ladies with their tiny yapping dogs and keep a sharp eye out for what they leave behind! Look out, too, for the street-cleaning machines, which resemble a cross between a golf cart and a toothbrush.

Paris, it should be said, is a much cleaner city now – an army of garish-green uniforms washes the streets endlessly, but the dogs still win. And, wherever you go, keep an eye out for the Eiffel Tower, which, thrusting skyward out of a landscape of classic architecture, was once described by writer Jean Cocteau (1889–1963) as the Notre Dame of the Left Bank.

Taking Paris easily

As a first-time visitor to Paris, you may already have a strong impression of the city from other people, literature and films, giving you high expectations. Paris can be a most daunting city, but don't be afraid to admit it, if your sense of

---

PRECEDING PAGES: merry-go-rounds pop up everywhere. **LEFT:** soaking up the atmosphere at the Louvre. **RIGHT:** relaxing in the Jardins des Tuileries.

duty to see as many sights, monuments, museums and galleries as possible is at odds with your inclination, your timetable and even your energy on what is supposed to be a holiday. Take it easy. Just as *Hamlet* is more than a sequence of quotations, so Paris is much more than a catalogue of sights.

A city of ideas

Connoisseurs of the capital often say that it is still a medieval city in essence. Some of its monuments are certainly medieval and its undying taste for bawdy high-living can be described as medieval but, essentially, it is an *everyday* city, briskly mundane in the midst of the breathtaking grandeur.

Honoré de Balzac (1799–1850), the great novelist, thought of Paris as a city of ideas, those that smile at you at street corners or splash you with mud from carriage wheels.

Where compression and excitement are concerned, the city of New York is quite similar to Paris, but New York's landscape of mighty monoliths gives the stroller the impression of being built from the sky down, whereas Paris was built from the pavement up. Balzac also compared Paris to an ocean, with uncharted depths ever-yielding new pearls and monsters.

PARIS EDICTS

Throughout the city streets you will come upon evidence of the essentially Napoleonic taste for edicts and statutes, simple instructions backed up by the date of the relevant law. Take, for example, the sinister and frequently encountered citation of a law preventing the pasting up of posters – it is still dated April 1943, the period of the German Occupation. Or even the prohibition against public drunkenness announced in the same edict as the forbidding of under-age drinking and displayed as a tobacco-yellowed notice in every bar, "*Protection des mineurs et répression de l'ivresse publique*". Very few take notice of the "*Défense de fumer*" (no smoking) signs.

Avoiding the traffic

Even the traffic of Paris has its place in French history. In 1610, two dozen or so attempts on his life having failed, King Henry IV was stabbed to death as his carriage was trapped in a traffic jam in Rue de la Ferronerie. Moreover, the great sweeping Grands Boulevards of Paris today were not built for the benefits of traffic, but for better control of a restive civilian population: narrow streets lent themselves nicely to barricades, whereas boulevards were better for baton charges.

The most conspicuous blockade these days is the parked car. Paris is the centre of that continental sport, which involves the nudging forwards and backwards of a line of parked cars to allow just one more to squeeze in. Among the signs you may notice on the street is the one which warns of the risk of towing away – yet all it says is that you may have your car towed away if your parking is *gênant*, a word meaning mildly annoying.

Never so hugely was a city map redrawn when Baron Georges Haussmann, Napoleon III's Prefect of the Seine, was ordered to rebuild Paris. Climactic

WHAT'S IN A SIGHT?

In the past, sights were rarely created to be sights. Even the Eiffel Tower, built to vaunt French technology at the 1889 World Fair, was all set to be dismantled, until it was discovered that it made a perfect radio mast.

Wander the streets

Paris is a compact city, worth a good walk – just as your feet tire, your soul gasps. On a practical note, the street names are well displayed. Curiously, the name plates have been designed to look as if they were in relief, with a kind of shadow marked on the borders.

It is easy to get lost in Paris, even in Haussmann's grand scheme – possibly even more so, since his passion for vista gives rise to lots of sharp-angled street

views and sweeping carriage-trots this way and that across the city were created by a splintering geometry of long avenues meeting in starburst junctions (Place de Ternes, Place Victor Hugo) or round a great building like an exuberant but organised dance (the Opéra, the Madeleine, even the Gare St-Lazare).

The most relaxing way to see the city on the move is to leave the car at home and travel around by bus (*see* Travel Tips, *pages 266–67*). From your seat by the window, you can watch Haussmann's drama unfurl around you.

LEFT: taking the lunch for a drag.
ABOVE: time out for a beer with the newspaper.

corners, which may be hiding small shifts of direction in the pattern, leading you off course. We expect old buildings to be askew or awry. Those tall, old houses on the south bank of the river, by Notre Dame on the Ile de la Cité, lean in on each other like drinkers over-filling a bar. Even today this quirkiness continues.

Out just beyond the city limits, in the business area known as La Défense, at the end of the line constituted by the Champs-Elysées and the Avenue de la Grande Armée, passing through the Arc de Triomphe, is the Grande Arche, the focus of the central esplanade of which is at a slight angle to the rest of the Triumphal Way. In fact, La Défense itself is a phenomenon: whereas most cities could do with a dose of old Paris, new Paris wanted its own high-rise area without submerging its past. La Défense expresses the Parisian taste for high-rise technology, just as the Eiffel Tower before it – and Notre Dame before that.

As you wander around Paris, once your eye has acquired the habit, there is plenty to notice: the grills around trees, the stray café chairs that all but block the narrowest passageway, the rolls of old carpet used to divert the morning rivers that flow down the gutters.

As for those gutters, they contain numerous, alarmingly-wide drain-holes that yawn right

of a long tradition of everyone, including the servants, having to speak Latin in the university precincts. This practice continued until Napoleon I stopped it at the beginning of the 19th century.

The Sorbonne is the oldest university in the world, and student life is conducted in the streets and cafés that were once frequented by such great literary figures as Jean-Paul Sartre, Albert Camus, Ernest Hemingway and Henry Miller. Aspiring writers and intellectuals are still drawn to the area in their droves – indeed, virtually every nation seems to have a poet or painter who has adopted Paris.

down into the underworld, which, in fact, is open to visitors – in Paris, the city's vast labyrinth of sewers are a popular attraction to many tourists!

Exploring the quartiers

For aspiring artists, this city's centre is Montmartre. Here they can tread in the footsteps of those who spent their poverty-stricken youth, a century before them, creating masterpieces that are now hanging in the prestigious museums around Paris.

For students, the area on the Left Bank, south of Notre Dame, is the focus of university life. It became known as the Quartier Latin as a result

PAVEMENT THEATRICALS

During the student riots of 1968 (violent enough but not as bad as the student riots of 1223), there was a rebellious slogan to the effect that under the pavements lay the beach – *sous les pavés la plage*. The gist of this was that freedom, symbolised by the beach, was represented by the sand, typically to be found immediately under the cobblestones. Such freedom, therefore, could be won by hoisting the cobblestones at the police. After the riots, most of the pavements were replaced by unlobbable tar. The revolutionary slogan has since been used by a car manufacturer, replacing "under" with "on", to advertise the easy ride of a new model.

Today's café clientele

If you take a break in a café outside on the pavement, the chances are you will be able to spot a good cross-section of Parisian life alongside you. Almost every café has the paragon of fashion and the scallywag reading Nietzsche, their attention momentarily caught by the smartest of businessmen making a brief call for a snatch of coffee and a private word to each other on their way, or by old cronies arguing over politics or *pétanque*. And then there are those with nothing much else to do but pass the time of day holding on to their café tables for as long as possible. The music of video games and, above

that, the roar of the traffic, provides a constant accompaniment to the coming and going of human life.

In the Marais (the web of streets to the east of the Centre Georges-Pompidou), one of the most characteristic and varied quarters of Paris, the ancient contrasts between artisans and aristocrats can still be sensed today. Here it is quite possible for an aristocrat to find himself living next door to a carpenter or cobbler. Wealth and a person's position in society was once defined by the width of his property in the Marais, rather

LEFT: a busker playing for his supper.
ABOVE: a serious discussion in the Place des Vosges.

than its height, as it was around the Grands Boulevards, where social standing was measured vertically – the finest apartments were situated on the first floor, the most rudimentary on the topmost. Today, amid the resulting jumble of old aristocratic mansions and workshops, you can often buy vegetables in one shop and the most chic of fashionable accessories next door.

The mish-mash of Marais streets, never quite at right-angles, almost intentionally seem to hide one of the finest, most serene town squares in Europe, the Place des Vosges, the last duelling ground of Paris.

A city to suit your mood

Most cities have a contrast between the seedy and the splendid: in Paris the mixture is like a chemical reaction whose by-product is energy, sheer energy. A hundred years ago, Montmartre was a seedy quarter that became the genuinely creative crucible of Europe, a shanty town that gave birth to Cubism and a gossiping madhouse of chattering poets.

You will not find much of the same energy now – and the seediness lies tucked away from a rather too presentable model village neatness – but if you take in the unique view across the whole of Paris, roofs shimmering beneath, a capital at your feet, you may understand the vaunting, almost arrogant fertility of that creative world. To the artists of the time it made sense to live in a shack in order to experience the low life, while looking down on a quilt of palaces and boulevards.

There is a street or square in Paris for every mood – and for all weathers. Paris has shifting weather, blue, fluffy-white or damnably grey. It can look its best shimmering after a downpour, or in the lazy early light before breakfast, when the smell of fresh bread and coffee lurks behind every café front. So, take a seat and bathe in the atmosphere of the city. Breathe in. Mind the dog. If the coffee tastes terrible, that is history too, because Casanova made *exactly* the same complaint centuries ago. ❑

ARCHITECTURE

A veritable textbook of architectural history, Paris is a living museum that displays an evolving heritage in which the new complements the old

Two thousand years of history and seven centuries of artistic brilliance have made Paris a city rich in architecture. Yet invasions, sieges and insurrections have irreparably destroyed a great number of the capital's architectural masterpieces.

Fortunately, the many famous monuments that we can enjoy today had a narrow escape in 1944. As Allied troops approached Paris, Hitler gave General Dietrich von Choltitz, the occupying governor of Paris, the order to blast every single historical edifice to pieces, so that the Allies' triumphant entry would be greeted by a field of smoking ruins. Charges of dynamite were laid under Les Invalides, Notre Dame, the Madeleine, the Opéra, the Arc de Triomphe and even at the foot of the Eiffel Tower. But, at the last minute, unable to perpetrate such sacrilege, von Choltitz refused to give the order and ultimately surrendered the city intact to General Jacques-Philippe Leclerc, liberator of Paris.

Despite the various devastations in its history, Paris has retained examples of all France's architectural styles, especially from the 12th century and the beginnings of the Gothic era onwards, creating a textbook of architectural history, a living museum. It requires little imagination to conjure up a sense of the past. Over the centuries, the best architects, sculptors, masons and painters have preserved this sense, while at the same time looking forward. This explains the extraordinary juxtaposition of different styles of architecture, complementary or contrasting but seldom jarring or in bad taste.

Roman remains

Nothing is left of the wooden huts occupied by the Gallic Parisii on the Ile de la Cité. However, thanks to the Romans' development of an extremely durable concrete, from stone quarried out of Mont Ste-Geneviève, their ruins – the site of their settlement, Lutetia – can still be found in the Quartier Latin. Several streets, such as the Rue St-Jacques and the Boulevard St-Michel are built on ancient Roman roads. Lutetia was not an important city, but it was equipped with the buildings necessary to Roman civic life – a palace, forum, theatre, arena, baths and temples. The vestiges of one of these baths can be seen in the garden at the Musée National du Moyen Age – Thermes de Cluny and the ruins of the arena (Arènes de Lutèce) have also survived.

NOTHING BUT THE BEST

For centuries, Paris has traditionally attracted the best architects, sculptors, masons and painters.

Destruction by the Vikings

Unfortunately, nothing is left of the Merovingian and Carolingian eras (6th–9th centuries), because the Vikings burnt and pillaged Paris on several occasions during this period.

Romanesque, with a propensity for ponderous and gloomy structures, left hardly a mark, either. One of the few remnants of this artistic and religious movement that spread throughout France at the turn of the first millennium is the steeple of the St-Germain-des-Prés church.

In the 12th century, Paris and the Ile de France turned to the newest rage in religious

THROUGH THE AGES

Architecture in Paris embraces a very wide spectrum of styles. Here are a few examples:

- ☛ Gothic: Notre Dame (1160–1345), Sainte-Chapelle (1245), Tour St-Jacques (1523)
- ☛ Renaissance: Cour Carrée facade of the Louvre (1549–56), St-Eustache (1532–1637)
- ☛ Classical: Versailles (1668), Les Invalides (1671–76), Place Vendôme (1698)
- ☛ Neo-Classical: Panthéon (1764–90)
- ☛ 19th century: Opéra Garnier (1862–75)
- ☛ Modern: La Défense, Louvre Pyramid, Opéra Bastille (all 1989)

PRECEDING PAGES: a fine example of wrought ironwork at Gare de l'Est.
LEFT: Gothic arches line the nave of Notre Dame.

architecture: Gothic. Lighter, more slender and luminous than previous architecture, Gothic coincided with the strengthening of the French crown and a fresh religious fervour inflamed by the Crusades. Gothic architecture is distinguished by pointed arches and the combined use of ribbed vaults with flying buttresses, a technique that allowed windows to replace walls and walls to soar towards the heavens.

Gothic marvels

The most beautiful religious edifice in Paris, the cathedral of Notre Dame epitomises the perfection of Gothic style. The construction of Notre

Hugo's novel, *Notre Dame de Paris* (*The Hunchback of Notre Dame*) and prodding by the Romantic movement; the restoration was to take almost 23 years.

Close by stands Sainte-Chapelle, a fragile-looking church in the High Gothic style, which differs from Notre Dame in that the vast stained-glass windows (the oldest in Paris) are supported by only a thin framework of stone. Nestled within the walls of the Palais de Justice, the church was built by King Louis IX in 33 months to shelter the Crown of Thorns he bought from Emperor Baudouin II of Constantinople and other relics he acquired later from Byzantium.

Dame began in 1163 on the site of a Romanesque church, which had been built on the foundations of a Carolingian basilica, which in turn had been built on the site of a Roman temple. It took 200 years and several generations of architects and craftsmen to finish it.

Like all medieval churches, Notre Dame was completely painted on the inside. The paintings were the way medieval man learned the Bible stories and the use of colour was meant to glorify God and breathe life into the sculptures.

The building began to decay during the 17th century, but restoration by 19th-century Gothic revivalist Eugène Viollet-le-Duc (1814–79) eventually started in 1841, as a result of Victor

An Italian influence

War in Italy, in 1495, brought the French into contact with Renaissance grandeur, and the style, characterised by a contempt for all Gothic forms and a rediscovery of antiquity, was imported to France. In architecture, the ribbed vault disappeared in favour of flat ceilings with wooden beams. Medieval fortresses gave way to genteel palaces and Greek-style colonnades were re-established.

Among Paris's main exponents of the Renaissance were architect Pierre Lescot (1510–78), whose finest work is the west wing of the Louvre, and Jean Goujon (1510–68), who sculpted the magnificent reliefs on Lescot's facade at the

Louvre and worked on the Hôtel Carnavalet (1544) in the Marais. Goujon's work can also be seen on Lescot's Fontaine des Innocents near Les Halles, which provides an example of Renaissance sensuality.

The Classical influence

At the end of the 16th century, while the Renaissance had succumbed to the Baroque movement in the rest of Europe, French architects were looking towards sobriety and Classicism. A desire for strength and

RECORD BREAKERS

Notre Dame took 200 years to build, whereas the neighbouring High Gothic Sainte-Chapelle, started 80 years later, took all of 33 months.

central garden. The Place des Vosges, commissioned by Henri IV in 1609, was the first and most elegant of the Classical-style royal squares. Edged with graceful arcades, the square started out as the Place Royale, until it was changed in the Revolution.

In grand style

The Sun King certainly left his mark on Paris and the Ile de France, imposing his personality in true grand style on the palace of Versailles. Started in 1668, the château symbolised

clarity, born of rationalism, dominated architecture. The Classical style is based on symmetry, simplicity of line and great, wide open perspectives. The Pont Neuf, the first bridge to be built without houses on it in 1606, and now the oldest in Paris, was one of the first examples of such architecture.

During this period, large squares were created, surrounded by uniform buildings and with a statue of the king in the middle of the large

LEFT: Place des Vosges, the first and most elegant of royal squares, built by Henri IV.
ABOVE: Notre Dame was black before it was cleaned in the 1960s with forceful jets of pure water.

the absolute power of the monarch and employed the top designers of the time – architects Louis Le Vau and Hardouin-Mansart, painter Charles Lebrun and landscape gardener André Le Nôtre. Other fine examples are the Palais du Luxembourg (1631) and the Hôtel des Invalides (1670).

After Louis XIV's death, building was kept to a minimum until the 1750s, when the neoclassical movement turned to forms lifted directly from antiquity, taking the utmost care to reproduce what recent progress in archaeology had brought to light. Jacques-Ange Gabriel built Place de la Concorde and the Ecole Militaire and Jacques-Germain Soufflot designed the Panthéon, originally a church and today a necropolis for the great and the good of France.

With the coronation of a triumphant Napoleon and the installation of a new Empire at the beginning of the 19th century came the triumphal arch (Arc de Triomphe du Carrousel and Arc de Triomphe) and the triumphal neo-classical Rue de Rivoli.

Baron Haussmann's legacy

With the exception of a few elite neighbour-hoods, post-Revolution Paris was a squalid city. Poverty-stricken communities, with their filthy, narrow alleyways and miserable, overpopulated

shacks, were constantly on the brink of revolt. For obvious sanitary reasons, but also to cir-cumvent the risk of riots, Napoleon III and the Prefect Baron Georges Haussmann began a sweeping urbanisation programme in the 1850s.

Medieval Paris all but disappeared. Whole quarters were razed and wide, tree-lined avenues, more difficult to barricade than nar-row alleys, took the place of grimy backstreets.

The city of Paris today is still strongly stamped with Haussmann's ideas. After clear-ing out slums and opening up the area around the Louvre, he concentrated on expanding the system of boulevards through the city centre, started by Louis XIV. A small hill then known

as the Butte St-Roch, occupied by windmills, a gallows and a pig market, was intended to be their centre. It is hard to picture that today as you stand on the level, busy Place de l'Opéra, looking at Charles Garnier's opera house, the Second Empire's most sumptuous construction.

Monsieur Eiffel's tower

The second half of the 19th century was very rich in creativity. Wrought-iron architecture made its debut with the Grand Palais, the Pont Alexandre III and, of course, the Eiffel Tower. Panned by the architectural critics during its construction in 1889 for the World Fair, the tower is now the universal symbol of Paris. It was originally designed to be a temporary exhibit, along with "a grotesque city of plaster, staff and pasteboard... buildings from an Asian temple to a Swiss chalet, from Kanaka hut to medieval Paris, Chinese pagoda to Montmartre cabaret", as one contemporary visitor remarked on a trip to the city. The tower symbolised the uneasy relationship between science, industry and art in Paris. As Gustave Eiffel's contro-ver-sial creation rose higher and higher, bets were placed on when it would topple over.

When the engineer himself climbed up to plant the French flag atop his iron latticework fantasy, the cheering crowds comprised ordi-nary Parisians who admired his vision; the snobbish aesthetes stayed away.

This was also an eclectic period. After being burnt down during the Commune of 1871, the Hôtel de Ville (town hall) on the Right Bank was rebuilt Renaissance-style, while the Sacré-Cœur was created in the antique tradition, and numerous churches toed the Gothic line. React-ing against these academic approaches and inspired by Japanese art, the Belgian Hector Guimard established the Art Nouveau move-ment. The sinuous plant forms and curving lines, natural and Baroque at the same time, were decried by some as "noodle style". Guimard designed several buildings in the 16th *arrondissement*, including the Castel Béranger (14 Rue de la Fontaine), and also the city's Métro entrances, many of which, such as Porte Dauphine and Abbesses, still remain.

The modern age

Both the modern movements of the 1920s and 1930s and Art Deco were born in the 16th *arrondissement*. Mallet-Stevens (Rue Mallet-

Stevens) and Le Corbusier (Maison Jeanneret, 8 Square du Dr Blanche) were the main artisans of the Cubic style of architecture, all pure lines and concrete. The Palais de Chaillot is a typical example of this grandiose, neoclassical architectural style.

From the 1960s, Paris underwent a transformation. Facades were cleaned, the Métro was modernised and old parts of the city, such as Les Halles, were demolished. New architectural projects were developed, keeping up with technical advances by building upwards

GREAT ADMIRERS

The Palais de Chaillot, built in 1937, made a big impression on the Third Reich and Soviet Russia.

glass, in the Cour Napoleon, is already world-famous. Lauded for its beauty and efficiency, the central pyramid has earned its place on the architectural stage of Paris.

The new Opéra Bastille, like Peï's pyramid, built in 1989, or the bankside Institut du Monde Arabe, designed in 1987 by Jean Nouvel, exemplifies the harmony of modern architecture in Paris by reflecting the neighbouring buildings and the ever-changing Parisian sky. Gothic architecture, in its time, held a mirror to society in much the same way.❑

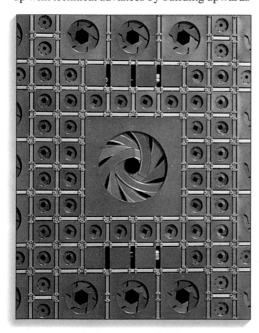

(La Défense and Tour Montparnasse), expanding indoor space (Centre Georges-Pompidou, La Villette, Bercy) and experimenting with new materials that capture, reflect and admit light.

In the 1980s, the Chinese-American architect I.M. Peï was employed to design a new entrance and orientation centre for the Louvre. His solution, an illusionistic "landscape" of pyramids in stainless steel and specially created polished

LEFT: Guimet's original Art Nouveau Métro entrance at Porte Dauphine.
ABOVE LEFT: one of the 1,600 light screens that filter light into the Institut du Monde Arabe.
ABOVE RIGHT: Reflections in the Parc de la Villette.

MITTERRAND'S GRANDS PROJETS

When François Mitterrand came to power in 1981, he initiated a *grands projets* scheme ensuring his mark would be left on the city:

- Le Grand Louvre (1981–97) renovation
- Cité des Sciences at La Villette (1986)
- Institut du Monde Arabe (1987)
- Gare d'Orsay conversion to museum (1986)
- La Grande Arche at La Défense (1989)
- Opéra Bastille (1989)
- Finance ministry building at Bercy (1989)
- Bibliothèque Nationale de France relocation to new buildings at Tolbiac (1998)

PARIS THROUGH PAINTINGS

The French capital has been a honeypot to artists for centuries, providing an infinite source of material for their canvases

The Russian painter Marc Chagall (1887–1985) declared "Paris was my heart's image – I should like to blend with it and not be alone with myself". In many paintings, especially those portraying lovers sky high in serene embraces, he did just that, wrapping the couple in warm colours as if in the evening

and provincial country, with a city that is sophisticated and worldly-wise.

In France, the establishment was firmly rooted in Paris, epitomised by the annual *salon* exhibitions, established by Louis XIVth's Académie Royale de Peinture et de Sculpture in the uninhabited Louvre in 1734. These exhibi-

air over Paris and giving flight to their calm passion across the rooftops of the capital.

A city of painters

Paris's reputation has not only developed as the city of lovers – if lovers need any city in particular – but more importantly as the city of painters. Apart from the obvious justification that it is a lovely place to paint, there are special reasons for this. Perhaps no other capital city has been the centre and focus of its whole nation's identity to such a degree for so long a time. Nor does any comparable country have such a unique divide between town and country as exists in France – a quintessentially rural

tions were all-powerful – sometimes an artist who had sold a given picture to a customer shortly before the opening of a *salon* would be obliged to take the picture back if it failed to be selected for the exhibition. Nevertheless, over the years, the *salon* jury continuously overlooked many great talents: Cézanne (1839–1906) was never accepted.

Paris as an artist's model

Thanks to the Montgolfier brothers' hot air balloon flight in 1783, Paris was the first city to be seen from the air and, 75 years later, to be photographed from on high – by French pioneer photographer and novelist Gaspard Nadar.

Moreover, with the reshaping of the city along starburst lines of avenues and junctions, an artist in Paris around 150 years ago may have felt that, as he created his Paris on canvas, the city itself was still being created around him.

Technology has always fascinated the French and the Eiffel Tower has not only provided a worthy subject for painters, but has also afforded an easily accessible aerial view as in no other city. For the Impressionists

PISSARRO'S VIEW

Towards the end of his life, Camille Pissarro (1830–1903) used to sit at windows on the top floors of houses painting the busy scenes below. His famous *Boulevard des Italiens*, bathed in morning sunlight, is absolutely full of atmosphere.

Studio life

In today's Paris, there is nothing like the system of studios that existed in the 19th century, when painters were apprenticed to masters. At that time, they learned to paint in an atmosphere sometimes deeply serious to the point of stuffy, or hilarious to the point of bawdy. Drawing was at the centre of the training, the nude the central subject of draughtsmanship. Mythological and generally heroic and historical subject

the railways were important, partly because they could take the train from the Gare St-Lazare up the Seine, but partly also because steam makes such a splendid haze over a field of vision.

The Eiffel Tower, placed beside all the other palaces and avenue apartments of Paris, stood out like a nude at a dinner party, and the sight of so blatant and jagged a thing that was yet so full of character appears to have had a liberating effect on all sorts of art styles associated with Paris, be it Cubism, Vorticism or Futurism.

PRECEDING PAGES: art on the Pont des Arts.
LEFT: Monet's Impressionist painting of Gare St-Lazare.
ABOVE: Edgar Degas's ballerinas.

matter was emphasised to such an extent that we may wonder that anyone ever thought of painting a simple view of a street.

Common sense did not always mix with high principles: Gustav Courbet (1819–77), who broke away from Classicism to lead a Realism movement, only wanting to paint what he could see with his own eyes, thought that life classes should extend beyond the human nude, to take in animals as well. However, instead of making excursions to the country, he had the animals brought to the studio – horses, cattle, the lot.

The aim of Edouard Manet (1832–83) was to make art belong to his own time and he became a forerunner for the Impressionists. But he did not like his studio, complaining that "everything that meets the eye is ridiculous – the light is wrong, the shadows are wrong…" Manet went out and about, painting life exactly and simply as he saw it, producing such masterpieces as the Buveur d'Absinthe, a true character study, and Musique aux Tuileries, a realistic portrait of Paris in the 19th century.

It was after Manet, in the early 20th century, that French painting – and the paintings of the many foreigners who came to live and work in Paris – became so domestic, be it rural or urban. From then on, studio life in the city changed completely. Artists rented their own space, where they lived as well as painted, and they met up with other leading lights in Paris to discuss ideas together.

First they gathered in Montmartre in a ramshackle building called the *Bateau Lavoir*, (so called because it looked like an old Seine laundry boat). It was in this humble setting that Cubism was born. Then they went to *La Ruche* (beehive) in the more sophisticated Montparnasse. Built from the remnants of the 1900 World Fair, a collection of studios was opened in 1902, which housed the likes of Picasso, Modigliani, Léger, Chagall, Soutine and the poet Apollinaire.

AN EYE FOR THE DANCING GIRLS

One of the most popular artists associated with Paris is Henri Toulouse-Lautrec (1864–1901), an aristocrat who led a Bohemian lifestyle in Montmartre. His artist's eye was a street eye, sharper than any in cafés, theatres, bars and brothels. And where was his art most often seen? In the street. His vibrant posters replaced layers of print wrapping the ventilation shafts and urinals of the capital. The painter also loved to entertain, always concocting new cocktails for his guests. His lover was Suzanne, the model for Renoir and Degas and whose son, Maurice Utrillo (1883–1955), became famous for his scenes of Montmartre.

The lure of the French capital

From the 1890s, as the city's fame spread, many artists flocked to Paris, a city of taste and filth, style and vulgarity, romance and prostitution, but above all, a city of tremendous energy. Talking of that time, one writer described the successful artist's lot: "A painter can become established more quickly than a notary's clerk: he does watercolours in albums, dresses like the Prince of Wales, paints slick portraits of ladies, leads the dancing. He pays his colour merchant in cash in order to get a discount, invests his money in the railways and, as soon as he is *hors concours*, marries the daughter of a wealthy if unscrupulous banker."

So obvious was Paris as the place to be at the end of the 19th century, that Pablo Picasso (1881–1973) used to claim that his journey there in 1900 was, in fact, just a halt on the way to London. It was as if he was afraid to admit to something as *obvious* as the lure of the French capital.

Although neither Picasso nor, to a lesser extent, Henri Matisse (1869–1954), two of the most influential painters of the 20th century, were known primarily for their landscape paint-

THE EIFFEL GARTER

Gustav Eiffel was also the inventor of the garter belt, which seems perfectly logical when you imagine his tower upside down. Doesn't it look like a stockinged leg?

Picasso's scenic paintings are mostly of the city during World War II, reflecting either the grey and depressing quality of life under an occupying army or the frantic relief of hope or news of victory. In his paintings of Notre Dame and the Ile de la Cité, we can detect his great sensitivity to the church's unique position, dominating an island. Picasso evokes from the church not only the intimate image of a woman, but also the inviolable heart of a nation.

ing, concentrating instead more on line and the human form, they could not resist Paris as a subject, especially Notre Dame.

Both artists' work tackles something of the intimate grandeur of the building, which is imposing not by size but rather by its intricate detail, not by scale but by rhythm. Clearly, these aspects of the church fascinated Matisse as he looked out at it from his studio and, from this, he produced one of his most abstract works, lush in its austerity.

FAR LEFT: Matisse's portrayal of Notre Dame.
EFT: Toulouse-Lautrec focused on Parisian society.
BOVE : Raoul Dufy's vision of Paris.

A charming vision

Raoul Dufy's vision of Paris is perhaps the most charming of all, for with deft simplicity he is able to conjure up the sheer jumble of impressions that is Paris. It is a touch as brisk as the city's traffic but as certain as the *joie de vivre* that is so peculiar to the place.

It seems typical that while Picasso travelled all the way from Barcelona to Paris to attend the World Fair of 1900, Dufy (1877– 1953) did not even take the trouble to stroll down the street to visit it. Dufy's pictures saunter in the shade, bask in the sun; his understanding is lazy, but it is understanding for all that and perfect for this romantic French city. ❐

PLACES

This section is a detailed guide to the entire city, with the principal sites cross-referenced by number to the maps

As Victor Hugo put it: "It is in Paris that the beating of Europe's heart is felt. Paris is the city of cities." Certainly, it is at the heart of France. In terms of urban sprawl, it is, in Europe, second only to London. Where matters of French administration, politics and cultural life are concerned, it plays an absolutely dominant role. It is also the world capital of chic. For all these reasons and more, Paris is so unlike much of the rest of France that it has been described as virtually a city-state in its own right.

Largely undamaged by two world wars, Paris has been created by centuries of inspired planning. Its street corners reek of history, its monuments and museums are well known to people from all over the world and its inhabitants are an endless source of controversy. In the French capital, every pavement is a theatre on which the drama of daily life is played out.

Perfectly preserved though it is, Paris is a city unafraid of change. I.M. Peï's pyramid in front of the Louvre and the massive development at La Défense are evidence of that. But there are regrets in this process of evolution – in the city where Voltaire was reputed to drink 40 cups of coffee a day at Le Procope, the café culture is threatened by the fast-food invasion, and the number of cafés has drastically fallen from a total of 12,000 at the beginning of the 1980s to fewer than 5,000 today.

Paris has a reputation for being a city of romance, a city of arts *par excellence* and a city of fun. There's endless entertainment here for the observant, who will learn as much about Paris and its inhabitants from walking the streets as from visiting the great museums.

The chapters that follow cover the key destinations on both banks of the Seine, as well as venturing further afield to outlying parks and markets, to Disneyland Paris and La Défense, and to destinations that can easily be visited in a day – the palace at Versailles, Monet's house at Giverny and the cathedral at Chartres.

This is a city that can easily be discovered on foot. But help is at hand for the weary: one of the beauties of Paris is it's superb public transport system – and it is thanks to the RER and SNCF that the region surrounding the capital is so easily accessible. ❐

PRECEDING PAGES: the view from Montmartre; village Paris; the historic booksellers, Shakespeare and Company; Henri de Miller's giant sculpture in the Jardin des Halles in front of the church of St-Eustache.
LEFT: the Eiffel Tower – a powerful sight by twilight.

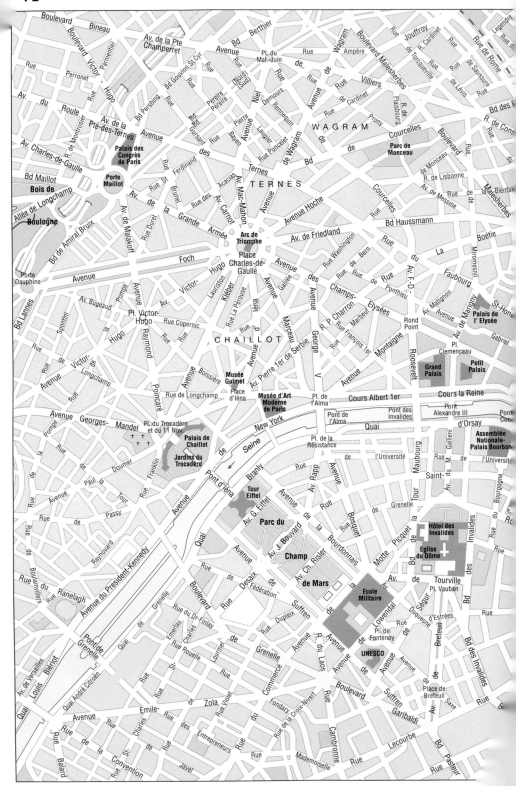

Paris

0   500 m

0   500 yds

MONTMARTRE

Cimetière de Montmartre
Moulin Rouge
St-Pierre
Basilique du Sacré-Cœur
Place de Clichy
St-Jean
Pl. Pigalle
Boulevard de Rochechouart
Gare du Nord
Gare de l'Est
Place du Colonel-Fabien
la Villette

Rue Notre-Dame de Lorette
Avenue Tredaine
Rue La Bruyère
Rue St-Lazare
Rue de Châteaudin
Folies Bergère
Rue Richer
St-Lazare
de Provence
Mathurins
Opéra
Ste-Marie-Madeleine
Bd des Capucines
Bd des Italiens
Haussmann
Bd Montmartre
Bd Poissonnière
Bd de Bonne Nouvelle
Bd St-Martin
Pl. de la République
Av. de la République
Boulevard Voltaire

Place Vendôme
Bibliothèque Nationale
R. des Petits Champs
St-Roch
Jardin du Palais Royal
Comédie Française
Palais Royal
Jardin des Tuileries
Jardin du Carrousel
Rivoli
Musée du Louvre
Bourse de Commerce
St-Eustache
Forum des Halles
Centre Georges Pompidou
St-Merri
Musée National des Techniques
MARAIS
Musée de l'Histoire de France
Musée Carnavalet
Pl. des Vosges
Place de la Bastille

Tuileries
Seine
Musée d'Orsay
Quai du Louvre
Pont Royal
Pont du Carrousel
Pont Neuf
Ecole Nationale Supérieure des Beaux-Arts
Institut de France
Palais de Justice
Hôtel de Ville
Hôtel d'Aumont
GERMAIN
St-Germain des Prés
St-Chapelle
Île de la Cité
Hôtel d'Aumont
R. St-André-des-Arts
Notre-Dame
Île St.-Louis
St-Sulpice
R. St-Sulpice
Boulevard
St-Julien-le-Pauvre
Quai de la Tournelle
Théâtre National de l'Odéon
Vaugirard
La Sorbonne
Germain
Palais du Luxembourg
Jardin du Luxembourg
Panthéon
Jardin des Plantes
Gare d'Austerlitz
Rue A.-Comte

Louvre and Grands Boulevards

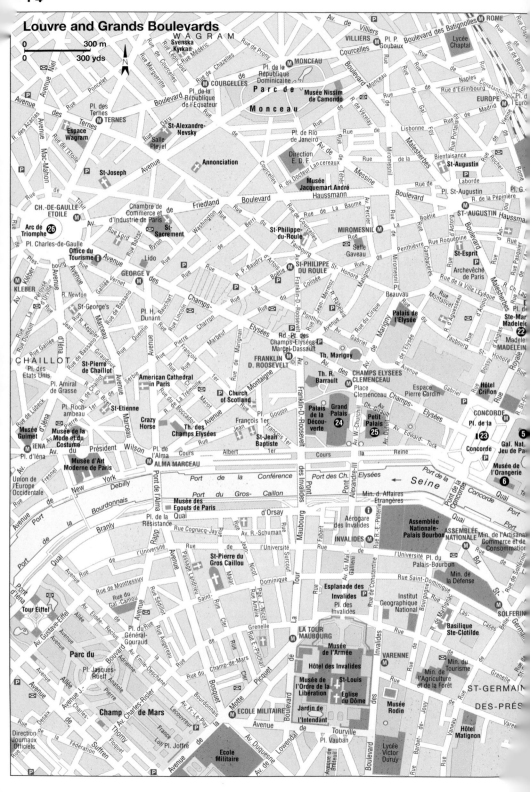

THE LOUVRE AND THE GRANDS BOULEVARDS

The royal part of Paris offers the world's largest museum of art, the ornamental Jardin des Tuileries, the elaborate Palais Royal, the opulence of the Opéra and elegant Champs-Elysées

O n the Seine's Right Bank expanses of beautifully laid out gardens stretch into ostentatious squares, and wide tree-lined boulevards overflow with designer boutiques and department stores, interspersed with royal palaces, arguably the world's most famous museum and an opulent opera house. The lairs of the most fashionable of fashion houses hide in between. Meticulously planned by Prefect Baron Haussmann, the elegant buildings, boulevards and open spaces engulf the visitor in 19th-century grandeur.

In this self-contained world, you can buy your luxurious outfit to wear to the luxurious restaurant which serves food bought from luxurious shops. At night, however, apart from the expensive sparkle of the Champs-Elysées and the area around the Opéra, this historically royal region is empty and strangely forlorn.

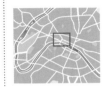

The Louvre – grand palace of art

Once the seat of royalty, the **Musée du Louvre ❶** (open daily 9am–6pm except Tues and some public holidays, Wed until 9.45pm; reduced entry fee Sun; first Sun of month admission free; tel: 01 40 20 51 51 or visit www.louvre.fr) has been the home of fine art since a colony of painters and sculptors moved into the empty halls after Louis XIV decamped to Versailles in 1682. The Louvre's art collection goes back even further, to 1516, when Francois I invited Leonardo da Vinci to be the Royal Court painter and he brought with him his masterpieces of the *Mona Lisa* and *Virgin of the Rocks*.

Originally built as a fortress in 1190 by King Philippe-Auguste to protect a weak link in his city wall, the Louvre was transformed into a royal château in the 1360s by Charles V, who established his extensive library in one of the towers. Successive monarchs added to it and destroyed parts until Louis XIV moved out leaving his extensions partly built. The squatters who consequently took up residence in the palace included Guillaume Coustou, sculptor of the *Marly Horses*, now one of the Louvre's main exhibits. A fine artistic reputation grew out of the decaying passageways and galleries and, in the 18th century, the fine arts academy, which had joined the Académie Française (*see page 197*) and other academic bodies in the royal apartments, set up a tradition of *salons* (*see page 98*) for artists to exhibit their work, lasting for more than 120 years.

During the Revolution, in a rare moment of creative fervour, the rebels decided to inaugurate the palace as a museum, ironically fulfilling the plans of Louis XVI, the king they had just beheaded. Opened in August 1793, the museum benefited from the growing collec-

LEFT: down the Champs-Elysées to the Louvre from the Arc de Triomphe. **BELOW:** postcards *circa* 1900.

tion of royal treasures, augmented by Napoleon's subsequent efforts to relocate much of Europe's artistic wealth, following victories in Italy, Austria and Germany. After Napoleon lost at Waterloo in 1815, many of the stolen masterpieces were reclaimed by their rightful owners.

Modern-day museum

In 1981, President François Mitterrand began a vast renovation of the museum, calling it the *Projet du Grand Louvre*. His first step was to move the Finance Ministry out of the **Richelieu Wing** to Bercy, in eastern Paris, to create more museum space. Opening in 1993, it doubled the size of the already enormous museum to make it unquestionably the world's biggest. Four years earlier, the controversial **Louvre Pyramid**, designed by the Chinese-American architect I.M. Peï over the new main entrance, was opened. A celebration of angles, the pyramid's 666 panes of glass are held together with stainless steel nodes and cables, reflecting and contrasting with and, to some minds, complementing the ancient curves of the surrounding main building. However, to traditionalists such modernism amid such historic beauty is a heresy. Occultists take comfort in the fact that the number of panes in the pyramid matches the sum of the numbers in the sun's magic square, advocating that it is a solar temple. It also forms part of the Royal Axis, or Triumphal Way, which lines up monuments, regal and triumphal, from the Louvre's Cour Carrée to the Grande Arche in La Défense.

Practical, as well as sparkling, the pyramid allows light to flood into the new underground area where you buy your ticket – if you don't already have a *Carte Musées* (*see page 278*) – and it also illuminates the area where shops, restaurants, cafés and an exhibition area, are situated. The exhibition area, called the

ABOVE: foundations of the Louvre fortress and keep discovered in 1984.
BELOW: underneath the Pyramid in the Louvre entrance hall.

Medieval Louvre, shows the palace at different stages of its development. It is also the new location for the Paris fashion shows (*see pages 54–55*). However, the pyramid entrance does become very congested, so try to avoid peak times such as Sundays or after 3pm, when ticket prices are reduced. You could also use the entrances at 99 Rue de Rivoli or Porte de Lions on the Quai des Tuileries, through which cars pass, and go down through the shopping arcade, **Galeries du Carrousel** under the arch, or approach it from the Palais-Royal–Musée du Louvre Métro. There is an underground car park (open daily 7am–11pm) off Avenue du Général-Lemonnier.

Map, pages 114/5

A tour of the treasures

From the central **Hall Napoléon**, escalators whisk visitors off to various parts of the building, which is divided into three separate sections: Sully (east wing), Denon (south wing) and Richelieu (north wing), with the exhibits on three levels in numbered areas. Although star attractions are well signposted, the free map provided is essential.

A good exhibition to start with is the **Medieval Louvre** *en route* to the Crypte Sully under the Cour Carrée, where the remains of **Philippe-Auguste's fort and keep**, and some of the artefacts discovered in the recent excavations to build the underground complex, can be seen. Pieces of Charles VI's parade helmet were found at the bottom of the well in the keep in 1984 and a replica of the helmet is now on display in the **Salle St-Louis**.

Up on the ground floor of the Sully and Richelieu wings are the **Oriental Antiquities**, which include the Mesopotamian prayer statuette of Ebih-il (around 2400 BC), which has striking lapiz lazuli eyes, and the black basalt Babylonian

ABOVE: *Venus de Milo* in Sully Wing.
BELOW LEFT: Louvre and Triumphal Way.
BELOW RIGHT: the Galerie d'Apollon.

The enigmatic smile of the Mona Lisa *was described by Lawrence Durrell as that "of a woman who has just dined off her husband".*

BELOW: view of the Jardin des Tuileries.

Code of Hammurabi (1792–1750 BC), one of the world's first legal documents.

On the south side of the Sully Wing you will find the graceful Hellenic statue *Venus de Milo* (2nd century BC), purchased by the French government for 6,000FF in 1820 from the Greek island of Milos. From here, head on into the Denon Wing to see the Etruscan *Sarcophagus of the Reclining Couple* (*see pages 134–35*). Continuing along the ground floor level, you will reach the Italian sculpture section and its famous masterpieces, such as Michelangelo's *Slaves* (1513–1520), sculpted in marble for Pope Julius II's tomb but never finished, and Canova's neoclassical *Psyche Revived by the Kiss of Cupid* (1793).

In the **Grande Galerie**, immediately above on the first floor, is the work of art that everyone wants to see for themselves, the *Mona Lisa* (1503) – *La Joconde* in French. The first incumbent in the Louvre, Leonardo da Vinci's small painting of a Florentine noblewoman rests securely behind glass since her knife assault several years ago. But don't ignore the many other masterpieces hanging in this gallery, including more by Leonardo and works by Raphael, Titian and Veronese, as well as Caravaggio's *The Fortune Teller* (about 1594).

On the same floor is the **French School of 19th-century painting**, with work by Romanticist Eugène Delacroix (*see page 192*), which starts at the top of the Escalier Daru opposite the *Winged Victory of Samothrace* (2nd century BC), the Hellenistic stone figurehead commemorating a victory at sea. The Spanish School, with masterpieces by El Greco and Goya, can be found close by.

The second floor of the Richelieu and Sully wings are completely given over to paintings and include Rembrandt's masterpiece of his second wife, *Bathsheba Bathing* (1654), and the Dutch painter Jan Vermeer's telling portrayal of domestic life in the 1660s, *The Lacemaker*.

The beautifully renovated Richelieu Wing houses a vast collection of French sculpture on the ground floor and is focused around two splendid sculpture courts, starring Guillaume Coustou's two giant *Marly Horses*.

Also part of the Louvre collection is the **Musée des Arts Decoratifs ❷** (open daily except Mon and Tues; entrance fee; for further details, tel: 01 42 60 32 14 or visit their website: www.ucad.fr) in the northwest wing. The Renaissance and Middle Ages galleries were renovated for the year 2000 and the rest of the museum is due to be renovated for 20002. The museum presents an exhaustive survey of interior design from medieval tapestries to extravagant Empire furniture and a marvellous exhibition of 20th-century design including Art Nouveau and Art Deco. Note especially the wonderful Art Nouveau bedroom by Hector Guimard, designer of the Métro entrances (*see page 133*). Further along in the Pavillon de Marsan, which with the Pavillon de Flore on the south side is all that is left of Catherine de Médicis' Tuileries Palace, is the **Musée des Arts de la Mode et du Textile ❸** (open daily 11am–6pm ; Wed till 10pm; weekends 10am–6pm; closed Mon; entrance fee). Here on display are the fruits of Paris fashion from the 16th century until today as well as a large turnover of temporary exhibitions.

Opened in 1999, in time for the millennium celebrations, the **Musée de la Publicité** (open 11am–6pm Tue, Thurs, Fri, until 9pm Wed, 10am–6pm weekends; closed Mon; tel: 01 44 55 57 50 or visit www.museedelapub.org) is also situated within the Louvre and well worth a visit. The new exhibition space, designed by architect Jean Nouvel, is home to a rich collection of posters and newspaper and radio advertisements, complemented by interactive displays, slide shows and videos.

Map, pages 114/5

Aristide Maillol (1861–1944) started sculpting at the age of 40, concentrating his efforts on large, bronze, nude women – 20 of which adorn the Tuileries.

BELOW: drama in stone in the Tuileries.

André Le Notre (1613–1700) is France's most celebrated gardener. Creator of the French formal garden, he designed those at Versailles, the Champs-Elysées and the Tuileries, where his family had gardened for three generations.

BELOW: part of Monet's *Les Nymphéas* hanging in the Orangerie.

A walk in the Tuileries

The **Jardin des Tuileries** ❹ offers shade, statues, fountains and a place to relax and pretend to read *Le Monde*. Once a rubbish tip and a clay quarry for tiles (*tuiles*, hence the name, the Tuileries), the garden was initially created, in 1564, for Catherine de Médicis in front of her palace, to remind her of her native Tuscany. In 1664, Louis XIV's celebrated gardener André Le Nôtre, redesigned the park with his predilection for straight lines and clipped trees. It was then opened to the public and quickly became the first fashionable outdoor area in which to see and be seen, triggering the appearance of the first deckchairs and public toilets. One of the earliest hot-air balloon flights was launched from this garden in 1783. Now, after several years of disruption, the Tuileries have been renovated as part of the *Projet du Grand Louvre*, reflecting Le Nôtre's original design and incorporating a new sloping terrace and enclosed garden.

Approaching the gardens from the Louvre, you pass through the **Arc de Triomphe du Carrousel**, the smallest of the three arches (the others being the Arc de Triomphe and Grande Arche at La Défense) on the Triumphal Way. Erected in 1808 by Napoleon to commemorate his Austrian victories, this arch is a garish imitation of Roman arches and the four horses galloping across its summit are copies of four gilded bronze horses, stolen by Napoleon from St Mark's Square in Venice to decorate his memorial. After his downfall in 1815, the originals were returned.

In front of the arch, where the Tuileries Palace used to stand linking the Pavillon de Marsan and the Pavillon de Flore, is a collection of sculptures of sensuous nudes, produced between 1900 and 1938 by Aristide Maillol (*see page 209*), adorning the ornamental pools. More works by sculptors such as Rodin and Le

Pautre, along with copies of ancient works and late 20th-century sculpture added for the millennium, can be found scattered around.

Continue westwards along the Terrasse du Bord de l'Eau, where Napoleon's children played under the watchful gaze of their emperor father, to the hexagonal pool – still a favourite spot for children with boats, and ducks with attitudes. Here, facing each other, are the twin museums of the **Galerie National du Jeu de Paume ❺** (open daily; weekday afternoons; Tues till 9.30pm; closed Mon; entrance fee; tel: 01 47 03 12 50) and the **Musée de l'Orangerie ❻** (closed for renovation until 2002).

Built by Napoleon III as a real tennis court, the Jeu de Paume, following the Impressionists' migration to the Musée d'Orsay (*see pages 211–12*), now houses temporary modern art exhibitions. The Orangerie is one of the city's hidden gems, a beautifully harmonious museum, containing some of the world's finest paintings. The list of canvases is impressive: 22 Soutines, 14 Cézannes – including one of *The Bathers* which was cut into three, then stuck back together again (look for the joins) – 24 Renoirs, 28 Derains and a pile of Picassos, Matisses and Utrillos. Yet the masterpieces of the museum are, undoubtedly, Monet's *Les Nymphéas* (*Waterlilies*), paintings of the Impressionist leader's waterlily pond in his beloved garden at Giverny (*see page 253*). Eight huge canvases drown the spectator in colour and movement, subtly displayed in a room purposefully built for them after Monet's gift to the state at the 1918 Armistice.

Down the Rue de Rivoli

The arcaded **Rue de Rivoli**, topped with neoclassical apartments, was built to commemorate Napoleon's victory over the Austrians at Rivoli, north of Verona,

Map, pages 114/5

The Tuileries Palace, which had housed Louis XIV, Napoleon Bonaparte, Louis-Philippe and finally Napoleon III, was burnt down by members of the Paris Commune in 1871 (see page 36), when three centuries of art went up in smoke.

BELOW: Rue de Rivoli, named after one of Napoleon's victories in 1797.

TIP

Each evening, 45 minutes before curtain-rise at the Comédie Française, 112 tickets are sold at low prices at the booth just off the square on Rue de Montpensier behind the theatre.

BELOW: playing on Daniel Buren's columns in the courtyard of the Palais Royal.

in 1797 but was completed well after the Emperor's demise. Planned for victory marches along the Triumphal Way, the street now contains souvenir and luxury shops, cafés and bookstores, including **W.H. Smith**, for English books and newspapers, and Angelina, a late 19th-century Viennese *salon de thé*, which once played host to the likes of intellectual novelist Marcel Proust and fashion icon Coco Chanel.

From the Place de la Concorde head east towards Rue St-Roch, or you can take the Métro to the Tuileries. The harmonious church of **St-Roch ❼** is on the corner of Rue St-Honoré, running parallel with Rue de Rivoli. André Le Nôtre is buried here. In 1795, Royalist insurgents were shot dead on the church steps on the orders of a young, up-and-coming artillery general named Napoleon Bonaparte and you can still see the bullet holes today.

A few minutes walk further on, you reach **Place André Malraux**, which has been a focal point of Parisian life since the Middle Ages. It was here that Joan of Arc stood at the gates of Paris in 1429, attempting to win back the capital from the English. She was struck by a sniper's arrow and taken to a nearby house (No. 4 on the square) to be bandaged. Her quest was in vain and 10-year-old Henry VI of England was crowned King of France in Notre Dame in 1431, while Joan was burnt at the stake in Rouen.

Adjoining the square, on Place Colette, stands the **Comédie Française ❽**, the French national theatre. Originating from Molière's acting troupe, the company has been established here since 1799. Napoleon passed a decree in 1812, still applicable today, placing it under state control with a director nominated by the government. But his interest in the theatre was far from passive, as he was having an affair with the company's leading lady, Mademoiselle Mars.

MOLIÈRE – A GREAT MAN OF COMEDY

Born Jean Baptise Poquelin in Paris in 1622, Molière, playwright, actor, director and stage manager, created 12 of the most durable satirical comedies of all time, including *Tartuffe* (1669) and *Bourgeois Gentilhomme* (1671). After studying law, he formed an acting troupe with members of the Béjart family in 1643, whose daughter he was in love with. The troupe had an unsuccessful start, but after Molière polished up his act in the provinces, they became Louis XIV's official entertainers. In 1673, at 51, Molière collapsed on stage while acting the title role in his play *Le Malade Imaginaire,* in which an old man feigns death; he died a few hours later. In 1680 the King merged his company with a rival's, creating a united Parisian theatre called the Comédie Française. The great thespian lived at 40 Rue de Richelieu and is commemorated by the **Molière Fountain** close by.

The Palais Royal – den of state

Stretching its elegant columns and arcades away from the Louvre, the **Palais Royal** ❾ is a place of repose and refinement. Built on the site of a Roman bath house by Cardinal Richelieu, prime minister from 1624, as a palace for himself, he left it to the Crown in 1642, when it became the childhood home of Louis XIV. At the beginning of the 18th century, the dukes of Orléans took up residence and the palace became a den of debauchery, as a result of the infamous "libertines' suppers" regularly thrown by the Regent, Philippe d'Orléans. Gambling and prostitution became commonplace as, by order of the Dukes of Orléans, police were forbidden to enter the palace precincts. In 1780, to compensate for his family's free spending, Louis-Philippe built shops around the palace, to let at exorbitant prices. After the Revolution, the palace was turned into a gaming house and, although Louis-Philippe moved back in 1815, gambling continued until after he became King in 1830. The Commune (*see page 36*) almost destroyed the palace in 1871 and the state took control, starting restoration work the following year.

Today, the Palais Royal houses government offices and in the Cour d'Honneur, the main courtyard, stand 250 black-and-white striped columns of varying heights, erected by artist Daniel Buren in 1986. Once a meeting place for some of the most important protagonists of the Revolution, the garden is now a tranquil oasis and in the arcades are art galleries and specialist shops, selling costumes, coins, porcelain and antiques. Hiding under the arches at 17 Rue Beaujolais is the most beautiful restaurant in Paris, **Le Grand Véfour**, which opened in 1784 and has fed the likes of Revolutionary Camille Desmoulins, the Emperor Napoleon and writers Alphonse Lamartine and Victor Hugo.

Map, pages 114/5

By 1830, suicides in the garden of the Palais Royal were commonplace, as gamblers sought certain escape from their huge debts. Prostitution was so rife that guidebooks were produced detailing the wares on offer.

BELOW: browsing in the arcades of the Palais Royal.

Exploring the palace streets

Directly north of the Palais Royal, beyond the Palais Royal vaudeville theatre, sits the **Bibliothèque Nationale de France – Richelieu** (open daily; closed Sun and pub. hols; free). Formerly home to every book published in France since 1500, most of the collection has now been rehoused in the massive, new, ultra-modern premises at Tolbiac, near the Gare de Austerlitz as part of Mitterrand's *grands projets*. The library's book collection is one of the biggest in the world and includes Charlemagne's illuminated bible and original manuscripts from Villon, Rabelais, Hugo and Proust. The Richelieu building is keeping the specialised departments of prints, drawings, maps, music and manuscripts. The main reading room, designed by Henri Labrouste in 1863, is an architectural masterpiece. Downstairs, the permanent museum, **Cabinet des Médailles et Antiques** (open afternoons; entrance fee), contains *objets d'art* from the royal collections taken during the Revolution.

Opposite the library, across Rue de Richelieu, is the charming small **Square Louvois**, containing one of the most beautiful fountains in Paris, which represents the four "female" rivers of France – La Loire, La Seine, La Garonne and La Saône. East of the library are the early 19th-century aristocratic, covered arcades **Galerie Colbert** and **Galerie Vivienne** . Recently renovated, both arcades hint at past grandeur, fitted out with intricate brass lamps, graceful glass canopies and marbled mosaic floors. Sip a strong coffee at the expansive copper counter of the refurbished Le Grand Colbert, an 1830s' brasserie at 4 Rue Vivienne and pop into No. 6 to check out Jean-Paul Gaultier's latest creations. Tea addicts will find a welcome repose at A Priori Thé, in the Galerie Vivienne, a *salon de thé* which spreads out into the gallery.

ABOVE: a hard day's shopping.
BELOW: the stylish, 19th-century Galerie Colbert.

From the Galerie Colbert, the Rue des Petits-Champs points eastward to the 17th-century crescents of **Place des Victoires** ⑫. This genteel square, guarded by a mounted Louis XIV, is now home to the elite of the Parisian fashion world such as Kenzo, Stefan Kelian and Thierry Mügler. On your way there, look out for **Willi's Wine Bar** (13 Rue des Petits-Champs), which offers a fine selection of wines and cheeses.

Heading south down Rue Croix-des-Petits-Champs for about five minutes, you will reach the most beautiful and atmospheric passageway in Paris, **Galerie Véro-Dodat** ⑬ (opposite Rue Montesquieu), with its polished mahogany facades, brass lamps and musty skylights. When it opened in 1826, the arcade was fitted with the new technology of the day, gas lighting. Le Véro-Dodat Bistro serves wholesome dishes, expertly executed by Monsieur Gomond and served by his wife.

A little further south on the Place du Palais-Royal is the massive **Louvre des Antiquaires** ⑭. Once a department store, it is now packed with antiques shops. This area, once so congested, was cleared on the orders of Napoleon following an attempt on his life in 1800, when he was First Consul. Two Royalists planted explosives in a cart, but the bomb missed his carriage. Not wishing to repeat the experience, when he became emperor, Napoleon razed 50 houses.

Along the Grands Boulevards

Stretching from the Opéra to the Place de la République, the Grands Boulevards are 3 km (2 miles) of wide avenues incorporating boulevards Haussmann, Montmartre, Poissonière, St-Denis and St-Martin. The city's strolling grounds since 1705, the Grands Boulevards are aptly named. Tree-lined, bustling and endowed

Map, pages 114/5

ABOVE: exotic sculpture for sale. **BELOW:** the genteel Place des Victoires.

Shirley MacLaine roamed the red light district around Boulevard St-Denis, observing Parisian low life for her role as a prostitute in the film Irma la Douce.

BELOW: publicity for the wax museum, Musée Grévin.

with huge department stores, cinemas and cafés that spill out on to the pavements, they represent a particularly colourful side of Paris.

The Grands Boulevards have a colourful past. When Louis XIV tore down Charles V's walls around Paris, he created wide, open spaces, bordered with trees, for his subjects. A raised road was constructed, four carriages wide, which became known as the "boulevard". By the 19th century, the west end of the thoroughfare was the reserve of the rich, and the east had become the playground of the workers of industrial Paris – vaudeville theatres, circuses, waxworks, bars and brothels competed side by side. By 1830, the theatres played so many tumultuous melodramas that the area became known as the "Boulevard du Crime".

This end still maintains a nefarious reputation – the area around Boulevard St-Denis hosts 80 percent of the capital's prostitutes. Actress Shirley MacLaine, perfecting her role for Billy Wilder's *Irma la Douce*, spent a week here, observing the life of a Parisian prostitute among the neon sex shops and massage parlours. Paradoxically, Rue St-Denis was the road taken by the Kings of France to Notre Dame for their coronation, as well as their final route north, for burial in the basilica of St-Denis (*see page 250*).

At 10 Boulevard Montmartre, vestiges of popular 19th-century entertainment can be found at the **Musée Grévin** ⓯ (open daily in school holidays; afternoons otherwise; entrance fee; tel: 01 47 70 85 05 or visit www.musee-grevin.com). A light-hearted waxwork museum, full of cheerfully incompatible figures – from Marie-Antoinette, Michael Jackson and National Front leader Jean-Marie Le Pen to Lara Croft and French goalkeeper Fabien Bartez, both added in December 1999 – and a hall of mirrors, it is set in an old theatre, whose original decor of sumptuous upholstery and polished brass has been preserved.

COUR DES MIRACLES

Place du Caire (off the Rue d'Aboukir) is rich in mementoes of Napoleon's campaign in Egypt, including sphinxes and hieroglyphics. It was here that the Cour des Miracles was established In the 1600s, described by Victor Hugo in his famous novel *The Hunchback of Notre Dame*, as the central meeting point for Parisian beggars. By day, these ruffians went out on the streets convincingly handicapped, blind and deaf. At night, they returned, shed their wooden legs and eye patches, and embarked on riotous orgies – hence the ironic miracles. The police did not dare enter this criminal enclave until 1667, when one brave police chief emptied it of the scurrilous beggars in 10 minutes, by threatening that the last nine to leave would be hanged.

Today, the square, just across from Métro Sentier, is the centre of a clothes manufacturing area and contains countless low-cost clothing shops.

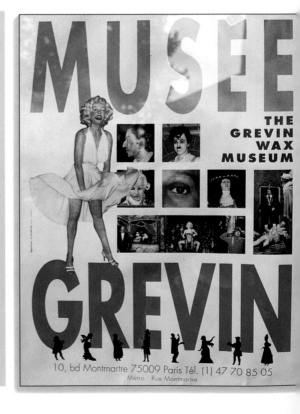

To the right of the museum is the **Passage Jouffroy**, with gift and bookshops. Across the boulevard, the **Passage des Panoramas** ⑯ is a bustling network of arcades. Stop at the window of Stern, the engraver, whose decor has not changed since 1840. The **Galerie des Variétés** still shrills to operatic tenors, reliving the golden years of the 1806 **Théâtre des Variétés** close by, and of Offenbach's finest arias. On emerging from the arcades head south towards the French stock exchange at the neoclassical, colonnaded **Bourse des Valeurs** ⑰ (afternoon guided tours daily; entrance fee) built in 1808 to Napoleon's specifications.

Going to the Opéra

Behind the Opéra runs the busy **Boulevard Haussmann**, which is laden with shops, including two main *grands magasins* (department stores). The green domes of **Printemps** compete with the sparkling cupola of **Galeries Lafayette** (*see page 71*). You can approach the Opéra from here or from the charming Boulevard des Italiens. On the left is **L'Opéra Comique** ⑱, once home to the popular 19th-century operetta composers of Offenbach's generation. In the adjoining Boulevard des Capucines, where the first motion pictures were shown in 1865 and where the music hall star Mistinguett used to live, is the **Musée du Parfum** ⑲ (open daily; closed Sunday; free). Here, in the former Théâtre des Capucines, is a fine collection of rare *objets* retracing 5,000 years of perfume.

Place de l'Opéra is not just a setting for Charles Garnier's magnificent opera house. Laid out by town planner Baron Haussmann during the Second Empire and criticised for being far too grandiose, this square is the intersection of six roads, and now the venue for a non-stop contest between pedestrians and traffic. Luxury shops and hotels line the busy square and the **Café de la Paix**, adjacent

Map, pages 114/5

BELOW: the Opéra lords over the chic Café de la Paix.

Beneath the auditorium of the Opéra lies an underground lake, draining water from the foundations. This inspired Gaston Leroux to write The Phantom of the Opéra *in which Erik, while working on the foundations, creates an underground palace on the lake.*

BELOW: Napoleon looks down over the Place Vendôme.

to the Opéra, ranks among the capital's most fashionable, most expensive and most crowded watering-holes.

Opened in 1875, the **Opéra** ⑳ (currently undergoing restoration to the front and back, although this does not prevent visitors from looking around the fabulous interior; tel: 01 40 01 22 63 for details) is predictably resplendent, with a team of gold leaf statues perched on the roof and monumental steps. Garnier who won the commission to build an opera house in a competition, intended it to be the model for a Napoleon III style of architecture but, as it broke away from the normal Classical vein of that time, it didn't get much of a following.

On the Rue Scribe side of the building, the Emperor's Pavilion now houses a library and museum. Initially, it enabled direct access from carriage to the royal box, thus reducing the risk of assassination. Underneath is an underground lake providing a perfect setting for many a tale – true or legendary. Inside, the deco is thickly ornate. If you cannot attend a performance, a tour of the interior will give you a glimpse of the pomp – Garnier's grand marble staircase and the masterpiece of a ceiling, painted by Marc Chagall in 1964. Now referred to as the Opéra Garnier since the opening of the Opéra Bastille in 1989 (*see page 165*) the theatre is the home of the Ballet de l'Opéra National de Paris, with opera and concert performances divided between the two opera houses.

From here, the Avenue de l'Opéra yawns down to the Palais Royal. Once the site of a slum neighbourhood, razed in the replanning of Paris, the avenue became a prestigious thoroughfare after its completion in 1878. Today, it contains tourist shops, whereas the Rue de la Paix, which leads south to Place Vendôme a short distance away, is one long, dazzling shop window for gold cards, where Cartier rubs shoulders with airline offices and the Hotel Westminster

AUSTERLITZ COLUMN

Napoleon had 1,200 cannons (captured in 1805 at the Battle of Austerlitz) melted down to make the column (right), which stands in the Place Vendôme, after the statue of Louis XIV was torn down during the Revolution. A copy of Trajan's Column in Rome, with Napoleon as Caesar on top, the 44-metre (140-ft) monument, decorated with battle scenes has proved a political yardstick. The fall of the First Empire brought the fall of the statue and, during the 100 days that Napoleon tried to regain power, a statue of Henri IV was erected there. Louis XVIII then hoisted a huge *fleur de lys* flag up on top of the column. Louis-Philippe reinstalled Napoleon, in military garb, to his perch, only for him to be toppled, supposedly by the painter Gustav Courbet, into a carefully arranged pile of manure during the 1871 Commune. The Third Republic restored it, requisitioning the exiled Courbet's paintings to pay for it.

The recently renovated expanse of **Place Vendôme** , which is dominated by Napoleon on top of his milky-green column, is ornamentally chic, resounding with every step of Italian shoes on polished marble. The 17th-century facades remained mere facades for half a century, following the construction of the square in 1685 as a display case for Girardon's statue of Louis XIV, which was replaced by Napoleon's Austerlitz Column. Like a film set, the walls had no buildings behind them, until, gradually, the rich and influential filled up the empty spaces.

Today, the square exudes concentrated wealth. Here are jewellers Boucheron, Van Cleef & Arpels. Here, too, are institutions such as the J.P. Morgan merchant bank, and **The Ritz** at No. 15. Hemingway once hoped that heaven would be as good as the Ritz; his ghost still haunts the bar, which is named after him – prices have unfortunately risen since Ernest's day. Now the hotel has earned world-wide notoriety through being where Diana, Princess of Wales, spent her last hours before her fateful car journey with the hotel owner's son, Dodi al-Fayed, in August 1997.

Place de la Concorde via La Madeleine's luxuries

Located close to Place Vendôme and reached via the chic Faubourg St-Honoré, the church of **La Madeleine** rises classically from the midst of the roaring traffic and expensive shops. Its temple facade is Athenian, and its interior gloomily Italian. It was almost a railway station or a bank before being dedicated in 1842.

In the surrounding Place de la Madeleine are the food halls of the rich and famous – Fauchon, Hédiard and La Maison de la Truffe (*see page 73*). Gucci

*A flock of fashion designers have their principal houses in **Rue Faubourg St-Honoré** (see page 72): Christian Lacroix at No. 73, Sonia Rykiel at No. 70, Yves St Laurent at No. 38 and Japanese Ashida at No. 34. For the best in scarves and leather goods, Hermès at No. 24 is worth saving up for.*

BELOW: Mohamed al-Fayed's Ritz Hotel in Place Vendôme.

Map, pages 114/5

ABOVE: guarding the Palais d'Elysée.
BELOW: the Unknown Soldier lies under the Arc de Triomphe.

stands proud on the western side. On the eastern side of the square is the charming Marché aux Fleurs Madeleine (open daily; closed Mon).

From La Madeleine, Rue Royale runs past the bullet-proof security of Maxim's restaurant to Place de la Concorde. In the **Hotel de Crillon** on the right, Benjamin Franklin signed the Treaty of Friendship between the newly formed United States of America and King Louis XVI in 1778. A few minutes away is the **Palais d'Elysée**, home of the French president.

Place de la Concorde ❷❸ was originally marshland, which offered the architect, Jacques-Ange Gabriel, much scope for grandeur. His square has been the site of many major historical events since its completion in 1763, most importantly, the decapitation of Louis XVI by Revolutionaries in January 1793.

The guillotine stood near the statue of Brest, representing one of the eight largest towns in France, where it still is possible to imagine Louis's calm words as the blade was raised: "May my blood bring happiness to France."

Standing majestically in the middle of chaos, the central obelisk was a gift from the Viceroy of Egypt in 1829 to Charles X. The 3,300-year-old column weighs 220 tonnes and took four years to reach Paris.

The Champs-Elysées – the world's most famous avenue

Since its recent facelift, with a new row of trees, underground parking and legislation banning the tacky facades of fast-food joints, the **Champs-Elysées** (Elysian Fields), the vast avenue from the Place de la Concorde to the Arc de Triomphe on the Triumphal Way, is looking elegant again. Once a bog, until Marie de Médici cut a carriageway through it in 1616, the avenue was landscaped 50 years later by Le Nôtre but, in 1814, the occupying Russians felled

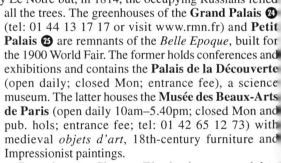

all the trees. The greenhouses of the **Grand Palais** ❷❹ (tel: 01 44 13 17 17 or visit www.rmn.fr) and **Petit Palais** ❷❺ are remnants of the *Belle Epoque*, built for the 1900 World Fair. The former holds conferences and exhibitions and contains the **Palais de la Découverte** (open daily; closed Mon; entrance fee), a science museum. The latter houses the **Musée des Beaux-Arts de Paris** (open daily 10am–5.40pm; closed Mon and pub. hols; entrance fee; tel: 01 42 65 12 73) with medieval *objets d'art*, 18th-century furniture and Impressionist paintings.

Crowning the Champs-Elysées is a memorial to megalomania, the **Arc de Triomphe** ❷❻ (open daily: Nov–Mar 10am-10.30pm daily; April–Oct 9.30am–11pm; closed pub. hols; entrance free; tel: 01 43 80 31 31). Commissioned by Napoleon in 1806, the ornately carved arch wasn't completed until after his death. Napoleon's chance to pass under the real thing came when his body was triumphantly returned to Paris for reburial in Les Invalides in 1840.

Beneath the arch, the Unknown Soldier was laid to rest in 1920 and, in 1923, the eternal flame was lit. It is rekindled each evening at 6.30, with a wreath-laying ceremony. In 1962, a man was arrested for frying eggs over the flame, but more daring deeds date back to 1919 when a biplane flew through the arch. From the top of the Arc de Triomphe, the view is breathtaking. Paris stretches to the horizon, humming and enticing.

The Métro

Deep beneath the streets of Paris there exists another city, a subterranean society with its own shops, cafés, market stalls, hairdressers, banking facilities, musicians, artists, beggars and pickpockets, even its own police force and its own micro climate. Temperatures here occasionally exceed 30°C (86°F), while wind speeds through the tunnels can reach up to 40 km (25 miles) per hour.

In Luc Besson's 1985 thriller, *Subway*, audiences had a glimpse of this surreal world and the kind of eccentric characters who have made the Métro their home. In real life, it is a sad statistic that every night around 1,000 people take refuge underground, most because they have nowhere else to go.

Construction of the Métro began in 1898. The first line, precisely 10.3 km (6.4 miles) long between Porte de Vincennes and Porte Maillot, opened on 19 July 1900. Within a year it had carried over 15 million passengers. Since then, the Métro has extended its routes in every direction and, today, it is widely hailed as the world's cheapest, cleanest and most efficiently run underground system, carrying over 3.5 million passengers daily along over 200 km (124 miles) of track to 370 stations on 14 metro lines, 5 RER lines and 2 train lines.

The massive station at Châtelet–Les Halles is the hub of the whole network. Five Métro lines and three RER commuter lines meet here, disgorging a quarter of a million passengers daily into its labyrinth of corridors. As you search this nightmarish warren for the exit, you may wonder if you will ever come up for air. Trudging the 75 km (47 miles) of corridors and 60 km (37 miles) of platforms, it seems unsurprising that the Parisian's average body weight is among the lowest in the industrialised world.

Métro stations abound in the city with no point being further than 500 metres (550 yds) away. Many entrances retain their Art Nouveau features, designed by the late-19th century architect Hector Guimard, whose work is recognisable by flowing lines and whiplash motifs, evoking the growth of plants. Two notable entrances still covered by his beautiful cast iron and glass pavilions are at the stations of Porte Dauphine and Abbesses.

Underground, the walls are mostly covered in white tiles, apart from a few stations such as St Michel, which has a mozaic ceiling, and Bastille whose platforms are decorated with scenes from the Revolution (*see page 164*).

The average Parisian commuter spends a year and four months of his or her life below ground. In an attempt to make this time slightly more bearable, the RATP (the organisation that runs the Métro network and the buses) organises a diverse programme of cultural events, from photography exhibitions to fashion shows, classical concerts to puppet theatre. Less organised are the buskers, profiting from the perfect acoustics.

Back home in Birmingham, England, or Knoxville, Tennessee, you may find yourself missing the whiff of that distinctive aroma of gorgonzola and old socks, so redolent of the Métro. Then you will know that Paris has truly worked its way into your heart. ❏

RIGHT: many of the Métro entrances retain their distinctive Art Nouveau features.

TREASURES OF THE LOUVRE

The largest palace in Europe, the Louvre has assembled an incomparable collection of old masters, sculptures and antiquities

One of the world's greatest museums, the Louvre is immense in scale, the size of its collections (over 36,000 pieces on display and over 410,000 in its collection as a whole) and the crowds that invariably throng its galleries (over 5 million visitors each year), make it one of the more challenging Parisian sights. It is impossible to try to see everything in one visit, although many people manage to cram in the edited highlights in one morning. This, however, does little justice to the wealth of exhibits, which range from European sculpture and painting to antiquities, decorative arts and objects.

HISTORY OF THE COLLECTION

The Louvre's collection was built up through patronage, gift-giving, requisition and other methods of appropriation.

François I (pictured above, by Jean Clouet) was a Renaissance king who amassed a fine array of mostly Italian contemporary and classical works, and patronised artists such as Leonardo da Vinci. Louis XIV made patronage a royal duty and added to the collection. Nationalisation of most French works of art after the Revolution led to the Musée de la Rèpublique being opened to the public in 1793. The greatest contribution to the Museum was made by Napoleon I, who brought back the spoils of his campaigns. Louis XVIII acquired works including the Venus de Milo, but in 1848 the Louvre once again became State property.

◁ **DYING SLAVE**
One of a pair of sculptures by Michelangelo, thought to represent the Arts, held captive by Death, after the death of Pope Julius II, a great arts patron.

▷ **THE BATHERS**
It is thought that Fragonard painted this canvas in the 1760s following his first trip to Italy. Fragonard was greatly influenced by Rubens in his use of colour, the fullness of his figures, and the painting's sensual and joyous theme was enhanced by the use of scumbles and glazes. Donated in 1869, the canvas is today part of the museum's comprehensive collection of European painting.

△ **OBJETS D'ART**
This 13th-century reliquary of St Francis of Assisi is one of the fabulous items found in the eclectic department of Objets d'Art.

▷ **ANTIQUITIES**
During the 18th and 19th centuries, antiquities were seen as the greatest art form, although the Louvre's core collection contains pieces which belonged to François I.

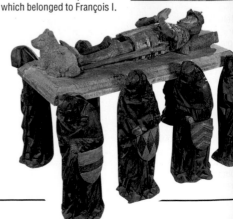

CASTLE, PRISON AND PALACE

The Louvre building, thought to be named after an area where wolves were hunted, has been enlarged and remodelled by French rulers for more than 800 years. The first building on the site was Philippe-Auguste's 12th-century fortified castle, known popularly as the "Tour de Paris", which contained the state treasury, archives and the royal storeroom. It also served as a prison. As medieval Paris grew, and the monarchy established other residences, the Louvre's importance declined.

In 1527, François I commissioned a Renaissance palace – the first example of French Classical architecture – to replace the château. By the end of the 17th century there was hardly an original stone left standing. The buildings surrounding the Cour Carrée predate 1715, and comprise the oldest parts of the building. In the 19th century, Napoleon I added the Galerie du Nord, and the buildings that flank the north and south sides of the Cour Napoleon date from the time of Napoleon III.

The most recent addition to the Louvre's landscape is I.M. Pei's dramatic glass pyramid, which has become the museum's 20th-century emblem.

ONTAINEBLEAU SCHOOL

16th-century painting of Duchess of Villars and rielle d'Estrée, attributed e School of Fontaine-u, is a fine example of the popular portrait genre. It ws the two sisters taking a . The Duchess, in a bolic gesture, is ouncing the future birth of sister's child, the itimate son of Henry IV.

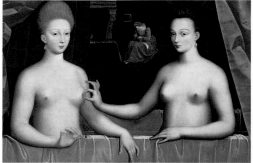

OMB OF PHILIPPE POT

ar of the collection of opean sculpture is this sual late 15th-century e by Antoine le Moiturier. ippe Pot was the Great eschal of Burgundy, an cial of considerable rank. imposing tomb, which formerly in the Abbey of aux, shows him dressed mour, being carried on a Id and supported by eight ping figures dressed in rning garb.

▽ **SARCOPHAGUS OF THE RECLINING COUPLE**
Standing more than a metre high, this painted terracotta sarcophagus is one of the most impressive of the museum's Etruscan treasures. It depicts in detail everything from the folds of the garments to enigmatic smiles. The base of the sarcophagus is a couch, used by guests at an Etruscan banquet.

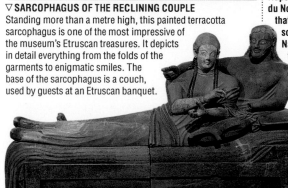

THE HEART OF THE CITY

The Gothic edifices of Notre Dame and Sainte-Chapelle rub shoulders with the dour Conciergerie on Ile de la Cité, at odds with the genteel mansions of Ile St-Louis and the fine modernism across the Seine

The Ile de la Cité in the middle of the Seine is the birthplace and topographical centre of Paris and has been its spiritual and legislative heart for more than 2,000 years. Invading the Parisii settlement already established here in 53 BC, the Romans built a prefect's palace, law court and temple to Jupiter on the island. Across the river on the Right Bank, the Hôtel de Ville has been the cauldron of political debate since the Middle Ages, while just to the north, the area of Les Halles fed the city's stomachs from AD 1110 until 1969. This is the core of the capital, an area which, in many ways, embraces the essence of Paris.

Notre Dame – seven centuries of magnificence

"The bells, the bells," shout crowds of giggling schoolchildren from the towers of the cathedral of **Notre Dame de Paris ❶** (open daily 8am–6.45pm; free; tel: 1 42 34 56 10), echoing the cry of Victor Hugo's infamous hunchback, Quasimodo. Gazing up at the cathedral's finely sculptured facade, it is very hard to imagine the building's poor condition when Hugo (*see page 159*) wrote his novel *The Hunchback of Notre Dame* in 1831. He and his Romantic followers (*see page 35*) were so appalled at the state of the building that, in 1841, they succeeded in triggering a massive restoration programme, headed by Viollet-le-Duc (*see page 92*). Taking 23 years, the meticulous architect repaired the cathedral's structure literally from the foundations to the roof tiles, recreated stained-glass windows by copying remaining ones and replaced sculptures destroyed in the Revolution, such as the Gallery of Kings, by studying those of other Gothic cathedrals. He scrubbed the whitewash off the interior walls and administered a protective coating to the exterior. He also added a sacristy to the south side, now the **Trésor de Notre Dame** (open daily; closed 11.45am–12.30pm; entrance fee) housing the alleged Crown of Thorns, other relics and manuscripts.

The church of "Our Lady" was built on the site of earlier pagan fertility worship by the Romans, venerating a Black Virgin. The conquering Frankish king, Clovis, erected a suitably impressive Christian basilica in the 5th century, which was replaced by a Romanesque church. By 1159, a young bishop, Maurice de Sully, decided that Paris deserved bigger and better. Work on the cathedral began in 1163 and took just under 200 years to complete, following plans by Pierre Montreuil, who was also the architect of Sainte-Chapelle.

Even before it was finished, Notre Dame had become the venue for national ceremonies: state funerals, thanksgivings and, in 1239, St Louis deposited in the cathedral the Crown of Thorns, and other relics acquired

Map, page 140/1

PRECEDING PAGES: imposing towers of the Conciergerie. **LEFT:** sculptured facade of Notre Dame by night. **BELOW:** one of the cathedral's exquisite rose windows.

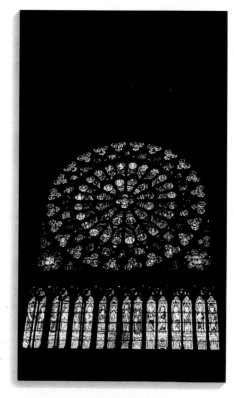

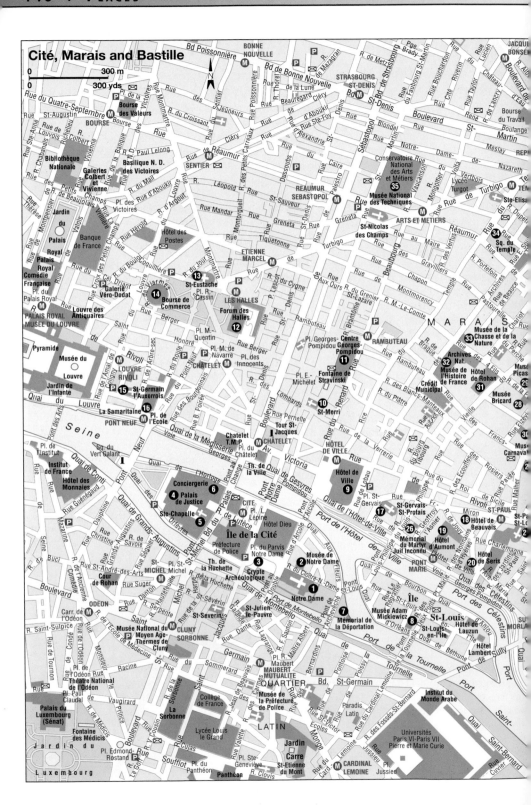

Cité, Marais and Bastille

on a Crusade, while Sainte-Chapelle was being built. Since then, Notre Dame has been witness to a string of historical events: in 1572, the cathedral's strangest wedding took place. The bride, Marguerite de Valois (a Catholic), stood at the altar, while the bridegroom Henri de Navarre (a Protestant), called in his vows from the doorstep. Later, in 1589, Henri was crowned in the cathedral, having decided to convert to Catholicism saying, "Paris is well worth a Mass".

Come the Revolution, Notre Dame was ravaged by enthusiastic citizens, who melted down and destroyed anything that hinted of royalty, lopping off the heads of the kings of Judah, along the top of the main portals – Viollet-le-Duc replaced the statues with copies in 1850 and the original heads were discovered in the cellar of a bank in 1977. They now reside in the Hôtel de Cluny (*see page 185*). The cathedral was then turned into a Temple of Reason and by the end of the Revolution was being used for wine storage.

By the time Napoleon decided to crown himself Emperor in 1804, the cathedral was in such a shabby state that bright tapestries were hung up to cover the crumbling decor. Pope Pius VII attended with reluctant obedience and, when he hesitated at the altar, Napoleon snatched the crown and to the crowd's cheers of "*Vive l'Empéreur!*" placed it on his head himself. In August 1944, at the thanksgiving ceremony for the Liberation of Paris, the Resistance hero and leader of the new government, General Charles de Gaulle, was shot at during the *Te Deum*.

Grand architecture

Notre Dame is magnificent from any angle, but its Gothic facade is particularly impressive. Viewed from out front on the **Place du Parvis**, the twin towers soar to the heavens with dramatic grace. The cathedral's three doors each have a distinct design – an asymmetry typical of medieval architecture. Originally, the stone figures were finely painted against a gilt background and were designed to illustrate the Bible to an illiterate populace. On the left, the **Portal of the Virgin**

The devilish gargoyles scowling down from the upper gallery are not medieval nightmares but the playful creations of the 19th-century Gothic revivalist architect Viollet-le-Duc.

BELOW: high-vaulted elegance of the central nave.

depicts the ark of the covenant and the coronation of the Virgin. The **Portal of the Last Judgement**, in the middle, shows the Resurrection, the weighing of souls and their procession to heaven or hell. The **Portal of St Anne** portrays the Virgin and Maurice de Sully. Above the doorways, the **Rose Window**, depicting the Virgin and Child in deep blues and rich reds, is a miracle of engineering. Picture the rickety scaffolding and the armies of stonemasons, who with simple measuring techniques constructed an intricate masterpiece that has lasted for 750 years. The glass, however, has been restored.

The ascent of the **Tours de Notre Dame** (open daily 10am–4.30pm; closed some pub. hols; entrance fee) is a religious experience for those who love heights and a taste of hell for claustrophobes with vertigo. From the top of 387 steps Paris stretches to the horizon. "Emmanuel", the 13-tonne bell of Notre Dame, is pealed only on state occasions. Dating from the 17th century, legend has it that the purity of the bell's tone is due to the gold and silver jewellery cast into its heated bronze by the most beautiful women of Paris.

A medieval cavern

Inside, edged with 37 side chapels, the cathedral is enough to inspire the most hardened atheist. Supported by flying buttresses, the vault of the chancel seems almost weightless, with stained-glass windows distributing rays of coloured light into the solemn shadows. The exquisite 13th-century north and south rose windows are the transept's two star attractions. The most spectacular north window still has most of its 13th-century glass but the south rose had to be reconstructed completely by Viollet-le-Duc. The 18th-century carved choir stalls depicting the life of the Virgin Mary, were commissioned by Louis XIV, who

as fulfilling the vow his father made 60 years earlier that he would build a high tar and devote the east chancel to the Virgin, if he were to have an heir. Louis III's statue stands behind the high altar, along with Guillaume Coustou's *Pietà*.

Outside on Rue du Cloître-Notre-Dame is the **Musée de Notre Dame de aris ❷** (open Wed, Sat, Sun; 2.30pm–6pm; entrance fee), which charts the istory of the cathedral and has exhibits of ancient pottery found beneath the arvis, Gallo-Roman artefacts, works of art and a cup, dating from the 4th century. In the **Crypte Archéologique ❸** (open daily; entrance fee), underneath e parvis, are excavations of buildings dating back to the 3rd century, including arts of a Lutetian house inhabited by the Gallic Parisii.

ainte-Chapelle – a venerable shrine

cross from Notre Dame rise the imposing walls of the Palais de Justice and e Conciergerie. At one time, the **Palais de Justice ❹** (open daily; closed weekds; free) was a royal palace and St Louis had his bedroom in what is now the rst Civil Court. In the 14th century, Charles V moved out, installing his parament there with full judiciary rights. A wander around the hushed corridors, ast fleeting black-robed figures, is a reminder of the tense days of the Revolution when a new judicial system was imposed and the public prosecutor, ouquier-Tinville, sent thousands to the guillotine. The present legal system has een passed down from Napoleon Bonaparte.

Confined within the walls of the Palais de Justice, **Sainte-Chapelle ❺** (open aily 9.30am–6pm, in summer 10am–5pm in winter; closed some pub. hols; ntrance fee; tel: 01 53 73 78 51) stands like a skeletal finger pointing heavenards – an ethereal counterpoint to the stones of the establishment. This mira-

Map, page 140/1

TIP

Each Sunday at 5.45pm, the organ master fills Notre Dame with classical music, soaring to paradise out of the 112-stop instrument. Classical concerts are also given in Sainte-Chapelle.

BELOW: the lower chapel of Sainte-Chapelle.

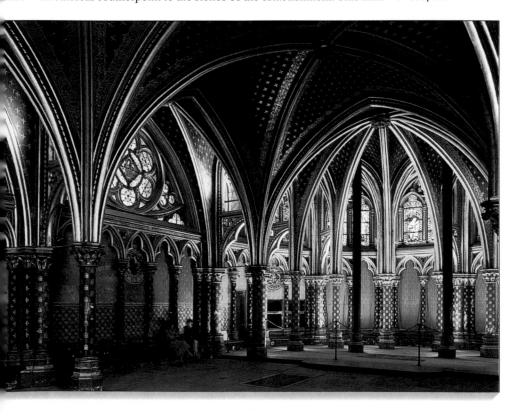

cle of High Gothic ingenuity is an obligatory pause on any visit to Paris. Completed in just 33 months by Pierre de Montreuil and consecrated in 1248, t chapel was built to house the Crown of Thorns, bartered from the Venetians St Louis. Seemingly constructed without walls, the chapel's vaulted roof is su ported by a thin web of stone, from which descend veils of richly coloured stain glass. A replica Crown of Thorns decorates the top of one of the pinnacles.

Built in two tiers, the lower chapel was designed for the palace staff and consequently smaller and gloomier. From the shadows, climb the spiral sta case into the crystalline cavern of the upper chapel. The soaring windows ca the faintest of lights, creating kaleidoscopes of colour. The 13th-century colou are sharply vivid and depict 1,134 scenes from the Bible, which begin by t staircase with Genesis and proceed round the church to the 15th-century ro window. Regular orchestral concerts are held in the chapel.

The Conciergerie – a place of retribution

Occupying the northeast wing of the Palais de Justice, the **Conciergerie** (open daily; closed pub. hols; entrance fee; tel: 01 53 73 78 50) looks like intimidating castle, its four towers rising insolently above impenetrable walls isn't hard to imagine this fortress as a merciless medieval prison – which it w (although much of the pitiless facade is 19th-century). It was originally built a palace, but when Charles V moved his residence to the Hôtel Saint-Pol, palace was used to house Comte des Cierges – hence the name, Conciergen The Comte was in charge of the king's lodgings and taxes until the Concie erie became a prison in the 14th century, when his job changed to that of ch gaoler. The Capetian palace came into its own during the Revolution, when

ABOVE: stained-glass perfection at Sainte-Chapelle.
BELOW RIGHT: replica of Marie-Antoinette's prison cell.

NOTABLE INMATES

A prison for four centuries, the medieval Conciergerie was host to many an inmate before the onslaught of the Revolution. Among those who were forced to take up residence there were the Scottish captain Montgomery, who fatally wounded Henri II during a tournament in1559 and Ravaillac, who assassinated Henri IV in 1610.

During the Revolution, inmates included Madame du Barry, Louis XV's favourite mistress, Marie-Antoinette, Louis XVI's wife (above), Charlotte Corday, who murdered the Revolutionary leader Marat, the poet André Chenier; and, finally, the public prosecutor Fouquier-Tinville, the judges of the Revolutionary Tribunal and even Robespierre himself.

housed nearly 2,600 prisoners awaiting the guillotine, including Marie-Antoinette. Ironically, her prosecutor, Danton, resided in the next cell before his trip to the guillotine, as, in turn, did his nemesis Robespierre. In the merry-go-round of retribution, 1,306 heads rolled in one month at Place de la Nation. To the west is the **Cour des Femmes**, a rough courtyard where the women were allowed during the day.

The tower at the back is called **Bonbec** (the squealer), for it was here, from the 11th century, that torture victims told all. At the front is the 14th-century **Clock Tower** containing the first public clock in Paris, still ticking today.

Inside, the original kitchens are still intact. They were built to feed up to 3,000 people using four huge fireplaces and have a Gothic canopied ceiling supported by buttresses. The adjacent **Salles des Gens d'Armes** is a magnificent four-aisled Gothic hall where the royal guards, or men-at-arms, used to live.

Exploring the island and river

Escape the shadows of the Revolution on **Quai des Orfèvres**, along the south bank of the island, now home to the *Police Judicaire* (CID), where goldsmiths (*orfèvres*) once fashioned Marie-Antoinette's jewellery. Beyond the Square du Vert-Galant and the statue of Henri IV, the river slides silently past the tip of the island, caressing wistful willows. **Pont Neuf**, bisected by the island, is the oldest surviving bridge in Paris. It was made of stone, rather than wood, and was the first bridge to be built without houses on it. In 1985, the American artist Christo wrapped up the whole Pont Neuf in brown paper.

You can return to the east end of the island via the colourful **Marché aux Fleurs** in Place L. Lepine opposite the **Préfecture de Police** and Haussmann's

Map, page 140/1

Vedettes du Pont Neuf (tel: 01 46 33 98 38) run cruises along the Seine lasting about an hour. Boats leave from the Square du Vert-Galant (métro: Pont Neuf) every half hour in the high season (see page 278).

BELOW: a river view of the Conciergerie.

Scooping the Poop

Since 1977, when opinion polls revealed that the cleanliness of the streets came top among Parisian concerns, the then new mayor, the proud and energetic Jacques Chirac, made it a priority to overhaul Paris's entire waste disposal and street-cleaning system. The city cleaners' distinctive green uniform and vehicles were introduced in 1980. An *école de la propreté* was added to teach new recruits the finer elements of street cleaning and, today, the green, gnashing wagons have become a symbol of the city.

Paris has one of the world's most efficient clean-up services, employing around 4,500 people to collect 3,500 tonnes of rubbish daily at an annual cost of 2 billion francs – about 10 percent of the city's annual budget. Representatives from abroad, including officials from Tokyo and New York, have rushed over for cleaning lessons.

The fact is that Paris faces a singularly challenging obstacle to maintaining clean streets:

déjections canines, of which no less than 20 tonnes are vacuumed off the streets daily by a team of mobile pooper-scoopers. The annual bill amounts to 42 million francs. Spread among the city's 200,000 dog population, that's 210 francs per dog.

Paris has an unusually large canine population – but then the Parisian pooch is not merely man's best friend, he is also an essential fashion accessory. Just as residents of Los Angeles define themselves by their cars and Italians by their wardrobe, so Parisians tend to express their personalities through their dogs. From the toy poodle prancing along the Faubourg St-Honoré in a tartan raincoat and matching ribbon to the muzzled German shepherd dozing on the Métro after a night's guard duty, Parisian dogs are as diverse and eclectic a breed as their owners.

In fact, the distinction between animal and human often seems blurred in a city where it is even a possibility that you'll see dogs seated at café tables. Far from being banned from shops and restaurants in France, almost every boutique or eating establishment worth its salt has its resident canine character, whose acquaintance it is advisable to make if you plan on becoming a regular customer.

Needless to say, this indulgence towards their pets does not translate well when it comes to teaching Frou-Frou the toutou (bow-wow) how to use the gutter.

Signs bearing sausage dogs and arrows have appeared at regular intervals on the capital's pavements, pointing to doggy latrines. When they failed to give results, a system of hefty fines was introduced. The new law is now enforced by an undercover cleanliness squad, the plainclothes *agents de propreté*, who patrol the streets and are instructed to swoop on sight – presumably watching where they put their feet.

Despite their valiant efforts, Paris remains a city where canny pedestrians keep an eye on the pavement. An estimated two serious falls a day are the result of what a man's best friend leaves lying around. If, during an unguarded moment, you too find yourself thus inconvenienced, take comfort: Parisians believe it brings good fortune. ❑

LEFT: praise for an essential Parisian fashion accessory.

Hôtel Dieu. Built on the site of a medieval hospital, which was the recipient of generous donations from Louis IX, the Hôtel Dieu, now a city hospital, was the scene of intense battles when the police resisted the Germans in 1944. In contrast to these forbidding structures, the market is a joyful array of small glasshouses selling flowers and plants underneath classical black streetlamps. On Sunday, the stalls become a bird market and the jabbering of parakeets fills the air.

On the north side of Notre Dame is the **Quartier des Anciens Cloîtres** (Ancient Cloister Quarter), one-time home and study area for 12th-century monks and scholars, belonging to the cathedral chapter, including the controversial philosopher and theologian Pierre Abélard, who got himself into hot water with Eloïse (*see page 27*). Around here used to be a warren of houses, until Haussmann razed the brothels, pawnbrokers and taverns, moving 25,000 inhabitants to the suburbs, to provide the present vista. As you pass along Rue de la Colombe, note the remains of the Gallo-Roman wall in the pavement.

On the eastern tip of the island lies the **Mémorial de la Déportation ❼** (open daily; closed noon–2pm; free; tel: 01 46 33 87 56 or visit www.paris.org/ monuments/martyrs.deportation). Within this rather bleak structure 200,000 crystals commemorate the 200,000 French victims of the concentration camps, overlooking the quays across the river where many of them lived.

Ile St-Louis – 17th-century elegance and tranquillity

Far from the madding video cameras, across the pedestrian Pont St-Louis, **Ile St-Louis** is a privileged haven of peace and wealth. The island's elegance is 17th-century and its mansions are home to Paris's elite. Turning right along the south bank, you will reach the **Musée Adam Mickiewicz ❽** (open afternoons;

Map, page 140/1

ABOVE: a decorative drainpipe on the Hôtel de Lauzun.
BELOW: a wider view of the *hôtel*.

The Tour St-Jacques was the belfry of a church on the pilgrimage route to Santiago de Compostela in Spain, in the Middle Ages. Pilgrims (above) carried gourds and a scallop shell with them as a symbol of St Jacques (St James).

BELOW: inside-out building of Centre Georges-Pompidou.

morning only Sat; closed Mon; entrance fee). Adam Mickiewicz (1798–1855) was a Polish poet, living in Paris, who devoted his work to helping oppressed Poles. The 17th-century building includes the Polish Library and memorabilia of the Polish composer Frédéric Chopin.

Continuing eastwards round the island to the north bank, you will pass **Hôtel Lambert**. Built in 1640 by Louis Le Vau, an advisor to Louis XVIII, it is the finest residence in the city, now owned by the Rothschilds. Further on, in **Hôtel de Lauzun**, fellow poets Théophile Gautier and Charles Baudelaire formed a hashish smoking society in 1845. Ironically, the house now belongs to the City of Paris, reserved for official guests. Behind, on **Rue St-Louis-en-l'Ile**, the church of the same name contains a plaque from the city of St Louis, Missouri, in America. Ile St-Louis's favourite attraction is edible: **Berthillon**, opposite the Pont St-Louis, purveys 100 flavours of the most delicious ice cream. **Brasserie de l'Isle St-Louis**, on Quai de Bourbon, is an institution among institutions, serving the likes of pop stars and politicians.

On the Right Bank of the Seine

To explore the Right Bank, **Place du Châtelet** is a good place to start. Flanked by its two theatres, the square is a meeting place for lovers above one of Paris's biggest Métro and RER stations. Northeast of the square stands the **Tour St-Jacques**, seemingly dropped there by mistake, but its chapel was destroyed during the Revolution. Scientist Blaise Pascal (1623–62) experimented with the weight of air from the top and it is now used as a weather station.

Opening out at the eastern end of Avenue Victoria is the wide esplanade of the **Hôtel de Ville ❾** (guided tours Mon only; tel: 01 42 76 50 49), which was

the scene of hangings and macabre executions in medieval times, site of the Paris Commune in 1871 and of the Liberation of Paris celebrations in 1944. Flanked by bare-breasted maidens and with a splendid Mansort roof in characteristic French style, the 19th-century building contains the majestic Salles des Fêtes (ballroom), a magnificent staircase and lots of chandeliers.

Heading north up Rue St-Martin, towards the Centre Georges-Pompidou about five minutes away, you pass the richly adorned church of **St-Merri ⑩**. The bell is the oldest in Paris, dating from 1331, and the 17th-century organ used to be played by the French composer Camille Saint-Saëns (1835–1921). Behind the church, the modern **Fontaine de Stravinski** is home to a colourful herd of spouting creatures – innovative fountains that suck and spit water, each named after a piece of music by the Russian composer (*see page 37*). **Le Café Beaubourg**, nearby, offers a trendy tipple in *avant-garde* surroundings. Westwards, down **Rue de la Ferronnerie,** is the spot where Henri IV was stabbed to death by Ravaillac.

Centre Georges-Pompidou – a modern experience

Known locally as Beaubourg and officially as the Centre National d'Art et de Culture, **Centre Georges-Pompidou ⑪** (closed Tues; open Mon and Wed–Sun 11am–9pm; entrance fee to galleries; tel: 01 44 78 14 63 or visit www.centre-pompidou.fr), looking like an airport terminal with the skin stripped off, caused an uproar when it was finished in 1977. But it has since attracted nearly 8 million visitors a year (the most visited cultural site in the world), who marvel at its pipes, tubes, scaffolds and the external escalators. The pipes are not just for show: the blue convey air, the green transport water, the yellow contain elec-

Map, page 140/1

ABOVE: viewing from the top of the Centre Georges-Pompidou.
BELOW: looking down on the entertainment outside.

In the Quartier de l'Horloge, a pedestrianised area just north of Centre Georges-Pompidou, is a huge Defender of Time clock in brass and steel. On the hour, a life-size soldier does battle with either the dragon of earth, the bird of the air or the crab of the sea. At six and 12, all attack.

tricity and the red conduct heating. The slightly sunken forecourt is a perfect stage for street entertainment.

Inside, the centre is cavernous, as all the infrastructure is part of the outer structure. The centre was renovated in time for the millennium, and the improvements include an extended entrance hall and ticket office, an educational area and the rehousing of the **Bibliothéque Publique d'Information** over three levels. In addition, the **Musée National de l'Art Moderne** is now spaced out over two floors – the fourth and fifth. Temporary exhibitions are shown on level six. Also on the sixth floor is a swanky restaurant.

The fifth floor covers the period from 1905 up to the 1960s. It shows work by Picasso, Matisse, Kandinsky, Klee, Klein and Pollock, and has sections on Dadism and Surrealism. The fourth floor is devoted to the wonderful comtemporary collection, from the 1960s up to the present day, and includes work by Andy Warhol, Xavier Veilhan, Claude Viallat, Verner Panton, Joseph Beuys, Gerhard Richter and Jean Dubuffet. Displays of 20th-century design and architecture, as well as installations, are now interspersed among the paintings. Also on show is a reconstruction of Brancusi's studio, **l'Atelier Brancusi**. The outdoor terrace looks over towards Les Halles, displaying sculptures by Tinguely.

Les Halles – a futuristic marketplace

West of Beaubourg, **Les Halles** (pronounced *Leyz Al*) has been a market area since 1183, when Philippe-Auguste erected permanent halls and ordered the city traders to close their shops for two days a week to do business at his own market. Reorganised under Napoleon III, who demanded that his architect, Baltard, build with "iron, nothing but iron!", the market consisted of 10 halls, resem-

BELOW: the Forum des Halles with St-Eustache behind.

FOUNTAIN OF INNOCENTS

The sole Renaissance fountain in Paris, the Fontaine des Innocents, created by Pierre Lescot and Jean Goujon, sits on the one-time site of the city's infamous cemetery, Les Innocents, just southeast of Les Halles.

Filled with corpses since the 12th century, the graveyard, encircled by a high wall, had become a putrid necropolis by the 18th century, as the dead – mostly paupers – were carried there amongst produce bound for the market at Les Halles. Gruesome tales abound about how people ground up the bones for bread, when Paris was under siege in 1590, and how they used the skeletons for firewood.

By 1780, the corpses were overflowing above street level and the area was teeming with rats, so the cemetery was finally closed and its inmates moved to the Catacombs, where their bones can still be visited (*see page 194*). Today, the square is a meeting place for the city's youth.

bling small railway stations, which were fed by vast underground storehouses, dark kingdoms of death and decay where cages of animals were piled amongst rotting fruits, ruled over by blind storekeepers. Up above, stallholders, restaurant owners, pickpockets, artists, prostitutes and police crowded the market.

The last night of the market, Thursday 27 February 1969, was a sad occasion for Parisians. The animated halls, so lovingly described by Emile Zola (1840–1902) in his novel *Le Ventre de Paris* (*The Belly of Paris*), were no longer suitable for 20th-century commerce and trading was moved to Rungis, near Orly Airport. Vestiges of the past survive in the scattered 24-hour bistros of the area. Make for Au Pied du Cochon (6 Rue Coquillère) for onion soup, snails and pig's trotters at six in the morning, or La Poule au Pot (9 Rue Vauvilliers) to partake of tripe with film directors and singers.

The present-day **Forum des Halles** ⓬ filled the large hole left after the market buildings were demolished. This vast underground commercial centre, four floors beneath Paris, is a monument to modernism. Above ground are glass-and-steel mushrooms housing cultural centres for contemporary arts and poetry, the **Pavillon des Arts** and **Maison de la Poésie**. The central courtyard hosts the odd concert around a suggestive Pygmalion statue by Julio Silva. Inside, the **Musée Grévin** (open daily, afternoons only Sun and pub. hols; entrance fee; tel: 01 47 70 85 05 or visit www.musee-grevin.com), a subsidiary of the larger Grévin museum on Boulevard Montmartre (*see page 128*), has waxwork displays illustrating the *Belle Epoque*, with a talking Victor Hugo and Gustav Eiffel, and the **Musée de l'Holographie** (open daily, afternoons only Sun and pub. hols; entrance fee) provides miraculous holograms to wonder over.

Back to the Seine

Outside the Forum, a pleasant park stretches westward towards the Bourse. In the northeast corner, a giant head and cupped hand, by Henri de Miller, attract children and pigeons to its benign seat, beneath the Gothic gaze of **St-Eustache** ⓭. The 100-metre (330-ft) long church, with Renaissance decoration, is one of Paris's most beautiful. Berlioz and Liszt played premieres here.

To the left, glass pyramids recalling the new Louvre entrance reflect the stones of St-Eustache. This is a new hothouse full of palms, papayas and banana trees. Metal walkways traverse the glasshouses to the Bourse de Commerce $ (open daily; closed weekends; free), a circular commercial exchange built in the 18th century.

Head back towards the **Rue St-Honoré**, a major 12th-century thoroughfare, at the **Fontaine de la Croix-du-Trahoir**. A little further on is the church of **St Germain-l'Auxerrois** ⓯. At midnight on 24 August 1572, the church bells rang as the signal to start the St Bartholomew's Day Massacre (*see page 29*), when thousands of Protestants were butchered on the orders of Catholic Catherine de Médici.

Behind, the edifice of **La Samaritaine** ⓰, one of the biggest and oldest department stores in Paris, spreads over five buildings joined by overhead walkways (*see page 72*). On the roof of the second building, which has an Art Nouveau facade, the terrace restaurant offers one of the finest views of Paris – at a reasonable price. ❑

Map, page 140/1

An ancient edict of Les Halles, stating that nothing hard could be thrown in the market – only mud and detritus – was obeyed with gusto. Dairymaids accused of giving short measures were stood in the square with a slab of the offending butter on their heads.

BELOW: organ grinder on the pedestrian Pont St-Louis.

THE MARAIS AND THE BASTILLE

Map, page 140/1

Steeped in political history, these two lively villages within a great metropolis offer medieval streets, museum-filled mansions and the city's oldest and most beautiful square

O n the Right Bank of the Seine, tucked behind the Hôtel de Ville and hiding away from the extravagance of the Grands Boulevards, the Marais and the area of the city around the Bastille are both proudly independent districts, possessing an intimate, animated charm that sets them apart from the more grandiose expanses to the west. Here live small communities with their own traditions, folklore and heroes.

The Marais (literally the swamp) was notable in the 13th century for the mosquitoes and frogs that infested the bogs on either side of Rue St-Antoine, the old, raised Roman eastern highway. First, Philippe-Auguste built a defensive wall, then with the arrival of monks and monasteries, the marshes were drained and Charles V constructed a new wall around Paris, which ended at the forbodding, newly completed Bastille fort, bringing the area into the city. When, as Regent, in 1358, Charles V moved from his royal palace on Ile de la Cité, as a result of the *Jacquerie* uprising (*see page 28*), he set up one of his residences on the Seine at St-Paul's, establishing the start of a royal influx into the quarter.

In 1609, Henri IV decided to build a sumptuous nest for his court at the present-day Place des Vosges (initially known as the Place Royale), shifting the political and financial focus from the Louvre. As a result, the finest architects and stonemasons in Europe descended on the Marais, building countless grand residences, or *hôtels*, for the nobility, each more impressive than the last. These classical walls sheltered *salons* – living-room intellectual societies – where the bright and beautiful of the day would pontificate, lounging on ornate divans.

PRECEDING PAGES: Hôtel de Ville in all its glory. **LEFT:** absorbed in a Picasso. **BELOW:** poised for a night on the town.

The fall and rise of the Marais

The pendulum of fashion swung away from the Marais after Louis XIV moved his court to Versailles in the 1680s and the nobility moved to the Ile St-Louis, then westwards to the Faubourg St-Honoré and the Boulevard St-Germain. During the Revolution, the area was abandoned to the people and the Marais's graceful *hôtels* tumbled into disrepair alongside the narrow streets, which became dens of iniquity.

In the 19th and 20th centuries, the quarter became a centre for small industries and craftwork, and successive developers dug up and widened its picturesque streets. In 1962, André Malraux, President de Gaulle's Arts Minister, set wide-scale renovation work in motion to preserve the Marais. Today, many of the *hôtels* are beautifully restored and, although the area maintains a rougher edge that adds to its charm, its former elegance is returning.

Catherine Beauvais, known as One-eyed Kate, was 40 when she "educated" 16-year-old Louis XIV under the benign gaze of his mother, Anne of Austria. When Louis's marriage procession passed under the balcony of the Hôtel de Beauvais many years later, Kate tipped the bridegroom a wink.

BELOW: a village tempo pervades the Marais.

Contained by **Rue Beaubourg** to the west and by **Boulevard Beaumarchais** to the east, the Marais is the historic home of the city's Jewish community and attracts a large number of gays; local cafés, bars and restaurants are animated day and night. Modern art galleries pepper the side streets and passageways, enticing the curious, and at night the ancient lamps exude a romantic glow.

A tour of the old *hôtels*

Behind the Hôtel de Ville (*see page 148*) stands the church of **St-Gervais-St-Protais** ⓱ (open daily; closed Mon; free) with a flight of Italianate steps and some monstrous-looking gargoyles. The church is famous for sacred music, possessing an 18th-century organ played by eight generations of the Couperin family and François Couperin (1668–1733) composed his two Masses for it. The church was shelled by Germany's Big Bertha as a parting shot at the end of World War I in 1918, killing over 100 worshippers.

Rue François-Miron leads away from the Place St-Gervais into the heart of the Marais. Houses along here were nearly demolished by World War II, but with careful restoration are now creeping back to their former glory. At the corner of Rue Cloche-Perce is a half-timbered medieval house and at No. 68, stands the **Hôtel de Beauvais** ⓲, built by Catherine Beauvais in 1654, with money and land from King Louis XIV, who had greatly enjoyed her favours as a teenager. She is also said to have entertained archbishops. More innocently, the composer Mozart stayed here on his first visit to Paris at the age of seven – before he too became considerably more profligate.

Neighbouring Rue de Jouy contains **Hôtel d'Aumont** ⓳, designed by the Versailles architect Louis Le Vau (*see pages 254–255*), renovated and enlarged

Map,
page
140/1

by the French Classical architect François Mansart (1598–1666) and decorated by Versailles painter Charles Le Brun (1619–90). With a formal garden designed by Le Nôtre (*see page 122*), the mansion is now the city's administrative court.

Further on down Rue Figuier stand the château-like turrets of one of Paris's few medieval residences, the **Hôtel de Sens** ❷⓿ (open weekday afternoons; all day Sat; closed Sun and pub. hols; entrance fee; tel: 01 42 78 14 60), which now houses the city's historical and fine arts library, the Bibliothèque Forney. Built at the end of the 15th century for the Archbishop of Sens, the mansion is military in style, with simple but immaculate gardens. Henri IV lodged his first wife, Marguerite de Valois (Reine Margot), in the *hôtel* when he could no longer put up with her promiscuity. Here she continued to leave a trail of broken hearts. When a jealous ex-lover murdered her current *beau*, Marguerite had him beheaded outside the house.

Behind the Hôtel de Sens back along the river, the resolutely modern **Cité Internationale des Arts** stands out amongst all the antiquated refinement; the building provides studios and a year's lodging for artists from around the world.

The Village St-Paul – a romantic spot

Opposite the Hôtel de Sens, the Rue de l'Ave-Maria intersects with the Rue des Jardins St-Paul, a block away. This leads into the **Village St-Paul** past two towers and ramparts, the remnants of the **Enceinte de Philippe-Auguste** (Philippe-Auguste's city wall), shadowing the antics of local schoolchildren. The restored village consists of a series of small courtyards and fountains, sheltering bustling antique shops and secondhand stalls. At night, it is romantically tranquil, beneath the halo of diffused light from the old streetlamps.

In the 18th century, Hôtel de Sens was the departure point for the Paris-Lyon stagecoach run – a route deemed so unsafe that passengers were encouraged to make a will before setting out on a journey.

BELOW: a trendy shop for those in the know.

For a true Parisian meal, Le Temps des Cerises in Rue de la Cerisaie, where 1,000 cherry trees used to grow, is a bistro that hasn't changed with the times, providing fresh market produce served by endearing, jocular waiters.

BELOW: Place des Vosges – a sought-after address.

On **Rue Charlemagne**, wooden walkways between the buildings have been restored as they were in the Middle Ages. Left along Rue St-Paul is an ancient passageway leading to the church of **St-Paul-St-Louis** ㉑, an amalgamation of two parishes and constructed by Jesuits, in 1627, copying the Gesù church in Rome. Here, the hearts of Louis XIII and Louis XIV were embalmed and kept as relics until the Revolution, when they were removed and sold to an artist, St-Martin, who crushed them to mix with oil for a varnish for one of his pictures. Later he gave what was left of Louis XIII's heart to the newly installed King Louis XVIII, in return for a golden snuffbox.

Before plunging into the area north of Rue St-Antoine, this may be a good point to stop for a meal, either at **Le Temps des Cerises** (*see left and page 275*) near the Place de la Bastille, or at **Le Beautreillis** (18 Rue Beautreillis). This is where Jim Morrison, lead singer of the Doors rock band, drank his last bottle of wine with his girlfriend Pamela Courson. He was found dead in the bath in her apartment across the street on 3 July 1971, officially from a heart attack.

To the Place des Vosges – an enchanting square

Rue St-Antoine is the ancient jugular of the Marais. Built wide and straight in typical Roman fashion, it became a site of jousting tournaments until, in 1574 Henri II was knocked off his horse by his Scottish Captain of the Guard, Montgomery, with a blow to his eye. In a drastic bid to save his life, Henri's physician, Ambroise Paré, ordered the immediate decapitation of every prisoner on death row and had their heads rushed to the surgery so that he could experiment on them in a bid to rescue his king. Needless to say he didn't succeed and Henri died 10 days later. The unfortunate Captain Montgomery lost his head, too.

Hôtel de Sully (open daily; closed pub. hols; entrance fee; tel: 01 44 61 20 00) at 62 Rue St-Antoine is one of the finest mansions in the Marais. Under the courtyard's grumpy statues, Voltaire was beaten with clubs by followers of the Count of Rohan, following a slanging match between the two at the Comédie Française (*see page 124*). Through the courtyard, temporary art exhibitions are housed in what is now known as the **Caisse Nationale des Monuments Historiques** (Historic Monuments Commission; tel: 01 44 61 21 50), which organises walking tours of Paris and guided tours of monuments and museums. Behind, the intimate garden is an unexpected surprise with clipped privet hedges *à l'anglaise*. A door in the back right corner leads to the **Place des Vosges** .

Initially called the **Place Royale**, this enchanting 17th-century square, with a garden surrounded by 36 arcaded residences, was constructed by Henri IV as a showcase for his court. Here courtiers paraded, preened and pranced. After the Revolution, when the melted-down statue of Louis XIII had been reforged and replaced, the square was named after Vosges, the first *département* to have paid its taxes promptly. Today, this is the most beautiful square in Paris and one of the capital's most sought-after addresses. The arcades house chic cafés, as well as Issey Miyake's boutique.

In the southeast corner is the **Maison de Victor Hugo** (open daily; closed Mon and pub. hols; entrance fee; tel: 01 42 72 10 16). The Romantic writer's house is a museum to the great man, containing manuscripts, pen-and-ink drawings and pieces of furniture knocked together by Hugo in his spare time.

On Sundays, the gardens are a playground for children and lovers, while ducks happily waddle in the dancing fountains. In summer, the arcades host classical concerts where, in 1763, Mozart gave his first recital. If you are hungry, and not

Madame de Sévigné was born at No. 1 bis Place des Vosges in 1626. Her claim to fame is through the letters written to her daughter, first published in 1726. She lived her final years in the Hôtel Carnavalet (see page 161).

BELOW: Victor Hugo's home in Place des Vosges is now a museum.

HUGO – MAN OF WORDS

Poet, dramatist, novelist, politician and leader of the Romantic movement, Victor Hugo (1802–85) lived at 6 Place des Vosges from 1832 to 1848. This was a highly creative period of his life in which he wrote critical essays, reviews and the major part of his dramatic works, such as *Lucrèce Borgia* (1833) and *Angelo* (1835). In 1841, after two attempts, Hugo was elected a member of the Académie Française (*see page 197*) and, in 1845, he accepted a political post under King Louis-Philippe. The 1848 Revolution threw Hugo into the thick of political struggle and he became a chief in the Democratic party against Louis-Napoleon. In 1851, he went into exile to the Channel Islands, where he wrote *Les Misérables* (1862). At the fall of the Empire in 1870, Hugo returned to Paris and continued writing there until his death.

Map, page 140/1

The Mémorial du Martyr Juif Inconnu (Memorial to the Unknown Jew) **26** *stands on Rue Geoffroy l'Asnier, south of the Jewish Quarter. Its eternal flame in an underground crypt is a poignant reminder of the Holocaust.*

BELOW: a beautifully preserved shopfront in the Marais.

poor, **L'Ambroisie** at 9 Place des Vosges is one of Paris's Michelin three-star restaurants. To be sure of a table you should either book a long time in advance or become a famous politician.

A turn around the Jewish Quarter

One of the city's most colourful areas, the Jewish Quarter is well worth a visit. Turning left from the Place des Vosges, Rue des Francs-Bourgeois leads a short way along sculptured walls past the Musée Carnavalet to Rue Pavée and the **Hôtel de Lamoignon 25**, at No. 24, where 60 people were murdered during the massacres of 2 September 1792 (including the Princess of Lamballe, whose head was presented to Queen Marie-Antoinette on a spike). Built *circa* 1584 for the Duchesse d'Angoulême, the *hôtel* now houses the city's historical library.

Rue des Rosiers, a little further on, is the heart of the district: a narrow extravaganza of kosher delis, falafel stands, old men on motorbikes selling watermelon and tiny shops packed with religious artefacts. In the 13th century, King Philippe-Auguste moved the Jewish community living by Notre Dame to the Marais and more arrivals came from Russia, Poland and central Europe in the 19th century. After the Holocaust in World War II, numbers swelled again in the 1960s, when Algeria became independent and immigrants from North Africa moved in.

Here, on 16 July 1942, French police arrested every man, woman and child in the district and sent many of them to concentration camps. More recently, in 1982, the world-renowned **Jo Goldenberg's** restaurant and deli, at 7 Rue des Rosiers, suffered a bomb attack, for which France's extreme right got the blame.

For less expensive fare and a bustling ambience turn the corner to **Chez Marianne** (2 Rue des Hospitalières-Saint-Gervais), where the owner André

Map, page 140/1

Jornot writes his saying-of-the-week on the restaurant window. Gems include: "Man is a dung-heap where the Lord seeks to grow a rose". Next door, children kick footballs on a small square – the site of a primary school whose pupils were all sent to Buchenwald camp.

The mansions of Carnavalet and Picasso

To experience the diverse collection of museums in the Marais retrace your steps back to the **Musée Carnavalet** ❷ (open daily 10am–5.40pm; closed Mon and pub. hols; entrance fee; tel: 01 42 72 21 13). Occupying two mansions, the main 16th-century Hôtel Carnavalet and the neighbouring 17th-century Hôtel le Peletier, the museum covers the history of Paris and contains well-displayed exhibits that trace the evolution of the capital in paintings, sculpture and costume. Madame de Sévigné, who wrote the illuminating *Letters* (*see page 159*), lived in the Hôtel Carnavalet between 1677 and 1696 and there is a gallery devoted to her life. From here, organised walking tours of the Marais visit those parts other guides do not reach.

Head northwards to Rue du Parc Royal, lined with magnificently restored 17th-century mansions, and in Place de Thorigny, a few minutes' walk away, is the **Musée Bricard** ❷ (open daily; afternoon Mon; closed noon–2pm and at weekends, Aug and pub. hols; entrance fee) in an elegant house built by Libéral Bruand, the architect of Les Invalides (*see page 210*). This is a fascinating lock and key museum, with exhibits including knobs and knockers from Roman times.

Opposite, Rue de Thorigny leads to the **Musée Picasso** ❷ (open daily 9.30am–5.30pm; closed Tues and some pub. hols; entrance fee: tel: 01 42 71 25 21 or visit www.oda.fr/aa/musee-picasso) in the beautifully restored **Hôtel Salé**,

ABOVE: a reminder of the German occupation.
BELOW: Hôtel Carnavelet – home to the museum of the history of Paris.

5 Rue de Thorigny. Following his death in 1973, Pablo Picasso's family was faced with an enormous inheritance tax bill and so, in lieu of payment, they donated to the French nation a large collection of his works, comprising 200 paintings, more than 3,000 drawings and 88 ceramics, along with sculptures, collages, illustrated books and manuscripts, plus his own private collection of work from contemporary artists. Laid out in chronological order, the exhibition covers his long and prolific career in a superb setting and provides a conclusive tour around the genius of this 20th-century artist whose motto was, "I do not seek, I find". Giacometti's stunning ironwork completes the artistic decor. In the summer, among the statues in the garden, a small outdoor café serves tea to weary art lovers.

A cluster of museums

Passing back through Place de Thorigny, down Rue Elzévir, **Musée Cognacq-Jay** ③ (open daily 10am–5.40pm; closed Mon and pub. hols; tel: 01 40 27 07 21) can be found a few minutes' walk away in the exquisite Hôtel Donon. The mansion houses the art collection of Ernest Cognacq, founder of the Samaritaine department store (*see page 151*), and his wife Louise Jay and includes works by Rembrandt and Canaletto.

A little further west, at the end of Rue Barbette, is the stunningly restored **Hôtel de Rohan** ③, which is unfortunately only accessible when housing temporary exhibitions. If closed, take a look in the courtyard at the magnificent sculpture of the *Horses of Apollo* over the stables.

Turning right on to Rue des Francs-Bourgeois a few minutes' walk southwards, you will see, on your left, the austere facade of the **Crédit Municipal**, the

ABOVE: Portrait of
Marie-Thérèse
Walter, in the
Musée Picasso.
BELOW: children's
hour, Musée Picasso.

A SPANISH GENIUS

B orn in Málaga in Spain, Pablo Picasso (1881–1973) finally settled in Paris at the age of 23, having studied art in Barcelona and Madrid. However, he never lost his Spanish touch as his work so often revealed. A leading figure in modern 20th-century art, his work developed through many phases, including a Blue Period, when he painted his *Self Portrait* (1901), and Cubism, a primitive and monumental form of art, which he also explored in sculpture. In the 1920s and 1930s, Picasso produced his most abstract work and, in 1937, he painted *Guernica*. He remained in Paris, in the Rue des Grands-Augustins, during World War II moving to the South of France afterwards.

Picasso died in Mougins, leaving behind him a massive collection of paintings, sculptures, drawings and ceramics, along with a large collection of works by his contemporaries such as Matisse, Braque, Cézanne and Rousseau.

tate pawnbroker. Nicknamed *Ma Tante* (My Aunt), the lending facility was opened in 1777 and you can still obtain cash on the value of objects surrendered o its charge.

Opposite the house of the poor stand the houses of the rich, namely the **Hôtel le Soubise**, home to the **Musée de l'Histoire de France** ❷ (open afternoons; closed Tues and pub. hols; entrance fee; tel: 01 40 27 62 18). This early 18th-century mansion has rooms handsomely decorated in the Rococo style. Here, oo, are the **National Archives** in which over 6 million official documents, on 290 km (180 miles) of shelving, demonstrate the French nation's love affair with he rubber stamp.

Rue des Archives leads up to Paris's finest collection of stuffed animals in the **Musée de la Chasse et de la Nature** ❸ (Hunting Museum; open daily; closed 12.30–1.30pm; closed Tues and pub. hols; entrance fee) in one wing of Hôtel Guénégaud, which bears witness to the French aphorism: "If it moves, shoot it".

Quartier du Temple – a town within a town

To the north of the Marais, about a 10-minute walk up Rue des Archives, the **Quartier du Temple** was once the headquarters of the Knights Templar, where 4,000 people lived out of bounds to the authorities. A 13th-century secret society of soldiers, originally formed to protect pilgrims in theHoly Land, the Knights Templar owned much of France and were in charge of the royal treasury until 1307, when Philippe the Fair burnt their leaders at the stake on an island in the Seine and the society was forced to go underground.

With the Revolution, the Temple Tower (no longer standing) became the most famous prison in France and was where the Royal Family was impris-

Map, page 140\1

TIP

Le Domarais, at 53 bis Rue des Francs-Bourgeois, is a French restaurant that offers spectacular decor and unique dinner entertainment; its circular 17th-century dining room is overlooked by a balcony where musicians perform.

BELOW: 17th-century Hôtel Salé, housing the Musée Picasso.

When the victims of the 1830 and 1841 revolutions were lying in state in the Louvre before burial under the Colonne de Juillet, legend has it they were joined by two Egyptian mummies, surplus to the museum's needs, who subsequently also received full military honours…

ABOVE: plan of the Bastille prison.
BELOW: in the Métro.

oned, at first in luxurious apartments and later in the dungeons. It was from here, in 1793, that Louis XVI went to the guillotine. His son, Louis XVII, stayed on, but mysteriously disappeared, aged 10, in 1795.

The Temple Tower was eventually razed by a superstitious Napoleon and Haussmann replaced it with a wrought iron, covered market, the **Carreau du Temple**, which still sells inexpensive and secondhand clothes and cloth by the metre. Along the tree-lined Rue Perrée lies all that remains of the Temple fortress, the **Square du Temple ㉞** garden, which resounds to the sound of ping pong balls on two outdoor tables.

Not far from the Temple district, about another 10 minutes along Rue Réaumur, is France's most prestigious technical college, the **Conservatoire National des Arts et Métiers**, which houses the **Musée National des Techniques ㉟** (National Technical Museum, refurbished in 1998). Immortalised in Umberto Eco's finale to his novel *Foucault's Pendulum*, in which bizarre ceremonies take place under the pendulum, the museum includes such innovations as Volta's battery, Pascal's adding machine and Blériot's aeroplane.

To end a visit to the Marais head down Rue du Temple past the jewellery boutiques (about a 10-minute walk) to No. 41 and its courtyard. Once the headquarters of the Aigle d'Or, the last stagecoach company in Paris, it is now a bustling corner, where the **Café de la Gare** puts on alternative theatre and music and **Le Studio** is one of the best of the Tex-Mex restaurants in Paris.

The infamous Bastille

To the east of the Marais squats the **Bastille** district. Once a fearsome bastion of royal strength, the *quartier* fell into disrepair and disrepute after the prison

was destroyed during the Revolution. On 14 July 1789, when crowds stormed the prison, freeing the inmates – all seven of them – Louis XVI was unimpressed, recording in his diary, "Today – nothing." Following the dismantling of the Bastille, an enterprising workman made sculptures of the prison from the rubble and sold them to local councils, who were denounced as anti-Republican if they refused the high price demanded.

The medieval Bastille covered the present day **Place de la Bastille** 36 and the **Arsenal** complex to the south, at the junction of the Seine with the Canal St-Martin. The modern square is a wide, busy thoroughfare with the usual tall column in its midst – **Colonne de Juillet** – erected to victims of the 1830 and 1848 revolutions, who are buried underneath.

Dominating the square, the imposing modern **Opéra Bastille** 37 (open 11am–6.30pm Mon–Sat; tel: 08 36 69 78 68; box office at 130 Rue de Lyon,) has been the victim of much polemic from politicians, art critics and public alike. Although its appearance (half a goldfish bowl attached to a black triumphal arch) has shocked traditionalists, the opera house is gradually creeping into Parisian hearts. Opened on the bicentenary of the Revolution, recent seasons have included works by Wagner, Verdi and Puccini.

A buzzing mecca by night and by day

The Bastille is one of Paris's most rapidly changing quarters. Old crumbling streets are being gentrified and the old crumbling inhabitants are moving out. Some of the rebellious charm remains in streets such as Rue de Lappe and Rue de Charonne to the east of the square, yet the influx of the upwardly mobile has led to an epidemic of dimly lit bistro-bars that are full of serious souls dressed in

Map, page 140/1

Table tennis is the number one sport for the Chinese and Vietnamese who live in the Quartier du Temple. In 1914, the French government brought in 100,000 Chinese to replace the workers gone to war, among them was a boy named Deng Xiao Ping.

BELOW LEFT: in the spirit of Bastille Day.
BELOW: symbolic Colonne de Juillet.

TIP

A worthwhile walk is through the newly designed park of Boulevard Richard-Lenoir, which stretches north from the Place de la Bastille for several kilometres along the Canal St-Martin to Villette. Alternatively, you can do the same journey by boat from Arsenal Marina (Canauxrama departures April–Oct 9.30am and 2.45pm; tel: 01 42 39 15 00).

BELOW: Frédéric Chopin's grave in the Cimetière du Père-Lachaise.

black. Countless modern art galleries, small designer boutiques and trendy bars and cafés have sprouted up, particularly on Rue Oberkampf, Rue Keller and Rue de Lappe. At night, Rue de la Roquette becomes a buzzing mecca for the fashion gurus of Paris as they roar up and down on their Harley Davidsons, oblivious to the past when this street echoed to the cries of prisoners being beheaded at the corner of Rue de la Croix-Faubin – five stones from the guillotine block remain.

Le Balajo (9 Rue de Lappe) is a hot, trendy Latin dance hall, but be prepared to stand in line to get in. The **Théâtre de la Bastille**, on Rue de la Roquette (nothing to do with the Opéra – as the tatty decor proves), currently offers Paris's most challenging dance works. At 17 Rue de la Roquette, **La Rotonde** is a young, chic bar – a far cry from its past life as a brothel whose owner was shot dead by a blind accordion player. The elegant **Bofinger** (3 Rue de la Bastille), off the Place de la Bastille, claims to be the city's oldest brasserie, magnificently decorated. Get here early for a seat under the glass cupola.

The area is still lively during the day and addictive for anyone who likes people-watching. Off Rue du Faubourg-St-Antoine, you can wander through numerous passages of workshops manufacturing furniture, rugs and jewellery as they have for centuries. **Passage du Cheval Blanc** leads off from the Bastille with courtyards named after the months of the year. **Passage de la Main d'Or**, five minutes further on, is equally intriguing.

Wine lovers should not miss **Bistrot Jacques Mélac** (42 Rue Léon-Frot – *off the map*), towards the Cimetière du Père-Lachaise in the east. The vine that sprouts proudly from the bar sets the tone, and two signs on the wall state categorically, "Here, water is for cooking potatoes", and "Do not drink water, fish

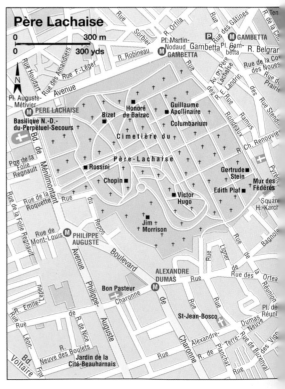

make love in it". The *patron*, Monsieur Mélac, produces 40 litres of wine annually, most of which he seems to consume himself, and The Wine Growers of Paris have their meetings here.

A trip to the Cimetière du Père-Lachaise

End your day as thousands of Parisians have ended theirs – in the **Cimetière du Père-Lachaise** (Métro Père-Lachaise). In the 17th century, a retirement home for old priests stood here and Louis XIV's confesser, Père Lachaise, was a generous benefactor. When the cemetery was built in 1803, the people were reluctant to be buried in it, as it was far from the city centre and unfashionable. Napoleon promptly dug up Molière and La Fontaine and buried them with pomp at Père-Lachaise, with the result that today the guest list is endless. A wander among the ornate graves is a unique experience.

Probably, the most visited grave is Jim Morrison's – graffiti ensures you will not miss it and security has had to be implemented to protect it from further vandalism. Other graves are harder to find, but a map can be purchased at the entrance on Boulevard de Ménilmontant: sempiternal residents include Chopin, Rossini, Bizet, Colette, Victor Hugo, Balzac, Apollinaire and Oscar Wilde, the latter under a fittingly inscrutable sphinx. Also at rest are Edith Piaf and American expatriates Isadora Duncan, Gertrude Stein and Alice B. Toklas.

The cemetery was the site of the last battle of the Paris Commune (*see page 36*) against French troops from Versailles on 27 May 1871. At dawn the next day, the remaining Communards were lined up against a wall and shot. They were buried in a ditch where they fell and the **Mur des Fédérés** (Federalists' Wall) is now a socialist shrine. Nearby are monuments to both world wars. ❑

Map, page 140/1

ABOVE: the French novelist Colette, one of the famous residents in Père-Lachaise.
BELOW: Jim Morrison's grave is the most popular.

MONTMARTRE AND PIGALLE

*Renowned for a colourful nightlife revolving around the Moulin
Rouge, Montmartre, once a haunt for writers and artists, still hums
with life in the steep, narrow streets under the opulent Sacré-Coeur*

Map,
page 172

The "village" of Montmartre occupies the highest point of Paris, nestling into a small hillside in the 18th *arrondissement*, north of the city centre. Extending from the sometimes seedy yet vibrant Place Pigalle in the south to the white cupolas of Sacré-Coeur, the village is an alluring huddle of small steep streets and hidden steps.

In parts, Montmartre resembles a country hamlet with its cobbled squares and gnarled inhabitants. Elsewhere, neon, fast-food, sex shows and tourist buses have tarnished the Bohemian atmosphere. Follow the golf hats and Montmartre will seem predictably commercial. Enter a narrow side street, down a deserted flight of steps and you will be alone, wandering in Paris's least Parisian and most charismatic quarter. Away from the crowds and indifferent food on Place du Tertre, numerous inexpensive restaurants greet the hungry wanderer.

How Montmartre got its name

Montmartre has always liked to be different. Legend has it that, in AD 287, the Romans decapitated St Denis, the first Bishop of Paris, and two priests on the hill. St Denis calmly picked up his head and walked off with it to where the basilica of St-Denis (*see page 250*) now stands. The hill became known as *Mons Martyrium* (Martyrs' Mound). As local bar owners point out, people have been picking their heads out of the gutters of Montmartre ever since.

In the 12th century, a Benedictine convent settled on the hill and 400 years later, Henri IV took shelter in it when laying siege to Paris in 1589. His only conquest of the campaign, it appears, was the 17-year-old abbess of the time. The last mother superior here was guillotined during the Revolution at the age of 82, despite her deafness and blindness, and the convent buildings were destroyed.

Revolution has been the district's speciality ever since St Denis's rebellious behaviour and, in 1871, its inhabitants seized 170 cannons to defend themselves after the fall of Paris to the Prussians. The Thiers' government sent in troops to recapture them but the generals were overwhelmed, lined up on the hill and shot – so beginning the Paris Commune (*see page 36*).

For much of the 19th century, Montmartre was mined for gypsum and still retained a country charm with its vineyards, cornfields, flocks of sheep and 40 windmills. This charm and the lofty isolation of the hill attracted artists and writers. Painters and their models frolicked in Place Pigalle, and people flocked to the Moulin Rouge. Impressionism, Fauvism and Cubism were conceived in the lofts, bars and dance halls of Montmartre.

When the Bohemians migrated to Montparnasse, the district was left to sex-shop owners, pawnbrokers and

PRECEDING PAGES:
one of the many
caricaturists in
Place du Tertre.
LEFT: Sacré-Coeur
on the Butte de
Montmartre.
BELOW: the notorious
Moulin Rouge.

TIP

The ideal way to see Montmartre is on foot, but the Montmartrobus and tourist train provide a less exhausting slice of the district and start from Place Blanche.

ABOVE: nightlife in *Gai Paree*.

cheap hotels and, for many years afterwards, Montmartre was synonymous wit[h] sleaze. Yet, today, the village is suddenly fashionable once more. Dingy stri[p] bars are being transformed into chic rock clubs, peep shows are becoming Amer[i] ican-style diners and the narrow streets roar with BMWs and Porsches.

The Moulin Rouge – a notorious dance hall

At Place Blanche, the **Moulin Rouge ❶**, with a red neon windmill, provides taste of tourist France to wealthy foreigners (the "French" dancers are selecte[d] from auditions in the US and the UK). The club's history is gloriously sca[n] dalous: Toulouse-Lautrec (*see page 100*) sat here during the *Belle Epoque* (*se*[*e*] *pages 36–37*), sketching the energetic cancan of Jane Avril. In 1896, the annu[al] Paris Art School Ball at the Moulin Rouge was the scene of the first fully nud[e] striptease, by one of the school's prettiest models. She was arrested, imprisone[d] and students went to the barricades in the Quartier Latin, proclaiming "The ba[t] tle for artistic nudity" – two students died in subsequent scuffles with polic[e.] The **Folies-Bergère** (Métro Cadet), about 2 km (1 mile) further south on R[ue] Richer (*see maps on pages 112–15*) has much the same fare. Next door to t[he] Moulin Rouge, modern hedonists gather at **La Locomotive**, a huge, train-shape[d] disco, ringing to rock, roll, and Europop. And a few doors away, on the Boul[e] vard de Clichy, the **Théatre des Deux Anes** offers typical Parisian cabaret.

The changing face of Pigalle

A little further east along Boulevard de Clichy lies **Place Pigalle ❷**, the gatew[ay] to Montmartre. Less artistic attractions abound in Pigalle, or "Pig Alley", as [it] was once known to American soldiers, for it has been the core of the Parisi[an]

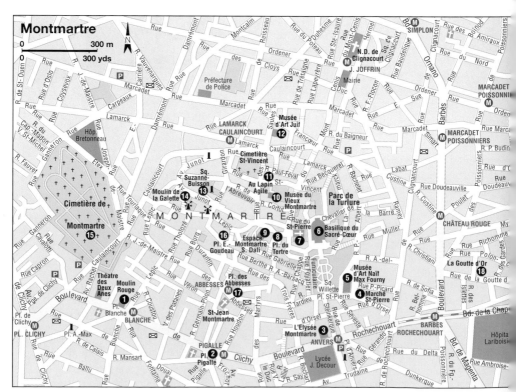

Montmartre

Map,
page 172

ex trade for several decades. Around the streets of Pigalle, tassled curtains pro-
ide glimpses of smoky interiors, slashed signs promote live sex shows and
ggressive bouncers attempt to persuade tourists into "naked extravaganzas".
eware – prices quoted are much lower than you will pay inside. Things are
hanging, however. The advent of Aids has drastically reduced custom, and a
efty increase in value-added tax, from 18.6 percent to 33.3 percent, has been
eliberately aimed at the sex trade.

The cabarets, which once occupied half the houses along Rue des Martyrs in
e 18th century are being taken over by hip clubs and trendy bars. At 72 Boule-
ard Rochechouart, the **Elysée Montmartre ❸** has come out of retirement to
ost up-and-coming rock groups. The old hall greeted Russian soldiers during
e Allied occupation of 1814. As they ordered their drinks (forbidden by the
ussian military authorities) they shouted "*bistro*" meaning "quickly", thereby
reating a Parisian institution. The *Belle Epoque* facade alone is worth the visit.

acré-Coeur – a church with a view

rom Boulevard Rochechouart, Rue de Steinkerque leads to Square Willette at
e foot of the hill, the top of which is called the "butte" of Montmartre. Here
front is the **Marché St-Pierre ❹**, specialising in clothing and cheap textiles
at often attract professional designers. Close by is the 1868 market hall
esigned by Baltard, the original architect of Les Halles (*see pages 150–51*).
ow a cultural centre, it houses the **Musée d'Art Naïf Max Fourny ❺** (open
aily; closed Mon; entrance fee), a museum exhibiting contemporary paintings
om around 30 countries, typified by simple themes and bright colours. The
uilding includes a children's **Musée en Herbe**, focusing on green issues.

TIP

If you plan to stay out
late, remember the
Métro closes at
12.30am, but for the
all-nighters it is open
again after 5.30am.
Night buses run on
some routes (*see
pages 267*).

BELOW LEFT: a
popular subject
for artists.

NIGHTSPOTS OF PIGALLE

Pigalle, which is cut
through the middle
by the Boulevard de
Clichy, is the centre of
Paris nightlife. Popular
venues include Folies
Pigalle (11 Place Pigalle), once a strip club
and now one of the most entertaining
nightspots; Le Dépanneur (27 Rue
Fontaine), the place to slam tequilas
around the clock in an imitation American
diner; Le Moloko (26 Rue Fontaine) is the
hang-out for models, bad boys and
transvestites – the kitsch dance floor,
smoking room and cocktail bar are open
all night. La Cigale (120 Boulevard de
Rochechouart) offers jazz, and for a trans-
vestite version of the Folies Bergères go
to Chez Madame Arthur (75 bis Rue des
Martyrs). Alternatively, Le Bar Jaune (6
Rue Germain, tel: 01 42 58 03 05) is a
laid-back, Bohemian hangout.

High up on the summit of the hill stands the impressive white bulk of th basilica of the **Sacré-Coeur** ❻, 35 Rue du Chevalier-de-la Barne (open dail 6am–11pm; entrance fee for dome and crypt; tel: 01 53 41 89 00). To get ther you can either walk up through the Square Willette, laid out in terraces in 1929 or take the *funiculaire* (cable car – Métro tickets are valid on it) alongside. Th domed basilica was conceived by a group of Roman Catholics in 1870 wh vowed to build a church to the Sacred Heart if Paris was delivered safely fror the Prussian siege – the heart of one of the men, Alexandre Legentil, has bee preserved in a stone urn in the crypt. The Church took on the responsibility of th project in 1873 and work started two years later. Paul Abadie, the architect i charge of the project, based his design on the Romano-Byzantine cathedral of S Front in Périgueux.

The bone-white colour of the building is due to its Chateau-Landon ston which secretes calcite when it rains, bleaching the walls. Its Byzantine austerit added to its symbolic censure of a popular uprising, has rendered Sacré-Coer one of the Parisians' least favourite monuments.

Completed in 1914 but not consecrated until after the war in 1919, the dom offers a stunning view over Paris, up 237 narrow spiral steps (this is the secon highest vantage point over the city, after the Eiffel Tower) and from the staine glass gallery beneath there is a good view of the cavernous interior which, apa from the massive Byzantine mosaic of Christ (1912–22) by Luc Olivier Mersc on the chancel's vaulted ceiling, has little else to offer.

Outside on the terrace, crowds gather together in the early evening to drir wine, strum guitars and watch the glittering lights of Paris, overlooked by statu of Joan of Arc and St Louis on horseback.

The Sacré-Coeur is dominated by an 83-metre (262-ft) belltower, built in 1895, holding one of the heaviest bells in the world at nearly 19 tonnes. Its clapper weighs 850 kg (1,900 lb).

BELOW: art and food in Place du Tertre.

On the "butte"

Next to the exotic Sacré-Coeur, the simple church of **St-Pierre de Montmartre** ❽ is the second oldest in Paris (after St-Germain-des-Prés, *see page 192*), dating from 1133, and the only remaining vestige of the Abbey of Montmartre, where the Bendictine nuns used to live. After the Revolution, the church was abandoned, until it was reconsecrated in 1908. If you are here on *Toussaint* (All Saints' Day – 1 November), visit the small, romantic graveyard behind the church, because this is the only day of the year that it is open.

Just to the west, **Place du Tertre** ❽ is the tourist honeypot of Montmartre, with its "authentic" bistros, and even more "authentic" craft shops. The square was once the site of the village hall and today it is ruled by the mighty franc. In the 19th century, artists began exhibiting their work here and now there are legions of mediocre artists on the square (two per square metre) who are voluble when selling their wares. Yet, despite this oppressive commercialisation, the square retains an animated excitement at night, lit up by fairylights.

From the Place du Tertre, quiet, winding Rue Poulbot leads through **Place du Calvaire** – the smallest square in Paris, which offers a spectacular view and is the intimate home of lovers and drinkers – to the **Espace Montmartre Salvador Dalí** ❾ at 11 Rue Poulbert (open daily 10am–6.30pm; entrance fee; tel: 01 42 64 40 10). A select collection of 330 sculptures and drawings of the surrealist Catalan painter are exhibited in unusual settings here, including his famous clocks representing "the fluidity of time".

A few minutes' walk further on, Rue des Saules passes the top of Rue St-Rustique, a quiet, rustically ancient street leading away from the buzz of the Place du Tertre, which contains the **Auberge La Bonne Franquette**, originally called

Map, page 172

On Christmas Eve in 1898, Louis Renault drove the first petrol-driven car to reach the top of the "butte".

BELOW LEFT: getting together in a bar in Montmartre.

A MASTER OF SURREALISM

A true eccentric, Catalan painter, Salvador Dalí (1904–89) was desparate to go to Paris in the 1920s, for it was considered to be the art capital and already conquered by fellow Spaniards Picasso and Joan Miró. After studying art in Madrid and mixing with such Spanish modernists as film director Luis Buñuel, he finally reached Paris in 1929. With the help of the two established, older artists offering him introductions and motivated by his "Catalan sense of fantasy", Dalí held his first Surrealist exhibition that very same year. Through Miró, Dalí met other Surrealists, many of whom he was to quarrel with later. Picasso once declared that Dalí's imagination reminded him of "an outboard motor continually running", and the painter himself wanted to "systemise confusion".

*Auguste Renoir
(1841–1919) was an
Impressionist who
loved to paint the
joyful and attractive
sides of Paris,
mainly using pretty
girls in colourful
clothes as subjects.*

BELOW: art for sale
in Montmartre.
BELOW RIGHT: sight-
seeing the easy way.

Le Billard en Bois, where Vincent Van Gogh and Auguste Renoir both painte
The crossroads outside the inn and other street scenes were immortalised b
Utrillo (*see page 100*) in his paintings. Other frequent vistors were Cézann
Toulouse-Lautrec (*see page 100*), Monet (*see pages 122–23, 253*) and Zola.

Old Montmartre

In Rue Cortot, the next street along, is the **Musée du Vieux Montmartre ◆**
(open daily; closed Mon; entrance fee), which chronicles the life and times of th
"butte" in an old rural residence. Originally the country home of Rozimund, a
actor in Molière's theatre company and whose death in 1686 was similar
Molière's while acting in *Le Malade Imaginaire* (*see page 124*), it also house
Renoir, Dufy (*see page 101*) and Utrillo. The museum is an evocation of pa
simplicity, gaiety and Bohemian living, with pictures by Kees van Dong
(1877–1968) and Dufy, reconstructions of Utrillo's favourite café and an artis
studio, yellowing photographs and a wonderful view over Paris. Composer Er
Satie (1866–1925) lived in the same street. His house is now a small museu
and a seven-person concert hall.

Nearby is the famous **vineyard of Montmartre**, cultivated since the Midd
Ages. At the beginning of October, the grape harvest attracts hundreds of vo
unteers and the streets host processions and parties. Around 300 litres of wine a
sold at auction, with the proceeds going to Montmartre pensioners.

The famous inn **Au Lapin Agile ⑪** (open evenings; closed Mon; entran
fee; tel: 01 46 06 85 87) stands opposite the vineyard at 22 Rue des Saules. Th
was the haunt of the bright and beautiful *circa* 1900: a restaurant-cabaret, whe
Renoir and the symbolist poet Paul Verlaine (1844–96) laid tables and Gu

laume Apollinaire sang with fellow Surrealist poet Max Jacob. Picasso paid for a day's meals at the Lapin with one of his *Harlequin* paintings – today worth several million pounds. The name of this small hut on the hill, shrouded with trees, originated from humorist André Gill's 1880 wall picture of a rabbit jumping over a cooking pot, which people called the "Lapin à Gill". Today, a tourist attraction, the inn, with smoke-stained walls, original paintings by Cubist Fernand Léger (1881–1955) and Gill, and old wooden tables, is still going strong. Get here by 9pm, and imbibe, sitting in the corner once inhabited by Picasso or Verlaine. A cabaret is provided, taking you back in time and encouraging audience participation.

Passing the **Cimetière St-Vincent** where Utrillo lies in peace, Rue des Saules leads to the **Musée d'Art Juif ⓬** (open afternoons; closed Fri and Sat; entrance fee), a collection of Jewish art, containing works by Soutine (1894–1943) and Pissarro, along with a Bible illustrated by Marc Chagall.

Tranquil Montmartre

Far from the helter-skelter animation of Pigalle and Place du Tertre, the west of Montmartre, on the other side of St Vincent cemetery, is a puzzle of small old streets and tumbledown houses. Take the steps from Place Constantin-Pecqueur, off Rue Caulaincourt, to **Square Suzanne-Buisson ⓭**, one of the most romantic corners of Montmartre with a terrace and antiquated lamps.

The square occupies the former garden of the **Château des Brouillards**, an 18th-century folly once inhabited by Renoir and the mad, symbolist poet Gérard de Nerval (who hanged himself in 1855, leaving a note saying, "Don't wait for me, for the night will be black and white"), and later turned into a dance hall.

Map, page 172

ABOVE AND BELOW:
Au Lapin Agile
where artists and
intellectuals used to
congregate.

The Dutch painter Vincent Van Gogh (1853–90) lived in Rue Lepic between 1886 and 1888. Here, he painted his Self-Portrait with a Gray Hat. *While in Paris, he taught himself the French Impressionist techniques, breaking away from his dark painting to make better use of colour.*

During the 19th century, the "château" could only be seen when the *brouillards* (thick fogs) of Montmartre lifted, hence the name. In the middle of the square, a statue of St Denis washes the blood off his head while watching the old men playing *boules*.

From the square, **Avenue Junot** is one of the widest and most expensive streets in Montmartre. Constructed in 1910, the avenue cut through the ancient *maquis* scrubland that used to cover the hillside, where windmills turned their graceful sails and goats scampered among the trees. The street's 1920s' Art Deco elegance has attracted the cream of Montmartre society – the singer Claude Nougaro lives in the big ochre house. **Le Hameau des Artistes** (No. 11) still provides artists' studios. **Maison Tristan Tzara** (No. 15) is named after the eccentric Romanian Dadaist poet who once lived here and was designed especially for him by the Austrian architect Adolf Loos.

Below, on the corner of Rue Girardon and Rue Lepic, is the last of the great windmills of Montmartre, **Moulin de la Galette** ⓲. Built in 1604, the windmill became an illustrious dance hall in the 19th century. The artists and writers living in Montmartre often hosted parties here and it was during one of these occasions that Auguste Renoir began sketches for his famous painting *Le Moulin de la Galette* (1866). Emile Zola held a party here to celebrate the success of his novel *L'Assommoir* (1877), set in La Goutte d'Or to the east of Montmartre. (The novelist lived just below the village on Boulevard de Clichy.) Earlier, in the 1814 siege of Paris, the four Debray brothers had fought fiercely to save their windmill from the Russians – one of them was subsequently crucified on its sails. Today, the windmill is better protected, as a notice proclaims "Residence under electronic, radar and guard-dog surveillance".

BELOW: an antique bookstall in Montmartre.

Map,
page 172

Picturesque Rue Lepic, leading from the windmill and past the Moulin de Radet, descends to Place Blanche. The old quarry road housed Vincent Van Gogh and his brother Theo, an art dealer, at No. 54 for two years in the late 1880s. During that time, Van Gogh is said to have presented his paintings at Le Tambourin, a seedy cabaret on Boulevard de Clichy, until the owner demanded that he remove them, as they disturbed her customers.

Au Virage Lepic (No. 61) is an ancient bar-restaurant that preserves the traditions of Montmartre – busy, inexpensive and animated by local singers and poets. Further down the hill, where the lively Lepic food market is held each morning, stop at **Le Lux** (No. 12) for a white wine or hot chocolate beneath the beautiful 1909 facade. **Le Restaurant** on Rue Véron, just off Rue Lepic, provides food as stylishly simplistic as its name and is much loved by the young and beautiful of the district.

The **Cimetière de Montmartre** ⓯, just west of Rue Lepic, reflects the artistic bias of the area. The tombs are elegantly sculpted and their inmates appropriately famous: here lie the 19th-century writer Stendhal, whose real name was Henri Beyle, novelist Alexandre Dumas, poet and critic Théophile Gautier, painter Edgar Degas, dancer Waslaw Nijinsky, composers Hector Berlioz and Jacques Offenbach, and Zola's bust (his body was moved to the Panthéon). Film director François Truffaut was buried here in 1984.

On your way back to Pigalle, cut down Rue des Abbesses and turn left into Rue Ravignan, just before Place des Abbesses, for a small detour to **Place Émile-Goudeau** ⓰, a particularly attractive square. At No. 13, modern art studios have replaced the wooden ramshackle building called **Le Bateau-Lavoir**, so named because it resembled a floating laundry. This artists' den housed Picasso and fellow Cubists Georges Braque and Van Dongen in the narrow ship-like corridors. Picasso painted *Les Desmoiselles d'Avignon* (1907) here in his chaotic studio, recalling the prostitutes of Barcelona, and Apollinaire and Max Jacob liberated verse-form in the rooms alongside. Unfortunately, the building burnt down in 1970 just as it was about to be renovated.

Turning left out of the square, take the Passage des Abbesses, a little further on, down to the picturesque **Place des Abbesses** ⓱ and the remarkable Art Nouveau Métro station, designed by Guimard (see *page 94*). Alongside the spiralling steps into the station is a mural painted by local artists. Just east of the square at 9 Rue Yvonne-Le-Tac, on the site of St Denis's decapitation, Ignatius Loyola and François Xavier founded the Jesuit order of the Society of Jesus in 1534.

Cosmopolitan Montmartre

To the east of Montmartre is the district of **La Goutte-d'Or** ⓲, vividly described by Zola in *L'Assommoir*. Today, the old workers' hovels are being razed for new developments. The conglomeration of Islamic butchers, African grocers, West Indian bakers, Jewish jewellers and Arab tailors is a never-ending spectacle of sight, sound and smell. Over 30 nationalities live side by side in the streets around Rue de la Goutte-d'Or, Rue Charbonnière and Rue des Poissoniers. Cut-price shopping at Tati on Boulevard Rochechouart. ❑

In 1911, novelist Roland Dorgelès played a joke on the Bateau-Lavoir Surrealists by tying a paintbrush to a donkey's tail and calling the result Sunset over the Adriatic, which he sold for 400F. Apollinaire, a keen follower of Cubism and an art critic, was not amused.

BELOW: oysters on the hoof.

THE LEFT BANK AND MONTPARNASSE

Map, pages 184/5

Writers, artists and thinkers have left their indelible mark on these areas since Roman times. Places to see include the Hôtel de Cluny, the Panthéon and the Jardin des Plantes, an oasis of natural history

Extending southwards, the Rive Gauche, or Left Bank, comprises several well-defined areas, with the Quartier Latin, an intimate puzzle of small streets and historic architecture between Boulevard St-Michel and the Jardin des Plantes, at its ancient heart. This has been the stamping ground of students for nearly eight centuries and, thanks to the concentration of academic institutions that grew up in the area, Latin was virtually the mother tongue until Napoleon put a stop to it after the Revolution. The elegant and chic hide in neighbouring St-Germain-des-Prés, the historical centre of literary Paris and existentialism on the west side of the Boulevard St-Michel. The once-Bohemian Montparnasse, to the south, is now host to a modern business centre, but still preserves its lively atmosphere at night.

The Rive Gauche maintains a roguish charm in its beautiful tree-lined boulevards, ancient, narrow streets, manicured parks and imposing monuments, as well as an intellectual arrogance that manages to stay just the right side of pretentious. This is the place in which to stroll, imbibe and look cool. Sit in the shaded parks by day and scan the menus in the fairylit streets by night. Be warned, though, this is not the area to go looking for typical Parisian cuisine.

PRECEDING PAGES: selling wares at the Marché Vanves on the Left Bank. **LEFT:** a chic student. **BELOW:** inside the Hôtel de Cluny.

The Quartier Latin – an area of rebellion

Settled by the Romans in 53 BC and a cradle of philosophy and art since the Middle Ages, the Quartier Latin conjures up contradictions and delights in paradox, epitomised by the words of student and poet François Villon in 1456, who declared "I laugh in tears." Villon debated with professors at the Sorbonne by day and drank with thieves in the brothels of St-Michel by night.

Villon's legacy of rebellion has survived. In 1871, the Place St-Michel was the headquarters of the Paris Commune (*see page 36*). Then in May 1968, demonstrations against deteriorating conditions in the Nanterre faculty led to students tearing up the old cobblestones of Boulevard St-Michel to hurl at the riot police. Hundreds of students were arrested, the University of Paris was decentralised, and the ancient cobblestones were buried under concrete forever (*see pages 39–40*). Protests, albeit subdued, still take place when roads are sometimes blocked by squatting students, eager to relive the glorious past of their revolutionary predecessors.

However, the Quartier Latin still remains a place of happy incongruity, where countless Greek *souvlaki* vendors stand amid traditional cafés spilling over the pavements, and new-wave cinemas front ancient academic facades.

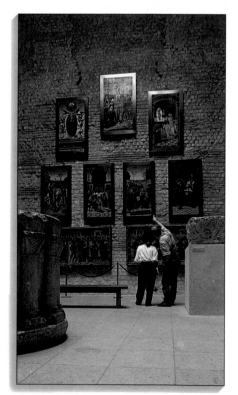

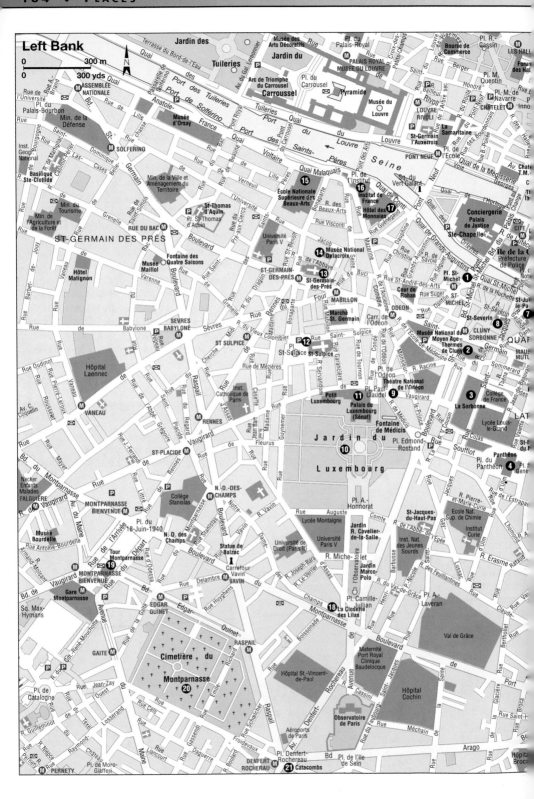

Left Bank

0 ——— 300 m
0 ——— 300 yds

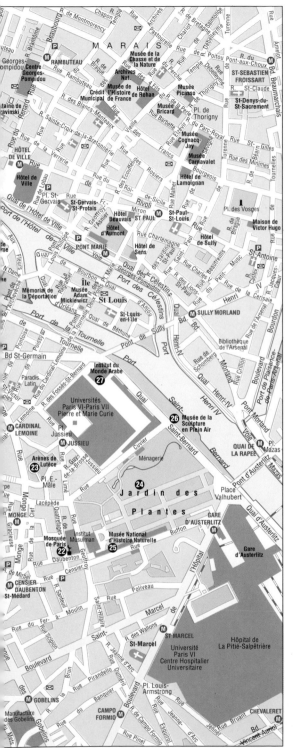

Along the Boul' Mich

Across the river from the palaces of justice and salvation (the Préfecture de Police and Notre Dame), **Place St-Michel** ❶ revels in recklessness. The fountain depicting St Michael and a surprised dragon often seems buried under scooters, lip-locked lovers and the ubiquitous *clochards* (tramps), sitting philosophically amid youthful chaos. Extending south, the grand **Boulevard St-Michel** ("Boul' Mich" to the initiated) will nourish the senses, the mind and the stomach, with an assortment of stalls, bookshops, alternative cinemas and fast-food joints.

By the crossroads of Boul' Mich and Boulevard St-Germain stands the fine 15th-century **Hôtel de Cluny**, which is home to the **Musée National du Moyen Age – Thermes de Cluny** ❷ (open daily 9.15am–5.45pm; closed Tues and pub. hols; entrance fee). Once the residence of the Abbots of Cluny, who rebuilt the mansion to how it is today, these Gothic walls house one of the world's finest collections of medieval artefacts. Many of the treasures reflect life in the religious communities such as illuminated manuscripts, embroideries, stained glass, liturgical vestments and church furnishings.

Among the numerous tapestries is the exquisite, 15th-century **La Dame à la Licorne** (The Lady and the Unicorn) on the first floor of the rotunda. The six panels are beautifully worked in the *mille-fleurs* style of design, using rich, harmonious colours. The museum also includes 21 of the original heads of the Kings of Judah, dating from 1220, from Notre Dame cathedral, which were vandalised during the Revolution (*see page 141*).

Here, too, are the remains of a huge **Gallo-Roman bath house** complex, which is believed to have been built in AD 200 by the guild of boatmen (*nautes*), as their unusual symbol of carved ships' prows were found on the arch supports of the *frigidarium* (cold bath house). As elsewhere in their empire, the Romans decided to civilise a barbarian people with hot baths and mindless violence, but the barbarians got the better of them 100 years later when they ransacked the joint.

ABOVE: a section of the six-panel, 15th-century tapestry, *La Dame à la Licorne*, in Hôtel de Cluny.
BELOW: university chapel in Place de la Sorbonne.

The Sorbonne – the oldest university in France

In a reversal of history, Greeks now seem to have overrun Romans in the streets leading from the Cluny baths, where Greek restaurants of dubious pedigree vie for custom with a ferociousness rarely seen outside Athens. Continue south down Boul' Mich a little way to the eternal pulse of the Quartier Latin, the **Sorbonne ❸** (open 9am–4.30pm Mon–Fri; closed weekends and pub. hols; free). Established in 1253 by St Louis and his confessor Robert de Sorbon, the oldest university in France has been rebuilt many times since its inception as a dormitory for 16 theology students, when it soon started to attract great thinkers from all over Europe.

In 1469, France's first printing press was set up by three Germans summoned by Louis XI, which encouraged the growth of intellectual life (*see page 29*). During the Revolution, the university was closed and allowed to become run down but, afterwards, Napoleon revitalised it and it grew once again to be the most important university in France. Now, since decentralisation in 1970, there are 13 universities in Paris and the Sorbonne has lost its force.

Entering from Rue des Ecoles, you can wander through the corridors and galleries, which are lined with meaningful paintings that reflect the university's long history. The 17th-century **chapel**, commissioned by Sorbonne alumnus Cardinal Richelieu and containing his marble tomb, overlooks the university's main courtyard. Above the tomb, beautifully carved by François Girardon, hangs a hat believed to be the cardinal's. Legend has it that the hat will fall when Richelieu's soul is released from hell.

Across Rue St-Jacques, in the next block, is the **Collège de France** (open Oct–Jun daily and Sat morning; closed Sun; free), set up by François I in 1530 on

Map, pages 184/5

the inspiration of the great humanist Guillaume Budé, to offer an unexpurgated education, unfettered by the intolerance and dogmatism of the Sorbonne. Today, the college still has its own say academically, although it is financially dependent on the state, and lectures are open to the public without charge. Next door, the **Lycée Louis-le-Grand** is the school in which Jean-Paul Sartre taught and from which the 19th-century poet and art critic Charles Baudelaire was expelled. Other old boys include Molière, Victor Hugo and Georges Pompidou.

The Panthéon – an ultimate resting place

A little further on, dominating the summit of Mont Ste-Geneviève, the **Panthéon** ❹, 5 Place du Panthéon (open daily Oct–Mar 10am–5.30pm; Apr–Sept 9.30am–6.30pm; closed pub. hols; entrance fee; tel: 01 44 32 18 00), is the sort of domed-and-colonnaded monument famous people would die to be buried in. Inspired by Rome's Panthéon, it was conceived following Louis XV's rash vow to build a church should he recover from illness in 1744. Money was short, however, and so public lotteries were organised to raise funds. Designed by neo-classical architect Jacques-Germain Soufflot (1713–80), the building was finished after his death but just in time for the Revolution, when in 1791 the church was designated a pantheon for the "Founders of Liberty", a monument to rival the royal mausoleum at St-Denis (*see page 250*). Thus Voltaire, who was transferred from the country, and Jean-Jacques Rousseau came to lie in the crypt and later Victor Hugo, Emile Zola and Louis Braille, inventor of writing for the blind; Nobel Prizewinning scientists Pierre and Marie Curie joined them in 1995. The body of the World War II Resistance hero Jean Moulin was reburied here in the 1970s.

After the Revolution, the use of the Panthéon yo-yoed from church to necropolis to church to headquarters of the Commune, until it finally became a civic building and lay temple in 1885. The interior is laid out in the shape of a Greek cross with the iron-framed dome towering above the centre. Frescoes depicting the life of Ste Geneviève line the south wall and her glorification is portrayed on the inside of the upper section of the dome.

Across Place Ste-Geneviève rises the richly ornate church of **St-Etienne-du-Mont** ❺ (open daily, closed noon–2.30pm and pub. hols; Jul–Aug closed Mon; free; tel: 01 43 54 11 79), which has a wonderful Renaissance rood (crucifix) screen. Playwright Jean Racine (1639–99) and the scientist Blaise Pascal (1623–62) are buried here and a marble slab near the entrance marks where the Archbishop of Paris was stabbed to death by a priest in 1857. To the right of the chancel is the shrine of Ste Geneviève who saved Paris from Attila the Hun in AD 451 (*see pages 25–26*).

Latin lanes

Heading back towards the Seine for a little way, the **Musée de la Préfecture de Police** ❻ is just across the Rue des Ecoles. This houses an intriguing jumble of macabre objects, weapons and documents. Cinema aficionados should pop into *Action Ecoles* or *Action Rive Gauche* (23 and 5 Rue des Ecoles) for quirky film classics, both in American and French.

By hanging his pendulum from the top of the Panthéon's dome in 1851, Léon Foucault (1819–98) publicly proved that the world was round and rotated. The pendulum is kept in the Musée National des Techniques (see page 164).

BELOW: a student meeting outside the Panthéon.

*The original
Shakespeare and
Company bookshop
was founded in 1921
in Rue de l'Odéon by
American Sylvia
Beach, who
shockingly published
James Joyce's*
Ulysses. *Throughout
the 1920s and 1930s,
her bookshop and
library was at the hub
of the literary world,
with regulars such as
Gertrude Stein,
Ernest Hemingway,
T.S. Eliot and Ezra
Pound. It closed
down in 1941 during
World War II.*

BELOW: a bookshop
for English readers.

Continuing on towards the Seine, you will reach **Place Maubert**, from where there is a network of small, medieval streets lined with a jumble of boutiques revealing their shadowy interiors to the curious. Quiet repose is to be found in the church of **St-Julien-le-Pauvre ❼**, off Rue Lagrange, (open daily; closed 1–3pm; free) in the shadow of Notre Dame. In the garden, you can sit under a 300-year-old false acacia, the second oldest tree in Paris (*see page 196*) and contemplate those who have done the same over the centuries. Behind is Rue du Fouarre, named after the bales of hay on which students used to perch during open-air lectures in the Middle Ages. The Italian poet Dante sat here in 1304.

Shakespeare and Company, at 37 Rue de la Bûcherie, parallel to the Seine, is Paris's most famous English bookshop, containing a range of literature, from the Bard to the Beatniks. Founded in 1956 by American George Whitman on similar lines to Sylvia Beach's original in Rue de l'Odéon, the shop attracted writers such as William Burroughs and James Baldwin. Today, it still closes at midnight, too soon for the addicted.

Le Petit Pont close by is a perfect spot from which to see the lights of the Seine at night. Here, the Quais St-Michel and Montebello offer picture-book views of the Ile de la Cité. By day, ancient bookstalls line the riverbanks, offering overpriced, antique volumes. Trial by Revolutionary council has been replaced with trial by jazz at **Caveau de la Huchette** (5 Rue de la Huchette). Danton and Robespierre selected guillotine victims in the cellars where jazz musician Maxim Saury now executes dixie stomps to great acclaim. At No. 10, a young Napoleon dreamed of power.

The beautiful Flamboyant Gothic church of **St-Séverin ❽**, in the next street, is famous for its mighty organ loft. The church has been a place of pageantry

since the Fourth Crusade set out from St-Séverin to conquer the Holy Land in 1204. In the adjacent cemetery, in 1744, the world's first gallstone operation was carried out on a death-row criminal, who was pardoned following the operation's success.

Map, pages 184/5

The Odéon – a bustling nightlife

Across Boul' Mich from St-Séverin, the Odéon district nestles between the boisterous Quartier Latin and the refined elegance of St-Germain-des-Prés. The antiquated charm of the streets that fan out from St-Michel Mètro belie the area's bustling nightlife, which is as inspired and dedicated as any in the city.

A short walk along Rue St-André-des-Arts takes you to Rue de l'Ancienne-Comédie, the next street along, where **Le Procope**, the first café to open in Paris and introduce coffee in 1686, is still doing good business. From here, it's worthwhile looking in at **Cour de Rohan** to see its picturesque courtyards with Renaissance facades. Behind is Rue du Jardinet, where the composer Camille Saint-Saëns was born in 1835.

Across Boulevard St-Germain stands the Revolutionary leader Georges Danton's statue at the **Carrefour de l'Odéon** marking his old house. Fellow Revolutionary Camille Desmoulins lived at No. 2 before storming the Bastille in 1789. Others plotted in neighbouring streets to the north, which now host some of the more bourgeois boutiques and apartments in Paris.

From here, Rue de l'Odéon, the first street in Paris to have pavements and gutters, runs parallel with Rue de Condé, where Beaumarchais wrote *The Barber of Seville* in 1773, a play whose theme of a common man usurping the nobility prefigured the rebellion of the man in the street.

Above: the guillotine, invented by Dr Guillotin near the Odéon.
Below: café *branché* on the Left Bank.

F. Scott Fitzgerald finished his most famous novel, The Great Gatsby *(1925), portrayed on screen by Robert Redford and Mia Farrow (above), at 58 Rue de Vaugirard, just south of the romantic Jardin du Luxembourg.*

BELOW: drawing in the Jardin du Luxembourg.

Place de l'Odéon is one of the livelier squares in Paris, especially at 2am. Here the **Théâtre National de l'Odéon** ❾ presents large-scale productions of foreign-language theatre, from the likes of Henrik Ibsen and Arthur Miller, while the smaller **Petit Odéon** within features *avant-garde* works. In 1968, the theatre was occupied by students who donned Roman helmets from the props department to protect themselves during battles with the police (*see pages 39–40*).

Jardin du Luxembourg – a Parisian favourite

No statistics exist relating exactly how many people have fallen in love in the **Jardin du Luxembourg** ❿, but if poets as miserable as Baudelaire and Verlaine had a good time here, the garden's magic is evidently potent. Young couples meet under the plane trees by the romantic Baroque **Fontaine de Médici** and stroll to the pool to watch children sail boats across the carp-filled water. Statues of the queens of France gaze down from the terrace, while the thwack of tennis balls disturbs the reverie of nannies pushing designer babies in designer prams.

On Wednesdays and weekends, the famous Guignol puppet show takes place in the **Théâtre des Marionettes**. More serious entertainment is located at the corner with Rue de Vaugirard, where wise old men take on earnest students at chess under the fragrant orange trees. There are 200 varieties of apple and pear tree in the garden and the beehives produce several hundred kilos of honey a year. Here, in the middle of the city, you can take bee-keeping lessons.

The Luxembourg neighbourhood was terrorised in the 13th-century by a bandit called Vauvert, who operated in an old ruin until he was evicted by Carthusian monks in 1257. As a result, they founded a monastery there, creating a vegetable garden and tree nursery still situated at the south of the garden.

The **Palais du Luxembourg**  (guided tours by arrangement in advance, tel: 01 44 61 21 69) was built for Marie de Médicis on the site of a mansion belonging to Duke François of Luxembourg (hence the name), in the style of the Pitti Palace in Florence. Unfortunately, she was banished by Cardinal Richelieu before it was completed in 1631. During the Revolution, the palace was used as a prison and in World War II the Germans made it their headquarters.

Now fortunate French Senators enjoy its Restoration interior and luxurious views of the gardens, for it is the seat of the *Sénat* (the Upper House of Parliament, as chosen by an electoral college of politicians). The even luckier President of the Senate gets to live next door in the **Petit Luxembourg**. American novelist Ernest Hemingway adored the Jardin du Luxembourg. His three principal residences during the 1920s neatly circumscribe the park, where he would saunter each afternoon. As he wrote later: "It was sad when the park was closed, and I was sad walking around it instead of through it."

From Petit Luxembourg, the Rue Garancière leads north to the imposing church of **St-Sulpice** ⑫, a short walk away. Apart from one of the finest organs in Paris and Eugène Delacroix's *Jacob Wrestling with the Angel,* modelled on the painter's own struggle with Art (*see page 192*), the great cavern of a church has little to offer. In front of the huge colonnaded facade, with mismatching towers, is a large square with an amusing fountain made by Joachim Visconti in 1844.

St-Germain-des-Prés – an elegant neighbourhood

The historical heart of literary Paris, St-Germain-des-Prés is an area stretching roughly from St-Sulpice to the Seine and encompassed to the west by Boulevard St-Germain. Its elegant streets house elegant boutiques, yet it still retains a

Map, pages 184/5

In Place St-Sulpice the Fontaine des Quatre Points Cardinaux shows four bishops at the cardinal points of the compass. A play on words, the name can mean the Fountain of the (compass) Cardinal Points or the Four Cardinals who Never Were.

BELOW: the odd towers of St-Sulpice.

LEFT BANK RENDEZVOUS

Café Voltaire (1 Place de l'Odéon), named after its most famous regular, was where, in the 18th century, Voltaire used to meet fellow philosopher Diderot to discuss their Enlightenment theories. The tormented 19th-century poets Verlaine and Mallarmé threw Symbolist ideas at each other there and, much later, the American writers Hemingway and F. Scott Fitzgerald extolled the café's "sudden provincial quality".

Writers between the two world wars spent hours at their favourite tables in Le Procope (13 Rue de l'Ancienne-Comédie) and existentialist writer Jean-Paul Sartre and his lover Simone de Beauvoir (*see pages 198–99*) consolidated the highbrow reputation of Les Deux Magots (6 Place St-Germain-des-Prés) in the 1950s. The Art Deco Café de Flore (172 Boulevard St-Germain) was another Sartre favourite. Today, politicians congregate at Brasserie Lipp across the road.

Place de Fürstenburg is one of the most romantic corners of Paris. The antique, white-globed street lamps and paulownia trees inspire poetry and black-and-white photography.

ABOVE: not everyone is academic on the Left Bank.
BELOW: all set for a good meal.

sense of animation, passed down from the 1950s (*see pages 198–99*), with crowded cafés spilling out on to the pavements. From St-Sulpice, head north to Boulevard St-Germain and the covered **Marché St-Germain** in Rue Mabillon, where both the vegetables and characters are colourful.

The church of **St-Germain-des-Prés** ⓭, close by, is the oldest in Paris, dating from 542 when it was originally a basilica for some holy relics. Ransacked and rebuilt over centuries, the resulting, heavily restored 11th-century building is an unsubtle blend of simple Romanesque and pretentious Baroque. In the small square alongside, Picasso's tribute to his friend, *Homage to Apollinaire,* stands under the steeple. Across the square, **Les Deux Magots** serves the best hot chocolate in Paris. Once the favourite haunt of the literati, the café is still popular – apparently, the waiters cover 12 km (about 7 miles) a day.

From the square, take Rue de Fürstenburg to the **Musée Delacroix** ⓮ (open daily 9.30am–5pm; closed Tues; entrance fee; tel: 01 44 41 86 50), where Romantic painter Eugène Delacroix (1798–1863) lived and worked for the last few years of his life.

Academia on the riverbank

From the charming Place de Fürstenburg, the streets to the Seine are awash with antique shops and art galleries, and the narrow Rue Visconti takes you to Paris's finest art school, the **Ecole Nationale Supérieure des Beaux-Arts** ⓯ (open daily; closed weekends; free), which includes two *hôtels* fronting on to the Quai Malaquais. From 1608, the school was a monastery until the Revolution, when it was used to store pillaged works of art. In 1816, the School of Fine Arts moved in and today holds public exhibitions of students' work.

Close by, and a dictionary's throw from the river, squats the imposing and majestic **Institut de France** , incorporating the **Académie Française** (*see page 197*). The illustrious academy, created in 1635, concentrates on safeguarding the French language and compiling *the* French Dictionary. From here you can cross the Seine safely to the Louvre (*see pages 117–21, 134–35*) by way of the pedestrian-only **Pont des Arts**.

Next door is the 16th-century **Hôtel des Monnaies** ⑰. When Louis XV installed the royal mint here, he commissioned the architect Jacques Antoine to build the workshops, completed in 1775. Antoine so liked his creation that he lived there until his death in 1801. It now houses the **Musée de la Monnaie** (open daily, Wed till 9pm; closed Tues morning and Mon; entrance fee), a museum of money and medallions and not for the easily bored. Along the Seine towards St-Michel is the **Quai des Grands-Augustins**. The oldest quay on the river, its facade is filled with antiquarian bookshops and antique dealers. Picasso lived for 20 years on Rue des Grands-Augustins, branching off the quay.

From art to business in Montparnasse

The once rural area around the Tour Montparnasse, southwest of the Jardin du Luxembourg, was christened Mount Parnassus (after the classical home of Apollo and his muses) by a local Dead Poets' Society in the 17th century, which gathered on quarry mounds to recite verse. Around the time of the Revolution, the district, then on the outskirts of Paris, became a pleasure ground as cafés, bars and dance halls sprang up everywhere. In the early 1900s, when the Bohemians decamped from Montmartre, young writers and artists such as Chagall and Léger set up studios in Montparnasse and were soon joined by Picasso.

Map, pages 184/5

TIP

Around the Ecole des Beaux-Arts – Picasso's old stamping ground – there is a notable concentration of art galleries, especially in the Rue de Seine, Rue des Beaux-Arts and the Rue Jacob.

BELOW LEFT: Tour Montparnasse – built for business. **BELOW:** view from the top of the tower.

La Closerie des Lilas, at 171 Boulevard du Montparnasse, was a favourite haunt of Jean-Paul Sartre (above). The mad 19th-century poet Gérard de Nerval used to walk his pet lobster on a lead at La Rotonde (No 105).

BELOW: busking in Rue Mouffetard.

Between the wars, the world was here – Lenin, Trotsky, Stravinsky, Man Ray, Cocteau and the Americans, including Gertrude Stein, F. Scott Fitzgerald and Hemingway – and Montparnasse became known simply as the Quarter. You did not have to live here to belong to it, as Hemingway's character Jake Barnes explains in *The Sun Also Rises* (1926), "Perfectly good Quarterites live outside the actual boundaries of Montparnasse. They can live anywhere, as long as they come to the Quarter to think." In fact, Hemingway wrote this novel at the **Closerie des Lilas** ⓲, (171 Bd du Montparnasse; tel: 01 40 51 34 50) one of the many trendy bars along Boulevard Montparnasse. The tables are inscribed with the names of its illustrious clients, including Lenin, Modigliani and Surrealist poet André Breton. Fittingly, Hemingway's plaque rests on the bar.

The Spanish Civil War (1936–39) brought this artistic era to an end as those with high socialist ideals went off to fight. After World War II, the philosophers such as Jean-Paul Sartre and Simone de Beauvoir moved in, patronising the same cafés clustered around the lively Carrefour Vavin, now Place Pablo Picasso, which still throbs with life well into the early hours. Close by, Rodin's dramatic **Statue de Balzac**, once despised, is now adored. Magnificent studios still exist along Boulevard Raspail (peek in at Studio Raspail at No. 216) and Boulevard Montparnasse (pass through to the second courtyard at No. 126).

The district is dominated by the **Tour Montparnasse** ⓳ (open daily; entrance fee), 59 storeys high, inaugurated in 1973 as part of a new business complex. The tower has one asset: from its top floor you cannot see the Tour Montparnasse. You can, however, get a great view of the city. Just below, before the **Place du 18 Juin 1940** – the date of General Charles de Gaulle's famous BBC speech urging the Resistance to keep fighting against the German occupation – is the

THE PARIS CATACOMBS

Several million skeletons line the miles of passageways of the Catacombs ⓴ (open 2–4pm daily, also 9am–11am weekends; closed Mon and pub. hols; entrance fee; tel: 01 43 22 47 63) under Place Denfert-Rochereau. The Roman quarries became ossuaries in 1785, when, over 15 months, cartloads of skeletons and corpses were removed from the overflowing cemeteries at Place des Innocents (*see page 150*) and other areas. Take a torch, and someone to hold your hand, as the inscription on the door reads "Stop. Here begins the empire of the dead". Not everyone has felt squeamish about fraternising with the dead. Wild parties used to be thrown here before the Revolution, and during World War II, the catacombs were the headquarters of the French Resistance.

Map, pages 184/5

Centre Commercial on eight levels, six of which are below ground with a shopping mall in the top three. Behind the tower is the modernised Gare Montparnasse from where thousands of Bretons emerged, fleeing rural poverty and famine in Brittany, during the mid-19th century. Consequently, Montparnasse is *the* place for crêpes, cider and wild bagpipe dances.

Heading east for a short way, stop for a drink at Le Café d'Edgar, a family-run, old-style café-theatre in **Rue de la Gaîté**, which, since the 18th century, has been lined with theatres and dance halls living up to its name. Further on is the densely populated, star-studded **Cimetière Montparnasse** ⓴ (open daily; free) which includes, among many others, the 19th-century novelist Guy de Maupassant (1893), the composer Saint-Saëns (1921), and the Irish playwright Samuel Beckett (1989).

Eastwards to Rue Mouffetard market

The area around Rue Mouffetard is one of the most ancient and colourful in France. Go via the beautifully restored square of **Place de la Contrescarpe** (Métro Monge, or a few minutes from Place du Panthéon eastwards along Rue de l'Estrapade). In the corner house (No. 1) François Rabelais (1494–1553) composed risqué rhymes, as did Villon, the century before (*see page 183*).

Just off the square, Ernest Hemingway moved into his first Parisian residence at 74 Rue du Cardinal Lemoine in early 1922 and he tells of the experience in his novel *A Moveable Feast* (1964). He idealised the area as a place of danger and excitement and although it has lost some of its edge, it has a refined charm.

Rue Mouffetard (*see pages 78–79*) is an intriguing blend of ethnic fast-food eateries and medieval passages. Walk down its cobbles in the early morning to

Singer and composer Serge Gainsbourg is buried in Cimetière Montparnasse with writers, poets, artists, composers, the Hollywood actress Jean Seberg, US photographer Man Ray and such industrialists as 2CV king André Citroën.

BELOW: Islamic Parisians.

Map, pages 184/5

one of the livliest street markets in Paris. On your stroll, note the ancient shop fronts and narrow passages. At No. 122, towards the bottom of the hill, the well carved onto the facade dates from Henri IV.

An Arab mosque and Roman ruins

From St-Médard, the Rue Daubenton leads to the green and white elegance of the **Mosquée de Paris** ㉒ (open daily, closed noon–2pm; closed Fri and Muslim hols; entrance fee) about five minutes away. Built in the Hispano-Moorish style in 1922 by three French architects, the mosque is a subtle reminder of Parisian ties with the Arab world and commemorates North African participation in World War I. Incorporating the **Institut Musulman**, the complex of buildings includes a museum of Muslim art, a large patio inspired by the Alhambra in Andalucia and an impressive selection of carvings and tiles. There is also a library, a restaurant and a *salon de thé*. Next door is a *Hamman* (Turkish bath).

Not far from the northwest entrance of the Jardin de Plantes is the ancient gladiatorial arena, the **Arènes de Lutèce** ㉓. The 15,000-seat arena, which was destroyed by barbarians in AD 280, was unearthed when building Rue Monge in 1869, and Victor Hugo (*see page 159*) led a campaign to restore it. Today, where gladiator fights were once popular spectacles, the arena serves as a children's playground and echoes to the clink of *pétanque* balls on shady afternoons

A walk through the Jardin des Plantes

A large verdant retreat from the bustle of the city, the **Jardin des Plantes** ㉔ (open daily 7.30am–8pm in summer, 7.30am–5.30pm in winter; entrance fee tel: 01 40 79 30 00), the city's botanical gardens, was opened in 1640 and was originally conceived as a medicinal herb farm for Louis XIII. Between 1739 and 1788, the park flourished under the curatorship of the Comte de Buffon, author of the 36-volume *Natural History*, who created a maze over a public waste tip.

Within the park is the **Musée National d'Histoire Naturelle** ㉕ (open daily; closed Tues and weekday pub. hols; entrance fee). Both the museum and its contents have been restored, which now present an impressive survey of evolutionary development, from a marine world to a large open space with stuffed animals exhibited in their natural habitats. Live animals can be seen in the **Ménagerie** which includes a Micro Zoo.

For a riverside stroll leave the park at Place Valhubert and head west to the **Musée de la Sculptur en Plein Air** ㉖ (open daily 10am–6pm; free; tel: 01 4 51 38 38), a park-cum-modern sculpture exhibition Also of interest is the high-tech **Institut du Mond Arabe** ㉗ (open daily; closed Mon; entrance fee) across Quai St-Bernard. One of Mitterrand's *grands projet* the nine-storey palace of glass, aluminium and concret was built by French engineers in conjunction with 2 Arab countries. The museum is a fascinating voyag around the Muslim world. A restaurant situated on th roof offers breathtaking views. For more traditiona Michelin three-star cuisine, reserve a table at **La Tou d'Argent** (15 Quai de la Tournelle).

In the 18th century, Parisians flocked to the cemetery of St-Médard, at the end of Rue Mouffetard, to the tomb of a young priest whose ghost was said to cure all ailments. Eventually, as more and more people came, Louis XV closed it with a notice: "On the King's orders, it is forbidden for God to perform miracles in this place."

EXOTIC PLANTS

When the Jardin des Plantes was being created in the 17th century, Louis XIV's doctor, Fagon, and botanists such as Tournefort and the three Jussieu brothers travelled far and wide bringing back seeds from around the world. The wild and wonderful collection of flora that resulted includes a 2,000-year-old American sequoia along with a Ginkgo biloba and iron tree from Persia. A laricio pine was grown from a seed brought back from Corsica in 1774 and the pistachio tree is almost 300 years old.

The oldest Lebanese cedar in France, planted in 1734, was brought from Kew Gardens in England by the Jussieu brothers' nephew, Bernard de Jussieu. The story goes that after dropping and breaking the pot the young cedar plants were in, he nurtured the seedlings in his hat until he could return. The oldest tree in Paris, the false acacia or Robinia, brought back from America in 1635, is also here.

The Académie Française

Traditionally seated at dinner parties above government ministers and just below cardinals and princes are the 40 members of the Académie Française, popularly known as the "*Immortels*". These chosen few are the watchdogs of the French language, compiling the *Dictionary of the French Language*, protecting it from the insidious onslaught of English (*franglais*) words, such as jogging, marketing and camping, despite their common usage in France. To be admitted to their ranks is the ultimate honour to which all *hommes de lettres* aspire.

The Académie shows the importance the French attach to their language. Yet, paradoxically, it is almost impossible to define. Simply put, it is uncertain what its members actually do. Even the *Immortels* themselves are confused about their role. Poet Paul Valbey said once, "We are what we believe we are, and what others believe we are, and neither we nor anyone else can say exactly what that is."

The Académie was founded in 1635 by Louis XIII at the prompting of Cardinal Richelieu. Its members were set the task of composing a dictionary and charged "to work with all possible care and diligence to give strict rules to our language and to make it pure, eloquent and capable of dealing with the arts and sciences". Louis XIV generously donated 660 volumes from his personal library, 40 goose quills and a lesson in equality. When one of the members, a cardinal, protested that his rank entitled him to a more comfortable seat than the chairs provided, Louis sent 40 of the now-famous *fauteuils* (armchairs).

In 1793, during the Revolution, the Académie was accused of being infected with "the incurable gangrene of aristocracy". Three members were guillotined, two committed suicide and three died in prison. Restored by Napoleon in 1803, it was re-established in the Institut de France (*see pages 193*).

A vacancy occurs only after a member's death. While eligibility is simple (candidates must be of French nationality), being elected is difficult. Voltaire was so desperate to be elected to the Academy, he was driven to write obsequious verses praising Louis XV. He even denied the authorship of his freethinking *Lettres Philosophiques* and finally made it on his third try. Victor Hugo was accepted on his fourth attempt in 1841.

Emile Zola was unsuccessful 24 times. The conservative *Immortels* disliked the realism of his novels and were wary of his courage in the Dreyfus Affair in 1898. Others who failed were the literary giants Diderot, Flaubert, Molière, Proust and Baudelaire. Women have been admitted since 1980, French-American author Marguerite Yourcenar being the first. Now there are two women members.

Not all members are geniuses – one is the author of a history of women's undergarments. As minor 19th-century novelist and *Immortel* Ludovic Halévy once said: "Some Academicians are talented, others aren't. The latter are especially worthy of respect because they made it without talent." ❑

RIGHT: immortalised in stone outside the Académie Française.

LEFT BANK IN THE 1950s

After World War II, artists, musicians, writers and philosophers converged on the quartier of St-Germain-des-Prés, making it the centre of the intellectual and artistic world

In Paris, the freedom of the period post World War II was characterised by an outpouring of literature and ideas. One of the most important to emerge was existentialism, which soon dominated French intellectual life. Developed by the writer Jean-Paul Sartre, this philosophy was based on the concept of a universe that was meaningless, or absurd, in which people were meant to find greater freedoms by assuming greater personal responsibilities. In attempting to change the world rather than simply examine it, existentialism represented a hope for the future. Its key figures included Sartre's life-long companion, Simone de Beauvoir, and the writer Albert Camus.

LEFT BANK CAFÉ SOCIETY

Existentialists lived in cheap hotels and gathered in local cafés, such as Les Deux Magots and the Flore. At times, the Café de Flore was like a classroom, with Sartre writing at one table and de Beauvoir at another. Even after the couple's popularity forced them to stop working in public, their followers, wearing the "existentialist uniform" of black sweaters and berets, continued to flock to the cafés to drink, gossip and argue over the latest literary offerings.

▷ **WRITERS' CAFÉ**
The Deux Magots, like its neighbour the Café de Flore, had a tradition of supporting artistic and intellectual social life. It took its name from the sign of a draper's shop that had occupied the site. Simone de Beauvoir (*above*) regularly came to drink coffee and write. Her favourite seat was the wall banquette next to the window.

▷ **THE TROGLODYTES**
Young Parisians packed the Left Bank's basement jazz clubs, to dance wild new dances such as the jitterbug and the mambo. The regulars were fondly known as *les rats*.

THE CLUBS OF ST-GERMAIN

Juliette Gréco (*above*) was the beautiful "face" of St-Germain-des-Prés. She was a young singer who helped to run Le Tabou, the first and most notorious of the clubs that appeared in the late 1940s.

The club's dance floor had just enough room for 20 enthusiastic couples to dance to the latest jazz. Smoke-filled and sweaty, it became the place to be after midnight, but its popularity proved its downfall; bad press about its supposedly wanton and hedonistic "existentialist" clientele attracted tourists, who soon outnumbered the beboppers themselves.

The club lasted only about one year, but other haunts such as the Vieux-Colombier and the Club St-Germain quickly sprung up to take its place. Perhaps not all existentialists fully understood the philosophy, but they all loved the music and dancing that was associated with it.

◁ LE JAZZ HOT
St-Germain-des-Prés was a jazz mecca. Its clubs attracted both top French musicians, such as Claude Luter, and American jazzmen including Miles Davis, Coleman Hawkins and James Moody (bottom right).

◁ JEAN-PAUL SARTRE
He was the epitome of a French intellectual and a prolific writer, communicating ideas through plays and novels, including *Being and Nothingness* and *Nausea*.

▷ ALBERT CAMUS
The "Humphrey Bogart of the Absurd", Camus dealt with existentialist ideas in novels such as *The Outsider* and *The Plague*.

THE EIFFEL TOWER AND LES INVALIDES

Map,
page 204

Enjoy a bird's-eye view from the top of the symbol of Paris and experience a rat's-eye view underground. In between, explore military splendour and the magnificent art of the Musée d'Orsay

The Tour Eiffel, or Eiffel Tower, stands in one of the most spectacular – and one of the quietest – areas of Paris. Commanding the palatial Faubourg St-Germain quarter, and most of the city, with its presence, the Eiffel Tower symbolises Paris. Used in James Bond and *Superman* films, among many others, and the focus of the French millennium celebrations, the tower is a world superstar. Whereas many monuments prove disappointing, it continues to impress, even though it has long been overtaken as the world's tallest building. Like some prehistoric behemoth stopping to drink at the riverside, it is the most impassive inhabitant of Paris, impervious to the daily chaos at its feet. From here, traditionally designed parks and magnificent buildings spread out on a grand scale, reaching across the Seine to the modern Palais de Chaillot, which complements the classical facade of the Ecole Militaire on the opposite bank. Wide avenues link up with the imposing Hôtel des Invalides and the Sun King's splendid, gilt-domed church, bordering an area peppered with sumptuous *hôtels* (mansions).

Now mostly dedicated to embassies and government ministries, the secret courtyards of Pierre de Laclos's *Les Liaisons Dangereuses* (1782) are still home to the nobility of Paris. Glimpses through the shuttered security are rare, but occasional open doorways reveal fountains, statues and soaring stairways. Rue de Grenelle and Rue de Varenne still retain an accessible charm, reflected in the streets leading to the Seine and the old railway station that is now bursting with fine art.

Palais de Chaillot – palace of museums

For the best view of the tower, start at Trocadéro across the river. From here, looking over the cascading fountains and gold statues of the **Jardins du Trocadéro ❶**, the tower is at its most magnificent.

Trocadéro was named in 1827, following the re-enactment on this spot of a French victory at Fort Trocadéro in Southern Spain. Earlier, Napoleon had started work here on a palace for his son, but the Battle of Waterloo (1815) had intervened. Today, against the backdrop of the Palais de Chaillot, the beautifully laid-out terraces and grassy banks of the garden, created after the 1937 World Fair, now play host to the capital's most flamboyant skateboarders and roller-bladers. At night, when the ornamental pool's huge fountains are lit up, the sight is spectacular.

Away from African street merchants selling "authentic" Senegalese and Camerooni plastic necklaces, wooden elephants and walking sticks, the neoclassical **Palais de Chaillot ❷** stands proud on the hill. Jacques Carlu's design for the 1937 World Fair, the curved-

PRECEDING PAGES AND LEFT: having fun at the foot of the Eiffel Tower.
BELOW: the altar in the Dôme, backed by a window into the soldiers' chapel.

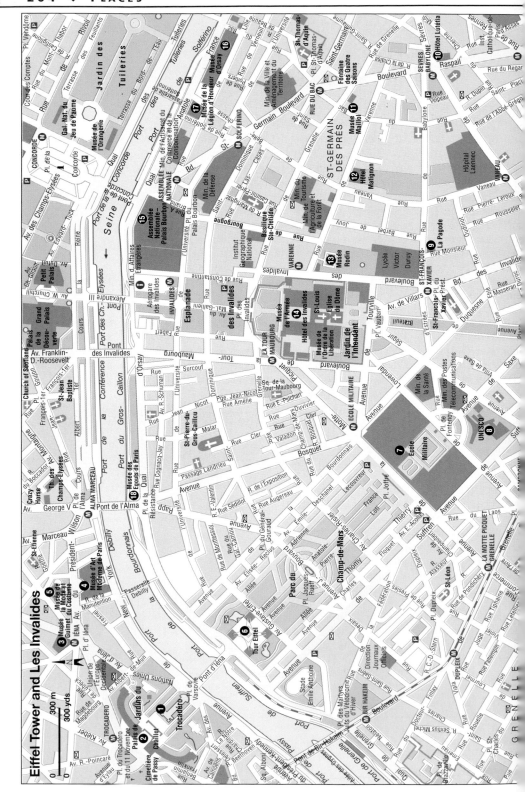

Eiffel Tower and Les Invalides

winged edifices, with a wide parvis between and a terrace in front, contain four museums and a 1,000-seat theatre.

Map, page 204

In the west wing is the **Musée de la Marine** (open daily 10am–6pm; closed Tues and 1 May; tel: 01 53 65 69 69; entrance fee) which charts French maritime history from wooden warships to today's mean machines in scale models, some of which are two centuries old. Among exhibits of underwater exploration, naval art, navigational instruments and mementoes of naval heroes is the windsurf board that crossed the Atlantic in 38 days in 1985.

The **Musée de l'Homme** (open daily 10am–6pm; closed Tues and pub. hols; tel: 01 53 65 69 69; entrance fee), or Museum of Mankind, has mummies, shrunken heads and exquisite rock crystal skulls from African, Aztec and Mayan collections, along with 400 musical instruments from around the world.

In the east wing is the **Musée des National Monuments Français** (open daily; closed Tues; entrance fee), dedicated to French monumental art with reproductions of monuments from around France.

For cinema addicts the **Musée du Cinéma Henri Langlois**, which was housed in the east wing and traced celluloid history with an exhibition of more than 5,000 objects, including several film sets, is currently in the process of being moved to the former American Center and is due to re-open in 2001.

Although about 10 minutes away in the opposite direction, the small **Musée Guimet ❸** in Place d'Iéna, is well worth a visit and is also in the company of two other worthwhile museums. One of the world's finest Asian museums, Guimet contains a superb collection of oriental art and will please lovers of silk, porcelain and jade.

Back on the Avenue du Président Wilson to the east, the Palais de Tokyo

ABOVE: a gendarme ready for business.
BELOW: Palais de Chaillot, a 20th-century palace.

TIP

Queues for the Eiffel Tower can be up to two hours long in the summer, so get there early. A double-decker lift from the second level is the only means of reaching the top.

contains the underrated **Musée d'Art Moderne de Paris** ❹ (open daily; close Mon; tel: 01 53 67 40 00; entrance fee), which is host to celebrity attractions such as Picasso, Matisse (*La Danse* – 1932), Modigliani and Soutine, and th world's largest painting, Raoul Dufy's *Fée de l'Éléctricité* (Fairy of Electric ity), a celebration of energy created for the 1937 World Fair.

Opposite is the **Musée de la Mode et du Costume** ❺ (open Tues–Su 10am–6pm during exhibitions; closed Mon and pub. hols; tel: 01 47 20 85 2: entrance fee) in the Renaissance-style Palais Galliéra, which has 12,000 outfi and 60,000 accessories dating from the 18th century to the present day exhibite in rotation twice a year.

The Eiffel Tower – a mighty symbol of Paris

Back at Trocadéro, cross the Pont d'Iéna, built by Napoleon to celebrate anothe of his victories, to the **Eiffel Tower** ❻ (open daily till 11pm, Jul, Aug till mic night; entrance fee). When Gustave Eiffel's icon of pig-iron girders was chose as the centrepiece to the World Fair of 1889, he claimed enthusiastically, "Franc will be the only country with a 300-metre flagpole!" But agitation overwhelme the artistic community of the time. The Opéra architect Charles Garnier and th novelist Guy de Maupassant were the most vocal opponents and Maupassai organised a protest picnic under the tower's four legs – "the only place out sight of the wretched construction".

However, the public (always a better judge) loved Paris's new tower and few years later it was being lauded by writers and artists such as Apollinair Jean Cocteau, Dufy and Utrillo. Surviving a proposal for its dismantlement 1909, when the placing of a radio transmitter at the top saved the day, the tow

BELOW: legging it up the Eiffel Tower.

THE TOWER'S VITAL STATISTICS

A t 321 metres (1,054 ft) high, including the masts, the Eiffel Tower was the tallest building in the world until the Empire State Building went up in New York in 1931. On hot days, the ironwork expands enabling it to grow as much as 15cm (6 inches).

A masterpiece of engineering, this world symbol of Paris is held together with 2.5 million rivets and the 10,100 tonnes of iron exerts a pressure of 4kg per sq cm (57lb per sq inch), the equivalent of the weight of a man sitting on a chair. Even in the strongest of winds, the tower has never swayed more than 12 cm (4 inches). Up to 40 tonnes of paint has to be used, when it is painted every seven years.

There are 360 steps to the first level, where there is an audio-visual presentation of the tower's history, and another 700 to the second. On the third level is Gustave Eiffel's sitting room.

s now swarmed over by six million visitors a year. The first two floors are
limbed by foot or by lift, and then another lift goes up to the top which, apart
rom being a meteorological station and aircraft navigation point, can hold 800
people at once. From here, the view is miraculous. At night, Paris appears as a
horizontal Christmas tree of dancing illuminations stretching to the horizon, and
he tower is transformed into a skeletal tableau, lit up by arc lights.

Map,
page 204

Ecole Militaire – military headquarters

From the Eiffel Tower, the gardens of the **Champ de Mars** spread down to the
impressive **Ecole Militaire** (military school) **7**. Once the parade ground to the
school where Napoleon practised triumphal marching in 1784, this park is now
a haven of peace, love and picnics. The first balloon filled with hydrogen rather
than hot air was launched from here in 1783 and the first anniversary of the
storming of the Bastille was celebrated here in front of a miserable Louis XVI.
At the far end is the imposing, 18th-century French military academy, still the
centre of French military know-how, where Napoleon, having been admitted to
the school on the recommendation that he would make a good sailor, graduated
a lieutenant.

Behind this university of war is the foundation for reconciliation and understanding, the headquarters of UNESCO **8** (open daily; closed 12.30–2.30pm and
at weekends, pub. hols and conference sessions). The graceful Y-shaped building was designed by an alliance of American, French and Italian architects.
Inside, 142 countries cooperate in educational, scientific and cultural projects.
A temple of modern art, its decoration is equally cosmopolitan, including Joan
Miró ceramics, Henry Moore sculptures, an Alexander Calder mobile and a huge

*As a cadet at the
Ecole Militaire,
Napoleon (above)
was told that he
would go far if
circumstances
allowed.*

BELOW: a mural by
Picasso in the
UNESCO building.

Picasso mural. The Japanese garden displays a spine-chilling relic from ou[r] nuclear age – a stone angel found after the atomic bomb blast at Nagasaki in 194[5].

Around the – very grand – houses

Before tackling the vastness of Les Invalides and if you enjoy a good walk, [it] may be an idea to explore the top-class area around it first, going via Paris'[s] most interesting cinema and tea house **La Pagode** ❾ in Rue de Babylone, abou[t] a 10-minute walk along Rue d'Estrées, where the tea is strong, the gardens tro[p]ical and the films up-to-date.

When Parisian nobility moved out of the Marais in the 18th century, and Ve[r]sailles tumbled, the rich and famous built new town houses across the river fro[m] the Tuileries. Beautifully preserved, they are now mostly behind heavily secur[e] gates, since only French ministries and foreign governments can afford the re[nt] (along with the odd Greek arms dealer). About 15 minutes further on, acro[ss] Boulevard Raspail (No. 45), stands **Hôtel Lutétia** ❿, its extravagant statu[e] facade fronting a deluxe four-star hotel where Charles de Gaulle enjoyed h[is] first night of married life. When the hotel was requisitioned by the Gestapo [in] 1940, the owner bricked up the vintage wine cellar and, even though the hot[el] staff were interrogated to reveal the whereabouts of the finest wine collecti[on] in the capital, no one talked.

About a five-minute walk along Boulevard Raspail towards the Seine, **R[ue] de Grenelle**, on the left, is bursting with beautiful buildings, including the Sw[iss] and Dutch embassies, the Ministry of Education and the National Geograph[ic] Institute. Just into the street on the left is the **Hôtel Bouchardon** where the po[et] Alfred de Musset lived between 1824 and 1839, before going on an orien[t]

voyage of discovery with George Sand. It is now the **Musée Maillol – Fondation Dina Vierney ⑪** (open daily; closed Tues; entrance fee), where the works of Aristide Maillol, whose sculptures adorn the Jardin des Tuileries (*see pages 121–22*), are on show, along with art from his contemporaries such as Cezanne and Degas. Dina Vierny, owner of the private collection, was an art dealer and model for Maillol. Next door, the grandiose **Fontaine des Quatre Saisons** was a monumental response to a local complaint about lack of water.

Map, page 204

Turning left up Rue du Bac, Rue de Varenne has a collection of fine old houses, the most famous being the residence of the French Prime Minister, **Hôtel Matignon ⑫**. It was here that the socialist leader Pierre Bérégovoy lived before his defeat in the elections in April 1993 and his subsequent suicide following the May Day celebrations.

Musée Rodin – a small man with a big talent

At the end of Rue de Varenne, next to Les Invalides, is the **Hôtel Biron**, housing the unmissable **Musée Rodin ⑬** (open daily; closed Mon; entrance fee), containing the best of the sculptor's work. Auguste Rodin's first work of critical acclaim was *The Age of Bronze* in 1877, a naked youth caressing his hair, modelled by a Belgian soldier. The establishment was shocked, maintaining that the statue was too lifelike to be regarded as art. A card stuck to the work at the Paris *salon* read "Beware – moulded from the body of the model". Eventually, the French government bought the statue and Rodin's reputation was made.

ABOVE: a sculpture of the sculptor Rodin himself.
BELOW: the ornate doors of Hôtel Biron.

Rodin came to live in the Hôtel Biron, owned by the state and ironically a former convent, in 1908 and stayed there until his death in 1917. He paid his rent with his best works, forming the basis of the museum, which overflows with

AUGUSTE RODIN – LOVER AND SCULPTOR

One of the world's smallest artists (at 1.65 metres/5 ft 4 in), Auguste Rodin was born in the Quartier Latin in 1840 and grew up wandering the markets of Rue Mouffetard (*see page 195*). Rejected by the Ecole des Beaux-Arts, he trained himself, visiting the zoo at the Jardin des Plantes and the horse markets on the Boulevard St-Michel for inspiration.

Further stimulus came from his incessant love affairs, which were interrupted only for a short while when the sculptor took holy orders. This was a reaction to the death of his sister in a convent, after she had been rejected in love by one of Rodin's close friends. Chastity did not suit him, however, and a year later he returned to his art. Some of his most famous works are *The Kiss*, *The Thinker*, *The Burghers of Calais*, *God's Hand* and the unfinished *Gates of Hell*, on which he worked from the 1880s until his death in 1917.

In the Dôme Church, Napoleon lies in six coffins, one inside the other. The first is white iron, then mahogany, two of lead, ebony and finally oak, on a base of green Vosges granite. When brought back to Paris after 19 years, his body was in perfect condition.

BELOW: the Hôtel des Invalides.

with his best works, forming the basis of the museum, which overflows with excellence. Here are *The Kiss* (removed from the Chicago World Fair of 1893 for being too shocking), *The Thinker* (reputedly Dante contemplating the *Inferno*), *The Burghers of Calais*, *The Hand of God* and other works. Recently restored to their white marble finish, the statues ripple with life, many being set outside in beautiful gardens of roses. Also included in the exhibition are works by Camille Claudel, the most famous of Rodin's countless mistresses.

Hôtel des Invalides

The **Hôtel des Invalides** ⓮ (open daily; closed pub. hols; tel: 01 44 42 54 52; free) is dramatic yet refined, as befits a one-time pensioners' retreat and mausoleum. Commissioned by war-loving Louis XIV as a retirement home for his soldiers in 1676, the buildings designed by Libéral Bruant once housed 4,000 men. It was here that revolutionaries seized 28,000 guns for the storming of the Bastille in 1789. The great courtyard, with its imposing arcades and array of captured cannons, now hosts the odd military parade and society wedding.

At the heart of Les Invalides lies the heart of an empire. The beautiful **Dôme Church**, the masterpiece of the Sun King Louis XIV's reign, contains the body of Napoleon. Returned to France in 1840, following much wrangling with the British, the little Emperor was given a state funeral during which a snowstorm enveloped the city. The interior of the Emperor's resting place is predictably over the top, with 12 damsels, symbolising his 12 military campaigns, guarding the polished oak coffin. High above the tomb, the dome, completed by Jules Hardouin-Mansart in 1706, is breathtaking, thanks in part to its new coat of gold leaf, regilded for the bicentennial celebrations in July 1989.

On the west side of the grounds is the **Musée de l'Ordre de la Libération** (open daily; closed pub. hols; entrance fee) in memory of the Resistance fighters who received the Order of Liberation, France's highest honour created by Charles de Gaulle in 1940, during World War II.

On either side of the Cour d'Honneur, the **Musée de l'Armée** (open daily; closed pub. hols; tel: 01 44 42 37 67; entrance fee) offers an extensive glimpse of man's inhumanity and skill at warfare from the Stone Age to World War II with a terrifying selections of weapons, armour and poignant reminders of the two world wars, including the original copy of Adolf Hitler's *Mein Kampf.*

Stretching to the Seine, the beautiful **Esplanade des Invalides** is another symmetrically designed garden much loved by strollers and sports fanatics. Along the west side is a series of *boules* courts. Opposite is a small air terminal.

From here, you can either go west along the Seine to the Place de la Resistance and the sewers (*see page 212*) or east to the Musée d'Orsay. However, take into consideration that you will need some time at both. Heading east, you pass the colonnaded **Assemblée Nationale–Palais Bourbon** ⑮ (open Sat at 10am, 2pm, 3pm; closed during sessions; proof of identity required), which is the Lower House of the French Parliament. The extravagant columns were grafted on to an 18th-century facade by Napoleon to complement La Madeleine across the river and now shelter an armed guard, protecting the 491 *députés* (members of Parliament). Outside, the view from **Pont de la Concorde** is stunning.

Musée d'Orsay – a transformed railway station

No visit to Paris is complete without a pilgrimage to the **Musée d'Orsay** ⑯ (open daily, Thur till 9.30pm; closed Mon and some pub. hols; tel: 01 40 49 48 14;

Map, page 204

BELOW: the Gare d'Orsay has been preserved as a lavish museum.

Map, page 204

TIP

Make a day of it at the Musée d'Orsay and take a break in the museum's restaurant or rooftop café.

BELOW: down under in the Paris sewers.

entrance fee). Considered by many as the most user-friendly museum in the world, the former railway station is spaciously arranged and sumptuously stuffed full of the most beautiful art from 1848 until World War I (which, by coincidence, is 95 percent French). The building, finished in two years in 1900, was almost torn down to make way for a hotel in 1970. Prompted by public outcry, government ministers fulfilled the prophesy of painter Edouard Detaille, at the opening ceremony in 1900, that the station would make a better museum. Its glass and iron construction was a triumph of modernity, rivalling Eiffel's tower, while the facade reflected the Palais du Louvre across the river. In the vast cavern of the interior, Orson Welles set his film of Kafka's *The Trial* (1962).

A tour of the Musée d'Orsay

It is difficult to get lost in this museum. Designed by an Italian, Gae Aulenti, and opened in 1986, the exhibitions are arranged on five levels, the central hall surrounded by terraces. As airy as the Louvre isn't, the museum's layout is deceptively approachable. How many have launched into an inclusive tour of its riches, only to be exhausted before even reaching the Impressionists on the Upper Level? Choose carefully, as this museum is a place to come back to.

The ground floor is dominated by the Academic School and its regimented style. In contrast, Edouard Manet's shameless nude – *Olympia* (1863), the first "modern" painting, stares insolently at her staid predecessors (the work was pronounced pornographic at the 1865 Paris *salon*). On the top floor is the museum's treasure trove. The Impressionists are bathed in soft light from the station's glass-vaulted roof, a setting they were painted for. Pass through galleries full of paintings by Monet, Manet, Renoir, Pissarro, Degas, Cézanne and Van Gogh. At the end is a small café under a large clock, from where a terrace high above the Seine offers appetising views over Paris.

The central aisle makes a perfect setting for sculpture (David, Rodin, Maillol *et al*), while Art Nouveau overflows from the middle floor, including the two towers at the east end, which present a bird's-eye view of the museum. For more information on favourite works visit the documentation room upstairs, where computers give details and video reproductions on all exhibits.

Anyone interested in medals and military decorations should visit the next-door museum, **Musée National de la Légion d'Honneur** ⑰ (open afternoons; closed Mon; entrance fee) tracing the history of France's most celebrated award, created by Napoleon I. The interior colonnaded courtyard is also a pleasant place to rest.

A trip round the city's underworld

For a surprisingly entertaining experience descend into the bowels of the capital at the Place de la Résistance next to Pont l'Alma. The **Musée des Egouts de Paris** ⑱ (open daily, 11am–5pm, Oct–Apr till 4pm; closed Thurs and Fri and last three weeks of Jan; entrance fee) is an excursion into the city's sewer system. Described by Victor Hugo in *Les Misérables* as the "other Paris" this network of tunnels follows the well-known streets above ground. Accompanied by a film and relevant odours, it is *the* alternative tour of Paris.

Café life

The café is the Parisian's decompression chamber, easing the transition between *Métro-boulot-dodo* – commuting, working, and sleeping. It provides a welcome pause in which to savour a *p'tit noir* (espresso) or an apéritif, to empty the mind of troublesome thoughts and to watch the people go by. The café is also the place to meet friends, have a romantic tryst or even to do business in a relaxed atmosphere.

The first café ever to open was Le Procope in 1686 (*see pages 189 and 191*) and the literati soon started to congregate there, keen to discuss ideas with each other. More establishments quickly sprang up all over the country and it wasn't long before there was at least one café in every village and hamlet where people kept each other company. During the 18th century, the neighbourhood "zinc", named after its metal counter, became part of the fabric of French life.

In Paris, each café developed its own character, attracting different types of clientele, and with the widening of the boulevards in the 19th century, the tables spilled out on to the pavements. By 1910, there were 510,000 zincs in France, but now café life is in danger of extinction. The figures are alarming: 4,000 French cafés disappear each year. Paris alone has lost 1,000 in five years.

While the invasion of fast-food restaurants is partly to blame (a nearby McDonald's, "*McDo*", can slash a café's profits by 30 percent), changes in the French way of life are also culpable. When customers move out to spacious homes in the suburbs, they tend to "cocoon", staying in to watch television and the local café eventually has to close.

Then there are the ageing proprietors to consider. The café is traditionally a family business but, today, fewer sons and daughters are prepared to take on gruelling 16-hour days with sparse holidays and little reward.

Sadly, even the atmosphere of remaining cafés is not what it was. Now there is formica where once there was marble. Piped muzak and the electronic beep of video games have replaced the song of the accordionist and the furious volleys of the "Baby-foot" players. Only the Gauloise-induced haze (attitudes to the 1992 smoking ban are casual) and the hazards of the lavatories (some are still holes in the ground) are the same.

Yet all is not lost. Authentic "zincs" are still to be found in Paris and many are thriving. Try the stylish Café de l'Industrie on Rue St-Sabin, La Palette on Rue de Seine or the tiny but lovingly restored Le Cochon à l'Oreille on Rue Montorgueil. For literary atmosphere order a *verre* (glass of wine) at Les Deux Magots, which has been home to almost every Paris intellectual from Rimbaud to André Breton. At the nearby Café de Flore, Sartre and Simone de Beauvoir wrote by the stove. "My worst customer, Sartre," recalled the patron. "He spent the entire day scribbling away over one drink." (*see pages 198–199.*)

But go soon. For, if you have never nipped into a French café to make a quick phone call, met your lover for an apéritif on a *terrasse* or negotiated the crouch of the *toilettes*, you cannot claim truly to know Paris. ❐

RIGHT: a rare zinc-topped bar, which were once so numerous, cafés were nicknamed *les zincs*.

LA DÉFENSE – A MODERN METROPOLIS

Map, page 218

Dominated by the Grand Arche, La Défense is a concentrated business area where architects' futuristic imaginations have been allowed to run wild and avant-garde works of art are everywhere

Heading west, crossing the city boundary at Porte Maillot, the historic avenues of Paris suddenly vanish. There, on the horizon, rises a futuristic metropolis, a city of gigantic glass blocks marching to the gates of the capital. "America-on-the-Seine", as Parisians affectionately refer to **La Défense**, is the city's newest attraction, enticing a million visitors each year to experience "Europe's premier business centre", the capital of French industry and finance, and one of the world's most *avant-garde* architectural sites.

Once a desolate commuter land of office blocks, La Défense has become a bustling 21st-century community set around a vast concrete podium, with an enormous shopping complex, high-tech entertainment centres and, as its focus, the Grande Arche, the crowning glory of President Mitterrand's "progressive vision for the 1980s" (megalomania is another description offered by right-wing publications). The Grande Arche has given La Défense the symbol it needed and connects this modern upstart to the ancient heart of Paris, via the historic Triumphal Way, running east through the Arc de Triomphe to the Louvre.

PRECEDING PAGES: the Grande Arche in line with the Triumphal Way. **LEFT:** art backs business in La Défense. **BELOW:** an open-air modern art gallery.

The development of La Défense

Since 80 percent of Paris is protected by preservation orders, new developments have to move out of the city, adding successive layers to the core, like an onion. When, in 1958, it was decided that Paris needed a business centre, a small hill overlooking the Seine was selected for development. It was called La Défense, because this was where citizens defended the capital against the Prussian siege of 1870–71. The first phase of building by EPAD (Etablissement Public pour l'Aménagement de la Défense) was completed in the late 1960s – a complex of office towers, not exceeding 100 metres (330 ft) high, huddled above a pedestrian zone with roads passing underneath. The RER line was extended, placing the city centre five minutes away. Then recession hit and bankruptcy threatened.

It was not until the recovery of the 1980s that La Défense finally took permanent root. New towers soared to nearly twice the height of the old incumbents and the business world moved in. Today, teething troubles over, the continuous construction, thousands of serious-faced business people and almost as many tourists make the district one of the fastest-growing and most adventurous in Paris. A "new spirituality" is being heralded in Paris's newest quarter.

It is not difficult to get to La Défense. Métro Line 1 cuts straight through the centre of Paris to end up beneath the Grande Arche, and the RER A line winds all

Avant-garde musician Jean-Michel Jarre gave a computerised concert extravaganza in La Défense on 14 July 1990, which was seen by two million people worldwide.

the way from Disneyland Paris (a journey of only 40 minutes) before branching out to the suburbs. In addition, 20 bus routes converge here, making this small district the most accessible in France and allowing 70 percent of the 110,000 workers to commute by public transport, 80 percent of whom spend less than an hour a day travelling.

La Défense, being a futuristic baby, loves statistics. There are 350,000 journeys to the district each working day, 66,000 parking spaces, 1,300 companies achieving an annual sales volume equivalent to France's national budget. Twelve of the top 20 French companies have headquarters at La Défense, such as Elf, Total and EDF, 13 of the world's top 50 companies are tenants, including IBM, Apple, Hitachi and Unilever. In the residential sector, 30,000 people live in the great apartment complexes to the west.

The Grande Arche – symbol of success

On 14 July 1989, the day of the bicentennial celebrations of the storming of the Bastille, leaders of the seven richest nations paid a visit to La Défense for the inauguration of the **Grande Arche ❶** (open daily; 9am–7pm; tel: 01 49 07 27 57; entrance fee). Previously, La Défense was a place to view from afar, with a certain traditionalist disdain. The spectacularly simple Grande Arche changed that, seducing both public and politicians alike, and today the view from its lofty summit is as famous as that from the Eiffel Tower. The magician behind this dramatic transformation was unknown Danish architect Johan Otto von Spreckelsen. It was his idea that most impressed President Mitterrand out of the 424 proposals submitted for a building at the "head of the Défense".

The Grande Arche is the grandest of François Mitterrand's *grands projets* (*see*

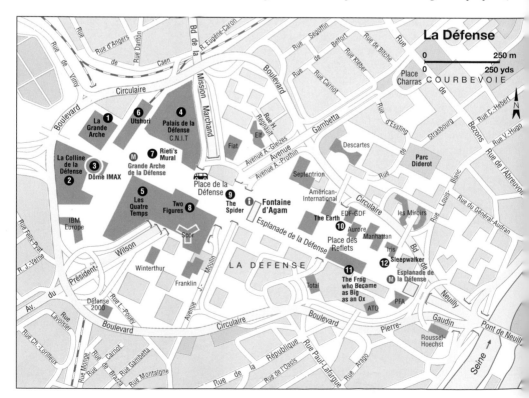

page 95). Entitled "The Arch of Man's Triumph", von Spreckelsen's design completes the Triumphal Way without enclosing it and forms a window out on to the new developments in the west. As the architect, who died two years before the arch was completed, said, "This is an open cube, a window on the world. The arch will see far, in all directions."

Map, page 218

Certainly, the view from the top is vast. Two glass bubbles whisk lines of visitors up to the roof at vertiginous speeds, through the symbolic "cloud", a canvas net suspended between the twin towers designed to cut down wind resistance. Funded by profits from rooftop tourists, the International Foundation for Human Rights, formed in 1989, has its headquarters in the top three storeys across the arch, where it holds exhibitions and conferences. On the roof terrace, Raynaud's **Carte de Ciel** (Map of the Sky) resembles an enormous sundial. Housed in the huge flanks is the Ministry of Transport and Public Works, a conference centre and numerous offices. At weekends, the majestic sweep of steps down to the parvis is dotted with families, children and tour groups.

Some notable buildings

Right next to the arch, **La Colline de la Défense ❷** (open afternoons, Sat till 10pm; entrance fee) is the district's most recent tourist attraction, created to cream off some of the coachloads of visitors heading for the arch. Wide steps lead past orange, blue and green cubes, designed by Piatr Kowalski to stimulate a "mental geometry". Inside is less intellectually demanding: to the left, the **Musée de l'Automobile** is a sparkling new display of the history of the car, exhibiting vehicles from pre-history to 1972, including the box-like hippomobile (horse-drawn), and the fantastical Rolls-Royce Phantom III. The museum is

ABOVE AND BELOW: the Grande Arche was the grandest of President Mitterrand's *grands projets*.

SIZING UP THE GRANDE ARCHE

From the Esplanade de la Défense at the entrance of the district, the great white arch seems two-dimensional. When viewed from the sides, the third dimension mysteriously appears, an illusion created by the arch's alignment six degrees off the axis of the Triumphal Way, or Royal Axis (a quirk shared by I.M. Peï's pyramid at the Louvre – *see page 118*).

The size of the arch is symbolic: measuring roughly 100 metres by 100 metres (330 ft by 330 ft), it has the same dimensions as the Cour Carrée at the Louvre. At 106 metres (348 ft) wide, the entire cathedral of Notre Dame could fit within the archway. The architect Otto von Spreckelsen's monumental vision also respects the historic pattern of Parisian arches. The Arc de Triomphe du Carrousel is 25 metres (82 ft) high, the Arc de Triomphe 50 metres (164 ft) high, so La Grande Arche is 100 metres (330 ft) high.

TIP

In the centre of the
Esplanade de la
Défense, the Info-
Défense provides free
information packages
and displays an
interesting scale
model outlining the
district's development,
past and planned. The
adjacent shop is rife
with arch souvenirs
and T-shirts.

BELOW: the Palais de
la Défense squats
next to the Bull
building (left).

surprisingly entertaining, even for those who aren't great lovers of automobiles. Alongside the memories of yesterday, more up-to-date models are displayed in the **Espace Marques**, which is a unique car showroom that allows prospective buyers or just the simply curious to view and test-drive the latest offerings available from top car manufacturers.

Dominating the "colline" is the immense silver globe of the **Dôme IMAX ❸**, the world's largest hemispheric cinema. Designed by the IMAX Corporation of Canada, the screen is 1,000 sq. metres (10,700 sq. ft), and shows pictures 10 times the size of a normal cinema image at a viewing angle of 180 degrees, with seats tilted at 30 degrees. Reservations for each show are recommended, although the dome is less crowded than its rival La Géode over at the Parc de la Villette (*see page 229*).

Opposite is the district's oldest resident, the **Palais de la Défense ❹**, the CNIT business centre, which has recently been given a face-lift. This curvaceous structure was built in 1958 as the focus of La Défense, but now seems rather dated. Its lofty concave dome is supported by just three pillars, the roof seemingly hanging in mid-air. Inside, recent refurbishment has created a high-tech bowl of glass offices, tapering outwards from the roof to the floor, interspersed with hanging gardens of small trees and shrubs.

Within this de luxe greenhouse, the **World Trade Centre** is the heart of the Parisian business machine, where market dealers, business service consultants and researchers plug into the network of 237 trade centres around the world.

Since 1981, **Les Quatre Temps ❺** shopping centre across the Esplanade de la Défense has provided a social focus for the complex, as well as a place to buy everything that the time-squeezed business person of today needs. It contains

three hypermarkets, 260 shops, 26 restaurants and nine cinemas, and greets 50,000 customers a day. Rumour has it that this is the biggest shopping centre in Europe: at La Défense, superlatives have become a way of life.

Map, page 218

Exploring the skyscrapers

The Esplanade de la Défense stretches from the arch to the Seine, providing a new strolling arena that seems to double up as a high-tech soccer pitch for local children, while the major roads pass underneath, unseen and unheard. On either side of this marble plateau rise forests of towers, including some of the most adventurous architecture in Europe.

The newest developments in the district are growing up behind the Grande Arche and are beginning to make the central buildings look prehistoric in comparison. Here, the Japanese architect Kurokawa has conceived an oriental response to the classical rigidity of Spreckelsen's arch – his **Tour Pacific** is gracefully curved and set on a convex arch. Next door, the **Société Générale** headquarters is formed of two semi-circular edifices, both of which are seemingly on the verge of rotating. The Tour Fiat's windows are wider at the top to prevent one of the tallest buildings in the complex looking narrower as it rises.

Further down on the north side is the **Vision 80** tower built on stilts in the Place des Reflets, behind which loom the **Aurore** and **Manhattan** towers. **Les Miroirs**, set around a fountain decorated with mosaics, is further back. At the entrance to La Défense, dominating the Seine, the **Tour Roussel-Hoechst** was the first skyscraper to sprout – a mere 34 storeys built in 1967 in blue-green steel and glass. Just behind, Willerval's PFA tower is a triangular temple of sleek glass pointing towards Paris.

BELOW: the Takis pool, where 49 spiral rods sway and light up at night.

A cradle of art

In honour of the defenders of Paris against the Prussians in 1870, a bronze sculpture, **La Defense de Paris**, was made by Barrias following submissions by 100 artists, including Rodin. The monument still stands at the heart of the district and represents a young guardsman and girl symbolising the valour of the innocent civilian population confronting the Prussians. Above it, the quarter's most amusing attraction, the **Fontaine d'Agam**, designed by Yaacov Agam, erratically spurts water by way of a series of 66 fountains, each shooting up at different levels and at different times and cascading over a multicoloured mosaic, often to computerised music. The small white building to the left of the fountains, mysteriously named **Art Gallery 4**, is the office of the artistic wing of La Défense and provides a free guide to works of art on the site. Take the brochure, and sip a glass at **Le Bistro de Vins**, with a ringside view of Agam's fountains dancing and wriggling, as you decide what to see.

The Tour Fiat has 45 storeys of tinted black glass above the Esplanade de la Défense. The Tour Elf behind matches it in height, its blue-tinted facades changing intensity according to the colour of the sky.

BELOW: Catalan sculptor Joan Miró's *Two Figures.*

Modern sculpture park

With more than 50 modern sculptures, La Défense is one of Europe's most interesting open-air art museums. The works are consistently interactive, complementing and contrasting with surrounding buildings, demanding the participation of even the most preoccupied passer-by. A good one to start with is Miyawaki's **Utshori** ❻ sculpture, commissioned by von Spreckelsen himself to sit alongside the Grande Arche – a series of pillars with nests of silver wires springing from them (the spectator is required to admire the space between the wires, according to Miyawaki).

At the entrance to the RER station, Rieti's 60-metre (200-ft) **mural** ❼ offers a

teasing choice between a painted kiss, a flock of birds, or a running woman, depending on the perspective of the onlooker. Across the parvis, Joan Miró's **Two Figures** loom above the square, marking the entrance to the shopping centre. These surreal beasts leer happily at the rigid angles of surrounding buildings and are a favourite site for photographs with the prosaically white arch behind. Facing Miró's anarchic couple, **The Spider** ❾ by Alexander Calder is one of the American artist's "stabiles" and his last work, comprising huge steel structures, painted red-orange. Inside the shopping complex, Beatrice Casadesus has created **Charlie Chaplin** and **Brigitte Bardot** in bas reliefs.

Outside once more, in the shadow of the EDF and Aurore towers, Derbré's **The Earth** ❿ is a beautiful bronze of two figures suggesting the rotation of the globe. More dramatically, Guy-Rachel Grataloup has decorated the foot of the **Tour Total** with an 850-sq. metre (9,000 sq. ft) ceramic of tree-like branches swirling skywards into mists of colour.

Further to the east along the esplanade is the happiest sculpture in La Défense – Claude Torricini's **The Frog who Became as Big as an Ox** ⓫. This corpulent frog is a favourite with children and you can drink water from his mouth. In the centre of Place de l'Iris, Henri de Miller's **Sleepwalker** ⓬ is contrastingly graceful – a slender figure with arms outstretched, standing on a smooth sphere.

End a visit to La Défense at sunset by the huge pool which overlooks the Seine at the entrance. This mirror of water is inhabited by 49 spiralling, swaying rods, designed by the Greek artist Takis. Each rod is crowned by a coloured light which blinks lazily as twilight gathers and the Arc de Triomphe in the distance turns soft pink. Here, at the gateway to one of the most modern developments in the world, the future somehow doesn't feel quite so bad. ❑

Map, page 218

Parc André-Malraux, beyond La Défense to the west, has 24 hectares (59 acres) of rolling lawns, a lake, botanical gardens, an adventure sandpit and is home to the Paris Opera dance school.

BELOW: one of the many works of art to be found dotted around the complex.

PARKS ON THE PÉRIPHÉRIQUE

On both sides of the city's busy ring road lie havens of leisure, from the ancient and tranquil royal Bois de Boulogne to the new André Citroën and Villette parks offering futuristic horticulture and fun

I n 1759 Voltaire declared, "We must cultivate our garden," and Paris has not looked back since. Here is a city where parks and gardens are a matter of philosophy, a touchstone for the state of mind and health of the capital, a reflection of the sinuous course of the city's history. The French quality newspaper *Le Monde* once asserted that "when we argue in favour of our gardens, we are arguing for the whole city".

Now, more than ever, Parisians are looking to their green spaces as an escape from the increasing congestion of urban living. While the 1980s may be remembered as the decade of the *grands projets* and monumental building (*see page 95*), the 1990s have seen the city's parks and gardens flourish. Derelict industrial sites are flowering and blossoming into suburban parks, with a fervour not seen since Haussmann's day. Never before has Paris been so green.

The Bois de Boulogne – a recreational paradise

Past the necklace of the Périphérique ring road to the west of Paris, the **Bois de Boulogne** (Métro Porte Maillot, Porte Dauphine, Porte d'Auteuil, Sablons) is one of the reasons that the 16th *arrondissement* alongside it is preferred by the wealthy as a place to live – Avenue Foch, perhaps the most expensive residential street in the capital, leads straight to park gates. Embraced by an elbow of the Seine, this 860-hectare (2,120-acre) expanse of woods and gardens has been the Sunday afternoon playground for generations of Parisian families. Historically, it has also had a reputation for love, as successive kings used to house their mistresses here and, after Louis XIV opened the woods to the public in the 17th century, it was noted that "marriages from the Bois de Boulogne do not get brought before the Right Reverend".

In 1852, Napoleon III had the surrounding wall of the royal hunting ground, built by Henri II, demolished and the park was remodelled on the Emperor's cherished Hyde Park in London. It now offers gardens, wild woods, horse racing at France's two famous racecourses, Longchamps and Auteuil, a sports stadium, boating, museums, restaurants, theatre and much more, making the park the main recreation area for Paris. However, it does have a reputation for being seedy at night.

A good place to start exploring the Bois de Boulogne is from the beautiful Art Nouveau Métro stop at Porte Dauphine (*see page 133*) and the best way is by bicycle, which can be rented (daily May–Sept; weekends Oct–Apr) near the **Pavillon Royal**, off the Route de Suresnes. A network of cycle paths and nature trails intersect the woods enabling easy access to the vast park and its scenic lakes and waterfall.

To the north is the **Jardin d'Acclimatation** (open

PRECEDING PAGES: the carefully laid-out gardens of the Espace Albert Kahn. **LEFT AND BELOW:** playing in the Bois de Boulogne.

The great novelist Honoré de Balzac (1799–1850) lived at 47 Rue Raynouard, east of the Bois de Boulogne (above), from 1840–47 under a false name and wrote 16 hours a day to pay his creditors. Now Maison de Balzac is a museum (open daily; closed Mon and pub. hols; entrance fee).

BELOW: playing Shakespeare.

daily; entrance fee), an amusement park for children, with a hall of mirrors, zoo, go-kart racing, a wooden fort, theatre and puppet show. Here, the **Musée en Herbe** (open daily; closed Sat morning during school terms; entrance fee) organises art exhibits and workshops for future Picassos. Also here is the **Musée National des Arts et Traditions Populaires** (open daily; closed Tues and some pub. hols; entrance fee) which portrays life in France before industrialisation, incorporating local customs, crafts and folklore with an audio-visual show.

Westwards, the **Parc de Bagatelle** (open daily; entrance fee) surrounds a small château constructed by the Count of Artois, later Charles X, who bet Marie-Antoinette he could build a house in three months. The bet was won at great cost, hence the ironic name "bagatelle". The gardens are magnificent with 8,000 roses blooming from June to October, a walled iris garden flowering in May and a display of waterlilies in August. Art exhibitions are held in the Trianon and Orangery during the summer season.

In the centre of the Bois, the **Pré Catalan** is the most romantic spot in western Paris. In spring, narcissi, tulips and daffodils carpet the manicured lawns, bathing the foot of the colossal copper beech, well over 200 years old, whose branches span over half a kilometre (550 yds). Le Pré Catalan restaurant is a big attraction offering sumptuous fare in elegant *Belle Epoque* surroundings. Nearby, the intimate **Jardin Shakespeare** (open for guided tours only, daily 3–3.30pm, 4–4.30pm; entrance fee) is planted with flowers, trees and shrubs that star in Shakespeare's plays such as Macbeth's heather, Mediterranean herbs from *The Tempest* and Ophelia's stream. In summer, open-air productions are presented in the leafy theatre.

On the eastern border of the park, between the Place de la Porte de Passy and

ROYALTY IN THE BOIS

From 1953 until their deaths in 1972 and 1986 respectively, the Duke and Duchess of Windsor lived in a truly magnificent house at 4 Route du Champ d'Entraînement, in the Bois de Boulogne. The twice-divorced American, for whom Edward VIII gave up the British throne in 1936, ensured that her husband was able to live in the manner to which he was accustomed, decorating the house in a style "fit for a king". After the Duchess died, Harrods owner, Mohamed al-Fayed took over the house, buying their personal collection of 40,000 items. The royal memorabilia finally went under the hammer in New York in 1998 after it had been postponed the previous September following the deaths of al-Fayed's son and Diana, Princess of Wales.

Porte de la Muette, is the **Musée Marmottan** (2 Rue Louis Boilly; open daily; closed Mon; entrance fee). The museum contains 65 paintings by Monet, which were donated by his son, Michel, in 1971 and include his celebrated *Impression: Sunrise* (1872), which gave its name to the Impressionist movement. Once home to Paul Marmottan, art collector extraordinaire, this beautiful 19th-century mansion also exhibits works by Pissarro, Renoir and Gauguin.

Parc de la Villette – futuristic fun

To the northeast of Paris, nestling against the Périphérique, the **Parc de la Villette** (Métro Porte de Pantin, Porte de la Villette; open daily; closed Mon; entrance fee) is France's third most visited site after Disneyland Paris and the Centre Georges-Pompidou. Built on the site of a huge abattoir, which was rendered obsolete by improved refrigeration techniques and poor design (the cows could not even get up the steps), 55 hectares (136 acres) of futuristic gardens surround a colossal science museum – Cité des Sciences et de l'Industrie – as well as **La Géode** (open daily; closed Mon; tel: 01 40 05 12 12; entrance fee), a giant silver ball housing a huge wraparound cinema, **L'Argonaute** (included in the science museum's entrance fee), a retired naval submarine and **Cinaxe** (open daily; closed Mon; entrance fee), a flight-simulator-cum-cinema, which is definitely not for the queasy.

The **Cité des Sciences et de l'Industrie** (open daily 10am–6pm; tel: 01 40 05 80 00; entrance fee) was designed by architect Adrien Fainsilber and built by the company that masterminded the moving of the temple of Abu Simbel in Egypt. This is not a museum for academics: the exhibits are interactive, with buttons, levers, keyboards and screens to keep mind and body alert. Begin at

Map, page 112/113

TIPS

At La Villette, combined entrance tickets are available at the Cité des Sciences et de l'Industrie. Combinations include Cité-Géode, Cité-Cinaxe and Cité-Géode-Cinaxe.

For guided tours of the city's parks and gardens, phone 01 40 71 75 23.

BELOW: La Géode – Parc de la Villette's wraparound cinema.

L'Univers with a spectacular planetarium and explanation of the inexplicable Big Bang. *La Vie* is an eclectic mix of medicine, agriculture and economics. A working meteorological station traces the day's weather in 240 cities across the world. *La Matière* reproduces a nuclear explosion and permits you to land an Airbus 320 and *La Communication* has displays of artificial intelligence, three-dimensional graphics and virtual reality.

Across the canal, the former cattle market now houses a cultural and conference centre in the immense 19th-century **Grande Halle**. Next door, the **Cité de la Musique** is an edifice of angles in two buildings designed by Christian de Portzamparc, holding the music and dance conservatory, concert hall and the **Musée de la Musique** (open noon–6pm, Fri and Sat till 7.30pm, Sun 10am–6pm; closed Mon; entrance fee), which contains over 4,500 musical instruments.

The gardens of the park are the biggest to be constructed in Paris since Haussmann's time. Designed by Bernard Tschumi and opened in 1993, they comprise several thematic areas such as the Jardin des Frayeurs Enfantines (Garden of Childhood Fears), with a huge dragon slide, Jardin des Brouillards (Garden of Mists), among sculptured streams, and the Jardin des Vents (Garden of Winds) growing multicoloured bamboo plants. Abstraction continues in the form of Tschumi's *folies*: red, angular tree houses minus the trees, each with a special function such as play area, workshop, daycare centre or café.

ABOVE AND BELOW: lots for children to do at Parc de la Villette.

Parc des Buttes-Chaumont – a mountainous creation

To the south of La Villette and on the city side of the Périphérique, **Parc des Buttes-Chaumont** (Métro Botzaris, Buttes-Chaumont) was built by Haussmann in the 1860s on the site of a rubbish dump and gypsum quarry. The uneven

ground provided a perfect setting for a wooded, rocky terrain and a lake has been created around an artificial 50-metre (150-ft) "mountain", capped by a Roman-style temple, with a waterfall and a cave containing artificial stalactites. Ice-skating, boating and donkey rides are also on offer and the puppet show or "Guignol" in the open-air theatre has been going for 150 years.

Map, page 112/113

The Bois de Vincennes – king of Parisian parks
On the southeast edge of Paris lies the **Bois de Vincennes** (Métro Château de Vincennes, Porte de Charenton, Porte Dorée; RER Fontenay-sous-Bois, Joinville), which is renowned for its château, racecourse and zoo. Philippe-Auguste enclosed the forest in the 12th century with a 12-km (7-mile) wall to protect the royal hunting ground. In 1370, Charles V completed the **château** (open daily; entrance fee), which over the centuries has served as a prison – incarcerating among others the philosopher Diderot and revolutionary Mirabeau – a porcelain factory and, under Napoleon I, an arsenal. Napoleon III started a restoration programme but the château was severely damaged by the Germans in 1944. Restoration is now complete and there is a museum in the 14th-century keep.

Just south of the château, **Le Parc Floral de Paris** (open daily; entrance fee) is a favourite with families who wander the Vallée des Fleurs, in bloom all year round, the pine wood and the water garden and take advantage of the adventure playground. Close by is **La Cartoucherie**, once an ancient arsenal, now a complex of theatres which resound to the sound of some of France's most *avant-garde* theatre companies, including the Théâtre du Soleil.

On the western side of the Bois is the **Parc Zoologique** (open daily; entrance fee). This zoo was all the rage when it opened in 1934, because the animals

When Henry V of England died of dysentery in the Château de Vincennes in 1422, staff boiled his body in the kitchen before shipping it back home for burial.

BELOW LEFT: the interactive Cité des Sciences.
BELOW: animal-friendly zoo at Bois de Vincennes.

Map,
page
112/113

La Ruche, designed by Gustave Eiffel as a wine pavilion for the 1900 World Fair and re-erected in 1902 as artists' studios in Passage Dantzig, is just west of Parc Georges Brassens. Residents included Fernand Léger and Marc Chagall. Now an historical monument, it is still used by artists.

BELOW: the site of the old Citroën car factory, now a park. **RIGHT:** boating in the Bois de Vincennes.

roamed free. Each enclosure is different, inspired by the animal's natural environment, and a giant artificial mound is home to monkeys, gazelles and goats.

At Porte Dorée, a few minutes walk away from the zoo, is the **Musée des Arts d'Afrique et d'Océanie** (open daily; closed noon–1.30pm weekdays, weekend mornings and pub. hols; entrance fee), one of the least known of Paris's museums, which houses a fascinating collection of African and Australasian art. Picasso used to come here to wander round the displays of Nigerian death masks, Algerian jewels and South Pacific fertility symbols, seeking inspiration. The star attraction is an impressive tropical aquarium with a crocodile pit.

To the west of Vincennes lies **Parc Montsouris** (Métro Porte d'Orléans; RER Cité Universitaire), the second of Haussmann's 19th-century parks, comprising 16 hectares (40 acres) of gently undulating grass and trees, much loved by Cubist Georges Braque and the exiled Lenin, who both used to live close by. On the day the park opened, the lake suddenly and inexplicably drained dry, and its engineer committed suicide.

New-age parks and horticulture

The far-flung southwest of Paris is the capital's most populated district and home to two of its newest parks. **Parc Georges Brassens** on Rue des Morillons (Métro Convention) was opened in 1982 on the site of an old abbatoir and is now a child's paradise with playhouses, rock piles, rivers and mini-lakes. It includes a garden designed for the blind: close your eyes, follow the trickling of fountains and smell the fragrant foliage. Braille signs give relevant information on herbs and shrubs. Along Rue des Morillons grow 700 vines, producing the annual *Clos des Morillons* wine (full-bodied, fine bouquet). At weekends, the ancient slaughterhouses host a giant book market.

Further west on the banks of the Seine, dereliction became creation when the site of the Citroën car factory on Rue Balard was turned into the **Parc André-Citroën** (Métro Balard, Javel – André Citroën). Here industrial buildings have become floral palaces – two huge glasshouses shine forth over the esplanade where children leap in and out of spurting fountains. Behind the glass lie two gardens – "black" and "white", side by side in botanical harmony. A series of six more colourful gardens completes the park – gold, silver, red, orange, green, and blue – with appropriately chromatic plants. Each garden is linked to a metal, a planet, a day of the week, and a sense: thus gold is linked to the sun, Sunday and the intangible sixth sense.

More traditional horticulture is found beyond the southeast of the Bois de Boulogne at the **Espace Albert Kahn** (14 Rue du Port, Métro Boulogne – Pont de St-Cloud) where the legacy of financier Albert Kahn takes the form of an extraordinary park, created between 1895 and 1910. Japanese, English and French gardens lie alongside an Alpine forest and North American prairie. The grass is cut at different levels, from "beatnik" style to "sailorboy". Kahn called the gardens "the vegetal expression of my thoughts concerning a reconciled world", an idea complemented by 72,000 photographs of world landscapes taken between 1910 and 1931 and exhibited on permanent rotation. ❑

DISNEYLAND PARIS

Map, page 250

Within easy reach of the city centre, this flamboyant slice of good, wholesome American entertainment provides fun for all, from a fairytale castle to the plunging delights of a runaway train

With twice as many annual visitors as the Eiffel Tower or the Louvre, Disneyland Paris ❶ is the most popular tourist attraction in Europe. Located at Marne-la-Vallée, 32 km (20 miles) east of Paris on a 1,943-hectare (5,000-acre) site one-fifth the size of the city itself, the land "where dreams come true", as Walt Disney put it, has finally taken off after a rocky start in 1992. Disney plan to open a film-linked park called Disney Studios in 2002.

Although hordes of school buses are the resort's staple diet, many of Disneyland Paris's attractions may also stimulate more sophisticated imaginations. The park is worth the detour from Paris, if only to glimpse France's most incongruous, yet enjoyable tourist mecca at the end of RER line A (a regular TGV train service takes 15 minutes from Roissy-Charles de Gaulle airport and there's a shuttle bus service from Orly airport, *see page 266*).

Following the success of Tokyo Disneyland, opened in 1983, Europe was scoured for a suitable site for another non-American venture. The Disney empire eventually chose the land of Napoleon (the UK was discounted, thanks to lack of land and inconvenient geography, as was Spain, due to infrastructural inadequacies and the all-eclipsing 1992 Barcelona Olympics). France was somewhat of a homecoming, suggest Disney officials, since Walt's family originally came from Isigny-sur-Mer on the Normandy coast – d'Isigny (from Isigny) evolved to Disney once in America. Generous financial incentives from the French government might also have influenced the final decision.

Disney has enjoyed a love-hate relationship with its hosts since the opening of the park in April 1992. President Mitterrand turned down an official invitation to the inauguration, saying it was not his "cup of tea". Publications such as *Nouvel Observateur* and *Libération* tripped over each other in their race to condemn "*la folie Disney*". Yet three and a half million visitors in the theme park's first year of operation were French.

PRECEDING PAGES: the four-star Disneyland Hotel at the main entrance. **LEFT:** Sleeping Beauty's Castle – the centrepiece. **BELOW:** riverboat ride in Frontierland.

Practicalities of Disneyland

With 40 attractions – 11 of them built since the opening – the whole site will not be fully developed, if present plans are maintained, until 2017, when there will be an MGM studio theme park, another new golf course and 13,000 more hotel rooms. But the resort is still impressive enough. Aside from the park itself, there is a complex of American theme bars, shops and restaurants known as Disney Village (*see page 241*), six hotels situated just outside the main turnstiles, a campsite and a 27-hole golf course.

Disneyland can be a daunting place, especially for mild-mannered Europeans unaccustomed to American-style fun. On popular days, the Magic Kingdom can receive more than 40,000 visitors (the park opens at

There are 150,000 trees in Disneyland, as many as in the whole of Paris. Many are North American varieties, such as Red Cedar, Honey Locust and Giant Sequoia, as well as exotic Judas trees, Monkey Puzzle, cacti and palms. The palms survive the winter insulated in foil painted to look like bamboo.

9am in the summer holidays and closes at 11pm). The best way to approach getting the most out of your time here is to decide on what you want to do in order of priority and get there early, as, by midday, lines of restless pilgrims at the most popular rides can be quite long. The longest wait can be up to 45 minutes, but the queues are well regulated and there is plenty to see while you gradually shift along. Heading round the park in an anti-clockwise direction avoids the bigger crowds, since the circular train chugs clockwise.

It does rain in Marne-La-Vallée, but most of the attractions have been built under cover and sheltered walkways lead from area to area, so the weather doesn't matter. Even the paint used is brighter than elsewhere in the Disney empire to counter grey skies. Eternally optimistic, Disney points out that rain leads to a stunning array of vegetation in the park, unrivalled by its developments in Florida and California.

The gardens are immaculate, as is the entire complex, with teams of roving cleaners ensuring nothing sullies the Disney brilliance. The code of cleanliness also extends to the employees across the board – from the managing director to the washer-up – who are not permitted facial hair, dangly earrings, tattoos or short skirts, causing intermittent disputes with French trade unions.

Getting your bearings

Disneyland Paris theme park is divided into five main areas, or "lands", each with attractions, restaurants and shops following a particular theme – a floor plan cloned from the other Disneylands in California, Florida and Tokyo. Designed by "Imagineers", the artistic and mechanical wizards who spend their lives thinking up weird and wonderful attractions, this is Disney's most technologically advanced park yet, benefiting from state-of-the-art robotics – the organisation's unique audio animatronics, where life-size, lifelike figures speak, sing and dance with gusto.

Once through the Victorian turnstiles, already humming along to ubiquitous Disney music, you enter **Main Street USA**, the first of the five areas representing 19th-century, small-town America. City Hall, on the left, is the central information centre, a contact point for lost children and property. Here, too, is the Main Street Station, from where the Disneyland train circles the park. The station is often quite crowded, so it is a good idea to get on the train at one of the other stations en route, such as Frontierland.

The bandstand in Main Street square is the best place from which to view the parades (weekends, and daily during the summer season) which traverse the park, passing around the bandstand and out through the large green gates to the right, between Discovery Arcade and Ribbons and Bows Hat Shop. These are Mickey's 11.30am parade, the 4pm Grand Parade and the night-time Electrical Parade, with illuminated floats lit up by 700,000 light bulbs. The park takes on an even more mystical face at night, with thousands of miniature lights blinking like fireflies. At weekends, and each summer night, the bandstand is also the best spot from which to view the five-minute Fantasia in the Sky firework display.

DISNEYLAND MADE EASY

Different types of passes are available and prices are reduced in low season during school term times.

The best option is a two- or three-day passport, so you can spread out your visit. It does not have to be used on consecutive days, has no date limit and is more economical. You could combine a two-day passport with a night in one of the resort hotels – during peak season, hotel guests are granted access to the park an hour before it opens. The Star Nights pass allows entrance after 5pm at a reduced rate in summer when it closes at 11pm.

Passports can be bought from the Disney Store and Virgin Megastore on the Champs-Elysées, from FNAC, and at the gate. A Combi-ticket, combining a return RER ticket and passport, is available from main stations on RER line A. For details, including accommodation, phone 01 60 30 60 30 in France and 0990 030303 in the UK, or visit www.disneylandparis.com.

Frontierland – the Wild West

Many of the most popular attractions in the park are found in **Frontierland**, to the left of Main Street. Frontierland evokes dreams of the Wild West and its centrepiece, **Big Thunder Mountain**, is a towering triumph of red rock reminiscent of every Western movie you have seen. The surrounding small town of Thunder Mesa represents a pioneer settlement of the late 1800s, including Cavalry Fort and Lucky Nugget Saloon, where Miss Lil entertains on a vaudeville stage. Get to Big Thunder Mountain roller-coaster early to avoid a long wait and enjoy a bird's-eye view of the park before you hurtle spectacularly around an old gold mine on a runaway train. Even the waiting area is consistent with this theme – the queue moves through a mining shack, with the smell of oil and grease in the air, past the foreman's office and water pumping station.

Meticulous detail plays a part in all Disney's evocations – researchers scour the United States for period pieces such as iron mine pulleys from Montana and Minnesota light fittings. Such detail helps ease the wait and encourages visitors to enter into the spirit of the attraction before they embark. Anticipation is heightened by glimpses of the ride as you shuffle along to take your turn.

Phantom Manor, home to some of Disney's most spectacular audio-animatronics, provides a high-tech rollicking ride through a haunted house. If the house itself seems vaguely familiar, it may be because it is copied from Norman Bates's abode in Hitchcock's *Psycho*. The "dead" tree outside is not actually dead, but specially treated by Disney botanists so that it grows no leaves. Inside are singing cowboy skeletons and holographic ghosts.

The **Rivers of the Far West**, an artificial lake in the middle of Frontierland, can be enjoyed by Mississippi paddle steamer, keelboat or Indian canoe. The

Map, page 250

BELOW: riding high in the Orbitron in Discoveryland.

Indian canoe station, verdant and full of birdsong (taped, but it fools the real birds) is a tranquil contrast to the roller-coaster ride. Also in Frontierland is the **Pocahontas Indian Village**, inspired by the Disney film of the same name.

Adventureland – pirates and shipwreck

From Frontierland, paths lead almost imperceptibly into **Adventureland**. Sparse scrub gives way to lush bamboo and flowers, and the twang of Wild West guitar fades into the beat of African drums.

Here is another top attraction, the unforgettable **Pirates of the Caribbean** (queues move quickly as a rule). As you descend into the castle, the air cools, water drips and the darkness is punctuated only by flickering firelight. The water ride, through tropical swamp to the open sea, is orchestrated by jovially barbaric Disney workers. The boats pass the **Blue Lagoon Restaurant**, serving Caribbean fare under a starlit sky. For the six-minute journey you remain spellbound by animated pirates invading a treasure-rich port – here, a singing donkey, there, an inebriated pig that taps its trotters in time to the music.

Rival to Big Thunder Mountain, the first-ever 360° looping roller-coaster created by Disney is **Le Temple du Péril**, near Explorers' Club Restaurant. Hold on to your stomach as the ore-carts plunge through rainforest and turn upside down above a mock archaeological dig inspired by the *Indiana Jones* saga. As with other top rides, get here early. Elsewhere, Adventureland offers the ultimate treehouse, **La Cabane des Robinson**, home of the Swiss Family Robinson; an **Adventure Isle** based on Robert Louis Stevenson's *Treasure Island*, complete with rope bridge and Ben Gunn's cave; and **Captain Hook's Pirate Ship** which, along with Skull Rock, acts as a playground.

ABOVE: Big Thunder Mountain gives a screaming good ride.
BELOW: tootling around on Main Street, USA.

Fantasyland – favourite fairytales

The most popular land for younger children is **Fantasyland**, containing Disney's emblem **Le Château de la Belle au Bois Dormant** (Sleeping Beauty's Castle), the centrepiece of the park. Unlike in Florida, California or Tokyo, here you can enter into the French-style château, where Sleeping Beauty's tale is told through rich tapestries and stained-glass windows. Underneath, through Merlin's Workshop, lies *La Tanière du Dragon* (the Lair of the Dragon), hiding a breathtaking 27-metre (88-ft) long creature that roars, curls its claws and hisses smoke. Next door, **Blanche-Neige et les Sept Nains** (Snow White and the Seven Dwarfs) leads children through the classic fairytale in the cars from the dwarfs' mine and terrifies them with a holographic floating witch's head.

Not even Disney executives can account for the popularity of **Peter Pan's Flight**, which is another site to visit early in the day before the tour buses arrive, where you can take a pirate galleon into the skies above London, as far as Never-Never Land. Next door, **Toad Hall Restaurant** is Disney's impression of Ye Olde English Pub, which now even sells beer, since Disneyland Paris relaxed its ban on alcohol in order to increase profitability. Nearby, the **Fantasy Festival Stage** puts on glittering musical revues featuring favourite Disney characters. Whimsical madness is found in Alice's **Curious Labyrinth**, another mecca for small children, and the crazily spinning **Mad Hatter's Tea Cups**. You control how quickly you feel sick by regulating the speed at which the cups spin.

More sedate amusement is found in **It's a Small World**, where national stereotypes live in a cheerful puppet kingdom of singing children, first designed by Walt Disney for Pepsi's stand at the 1964 World Fair and sponsored by France Telecom. The other big attractions are similarly supported by multinational

Map, page 250

BELOW: in the drink in Fantasyland.

DISNEY VILLAGE

Open until the early hours, the complex between the park and the hotels buzzes with shops, restaurants, nightclubs and a huge cinema complex. Dramatic entertainment takes the form of Buffalo Bill's Legend, a 90-minute Wild West show with Indian chiefs, buffalo and carousing cowboys. For eating, the LA Bar and Grill offers a pizza terrace and Beach Boys' music, while Key West provides seafood at the sign of the life-size shark, a source of endless fun for children. Upstairs, you can sip a Cyclone Special under an alligator at the Hurricane Disco until 3am. Annette's Diner is well priced and entertaining, and fills up early with families. A 1950s diner, it serves burgers and beer, brought by roller-skating waiters. The mood continues in Rock 'n' Roll America, a 1950s dance hall. Across the strip, Billy Bob's presents chicken and bluegrass. The area by the lake is more sedate and more expensive.

Map,
page 250

companies, such as IBM, Coca-Cola and Renault, in collaboration with Disney, and who receive advertising rights in exchange. It may be a small world – but it's certainly lucrative.

Discoveryland – high-tech wizardry

The final stage of the journey, unless you've decided to go anti-clockwise, is **Discoveryland**, providing an assortment of futuristic high-tech experiences. **Space Mountain** is a roller-coaster ride into outer space inspired by Jules Verne's novel *From the Earth to the Moon* and **Star Tours** offers a trip into space with George Lucas's *Star Wars* characters. To get there, you walk past hard-working robots complaining about the trials of life. Once at the ride itself, the five minutes spent in the air force-designed flight simulator are riveting as the spaceship crashes through meteors and engages in a laser battle with the enemy.

Next door's **CinéMagique** lets you sample Michael Jackson's feet in your face, with a 3-D motion picture of Captain Eo and his merry band of dancers. For a voyage through time in 10 minutes join the robotic timekeeper at the **Visionarium**, where a 360° screen provides a panoramic view of Europe, from the Swiss Alps to Gérard Depardieu's nose. The view of Paris *circa* 2200 is the most interesting and disturbing feature of the show.

ABOVE: Michael Jackson features in a CinéMagique film.
BELOW: luxury hotel outside the park.
RIGHT: Alice's Curious Labyrinth.

Beyond the rides – where to stay

The wider resort – **Disney Village** and the hotels (*see page 273*) – make up a celebration of "Americana", a direct response to Disney's vision of how Europeans view America. Continuing the cinematic motif of the theme park, the six hotels are Hollywoodesque in design. **Hotel Cheyenne** is the most imaginative – a film-set Western town, complete with saloon, sheriff's jail and wooden-planked stores. At the other "moderately priced" hotel, **Santa Fe**, Clint Eastwood grimaces down from a mock drive-in movie screen above reception. Designed by Antoine Predock, the hotel is a series of blocks recalling Mexican villages. Water runs in irrigation channels through desert landscapes, past a 1956 Cadillac buried in the sand.

The more expensive hotels, **Sequoia Lodge** and **Newport Bay Club**, overlook Lake Disney. One recalls Hitchcock's *North by North-West* in its pine surrounds and the other is a New England mansion straight from F Scott Fitzgerald's novel, *The Great Gatsby*. Across the lake, **Hotel New York** offers luxury rooms in a Manhattan-style skyscape designed by Michael Graves. Attached is the New York Coliseum Conference Centre, with capacity for 2,000 delegates.

But the jewel of the resort's hotels is, naturally, the four-star **Disneyland Hotel** sprawling across the main entrance. Its Victorian style whispers late 19th-century elegance and it is here that Michael Jackson comes to stay when he jets in to enjoy the park after hours.

Five kilometres (3 miles) from the theme park (you will need your own car) in natural forest is **Davy Crockett Ranch**, with 97 camping places for tents and caravans and 498 fully equipped cabins in rustic logger style. Set in a "pioneer" village, it provides sports facilities and bicycle hire.

TRIPS OUT OF TOWN

Visit Josephine's Malmaison or the royal Château de Fontainebleau, go cycling in an ancient forest or see the real waterlily pond that Monet painted – all within easy reach of Paris

Map, page 250

To visit many of the interesting places beyond the city limits, it is just a simple train ride, or you can hire a car (*see page 267*) to venture off the beaten track where your meanderings may lead to quaint old *auberges* serving hearty evening meals by the fire or lunch on a terrace overlooking a river. If time is limited, then a trip to Versailles is an obvious choice, but you could take a day or two to visit a town such as Rouen or Chartres further away, stopping at sights along the way. All of the noble forests of the Ile de France and surrounding regions are worth going to and are generously dotted with châteaux and monuments. SNCF trains are generally efficient and, on arrival at your destination, you will find the needs of visitors well catered for, with maps and information on tourist sights, hotels, restaurants and taxis. Some places can be reached by the speedy RER train (*see page 266*). In Compiègne and Fontainebleau, tour buses will take you into town or the countryside.

PRECEDING PAGES:
solemnity in the
Gothic Chartres
cathedral; Monet's
lily pond at Giverny.
LEFT: formal
Versailles in bloom.
BELOW: home with
the daily bread.

The shortest hops

Versailles ❷ (open daily; closed Mon and pub. hols; entrance fee; tel: 01 30 83 78 00), 23 km (14 miles) southwest of Paris, can be reached via RER line C5, which will drop you a short distance from the Sun King's magnificent château and gardens (*see pages 254–55*). You will have to pick and choose what to see as you will need much more than a day to take in everything. In the formal gardens on every Sunday from May to October, the fountains dance to music at 3.30pm.

Just half a day will suffice for a visit to **Sèvres ❸** (Métro Pont de Sèvres), southwest of Paris. Situated on the left bank of the Seine, the suburb has been famous for its porcelain for more than 200 years and the ceramics workshops, set in a sloping, wooded park include the **Musée Nationale de la Céramique** (open daily; closed Tues; entrance fee; tel: 01 41 14 04 20).

Further westwards, en route to **St-Germain-en-Laye ❹**, is the **Château de Malmaison** (open daily; closed 12.30–1.30pm and Tues; entrance fee; tel: 01 41 29 05 55) in Rueil-Malmaison (RER line A to La Défense-Grande Arche then bus 258), which was the favourite home of Napoléon Bonaparte's first wife, Josephine, and where she lived after their divorce. Napoléon used to come here to wind down between battles. Now, along with the neighbouring Château de Bois-Préau, it is an important museum of the First Empire with rooms kitted out as they were originally. The rose garden has also been nurtured in keeping with Josephine's day.

The wealthy bourgeois Paris suburb of St-Germain-en-Laye, just 5km (3 miles) away (at the end of RER line ❹), has perched above Paris since the 12th century and was once a royal retreat. The **château** (open daily;

During the Revolution, the tombs in St-Denis (above) were vandalised and the royal bodies thrown into a pit. However, they were secretly rescued and finally returned to their original resting places in restored tombs by Louis XVIII in 1816.

closed Tues; entrance fee; tel: 01 34 51 53 65), which still has a lovely Gothic chapel, was reconstructed under François I (his royal salamander and "F" can be seen in the courtyard) and again in the 19th century. Inside, you won't find any period furnishings or portraits, but rather a museum devoted to prehistoric and medieval times. The Gallo-Roman collection and the life-sized replica of the Lascaux cave drawings are favourite exhibits. The terrace gardens overlooking the Seine were designed by André Le Nôtre (*see page 122*) and later gave inspiration to the Impressionist painter Alfred Sisley (1839–99).

North of Paris, less than 4 km (3 miles) away, stands the basilica of **St-Denis** ❺ (Métro St-Denis – Basilique), the final resting place of France's kings and queens. Revered as an early masterpiece of Gothic architecture, the basilica (open daily; closed Sun morning; entrance fee; tel: 01 48 09 83 54) was mainly built by the charismatic Abbot Suger, close friend of Louis VII, in the 12th century on the site of an abbey church. According to legend, this is the spot reached by St Denis, first Bishop of Lutetia, when he walked out of Paris carrying his head, after having been beheaded in Montmartre (*see page 171*). Monarchs from as far back as Dagobert I (628–37) are buried here and the medieval and Renaissance sculptures, marking their tombs, are some of the finest in France.

North to Chantilly and Compiègne

Famous for horse racing, **Chantilly** ❻ – about 50 km (30 miles) away from Paris (SNCF from Gare du Nord) – offers a sumptuous palace, a magnificent park created by Le Nôtre and the splendid, 18th-century, palatial Grandes Ecuries, stables built by Prince Louis-Henri de Bourbon, who believed that he would be reincarnated as a horse. The château, nestling in a forest grove, is a real fairytale

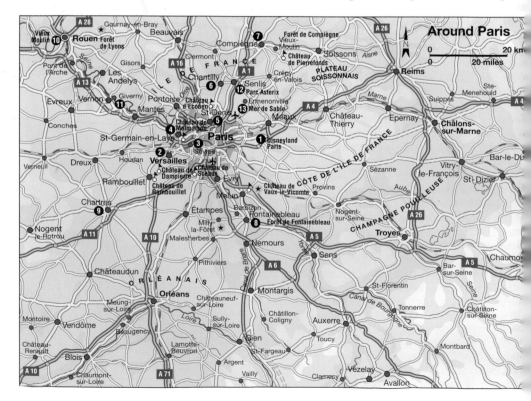

Around Paris

castle – white walls are topped by a blue-slate roof, and wild ducks bustle around its moat. Inside is the **Musée Condé** (open daily; closed Tues; entrance fee; tel: 03 44 62 62 62) with a comprehensive collection of works by Botticelli, Raphael, Giotto and Holbein.

You don't have to be a horse racing enthusiast to enjoy the **Musée Vivant du Cheval** (open daily, Wed–Mon afternoons; closed Tues; entrance fee; tel: 03 44 57 40 40) under the impressive dome of the Grandes Ecuries, with 30 horses of varying breeds on show and 31 exhibition rooms – these stables could once house 240 horses and 500 dogs. Riding displays are held on the first Sunday of each month. The Chantilly racecourse is the most fashionable in France and high society gathers here during June for the prestigious flat-racing trophies.

The town of **Compiègne ❼** – 30 km (20 miles) northeast of Chantilly and 80 km (50 miles) northeast of Paris (SNCF from Gare du Nord) – sits between the Oise River and one of the largest forests in France. The town's Hôtel de Ville has the oldest bell in the country hanging in its clock tower and *picantins* (little figures) strike every hour. The **Château de Compiègne** (open daily; closed Tues; entrance fee; tel: 03 44 38 47 00) was once the favourite residence of Napoleon III and the Empress Eugénie and contains three museums including one for cars.

If you enjoy walking, make your way on foot to **Les Beaux Monts**, just outside the town, for a spectacular view of the château and the Oise. From here, a round walk, lasting between one and two hours, has been marked out, guiding you through the beautiful Forêt de Compiègne, an ancient royal hunting forest full of old oaks and beech trees. By car or SNCF bus from Compiègne station, you can visit the **Musée Wagon de l'Armistice** (open daily; closed Tues; entrance fee) in the Clairière de l'Armistice (Armistice Clearing), where the signing of the 1918 Armistice between France and Germany took place and where Hitler humiliated the French by making them surrender on 22 June 1940.

On the eastern edge of the forest is Napoleon III's unusual hunting palace, the **Château de Pierrefonds** (open daily; closed 11.45am–2pm and Tues; entrance fee; tel: 03 44 42 72 72). Entirely reconstructed in the 19th century, in medieval military style by Viollet-le-Duc, with drawbridge, moat and towers, it is a remarkable architectural oddity, as inside the fanciful architect allowed his Romantic imagination a free rein.

Southeast to Fontainebleau

En route to **Fontainebleau ❽**, 40 km (25 miles) from Paris, is the luxurious 17th-century **Château de Vaux-le-Vicomte** (SNCF from Gare de Lyon to Melun; Feb–mid-Nov: open daily; entrance fee; tel: 01 64 14 41 90). Built by Louis XIV's powerful royal treasurer, Nicolas Fouquet, a devoted patron of the arts, the impeccable house along with a beautiful garden *à la française*, the first created by Le Nôtre, was his undoing. Jealous advisers whispered to the King that Fouquet had paid for it with treasury funds. After a grand housewarming party for the young monarch, Fouquet was imprisoned at Vincennes and the upstaged Louis set out to build something even more splendid – Versailles – using the very same architect and designers. The château, grounds and furnishings provide an intriguing visit. One room

Map, page 250

TIP

The SNCF runs a bike rental service (Train + Vélo) at many of its stations – when you buy your train ticket you can reserve a bike which will be waiting at your destination. This is the best way to visit Monet's house in Giverny or to explore the Fôret de Lyons.

BELOW: a royal stag in Fontainebleau.

Forgotten by industry, spared by wars, the medieval, walled town of **Provins** *(SNCF Gare de l'Est), 75 km (45 miles) east of Paris, seems to be under a spell. Once a Roman outpost perched above the Voulzie River, it grew to become the powerful seat of the medieval counts of Champagne and the third largest city in France. Every June, the town holds a crimson rose and medieval festival.*

BELOW: the apse in Chartres cathedral.

traces the history of its various owners, others are decorated in sumptuous period style, with coffered, painted ceilings and Gobelins tapestries, and the kitchen equipment is fascinating. The candlelit tour on Saturday evenings (May–mid-Oct) gives an added atmospheric dimension.

Melun sits on the edge of the **Forêt de Fontainebleau**, once a royal hunting ground and now, due to some giant rock formations, the haunt of cyclists, mushroom hunters, birdwatchers, picnickers and rock climbers. The town of Fontainebleau (SNCF from Gare de Lyon) lies just 15 km (9 miles) away and is dominated by the first purpose-built royal **château** (open daily; closed 12.30–2pm and Tues; entrance fee; tel: 01 60 71 50 70), residence of French sovereigns from François I to Napoleon III. Each one has added something to the palace, creating a mixture of styles, but Napoleon I outdid them all by building an ornate throne room – his *grands appartements* are definitely worth seeing.

If you are driving, **Barbizon**, 7 km (4 miles) away on the eastern edge of the forest, is a village that has attracted landscape painters since the 1840s, when Théodore Rousseau (1812–67) and Jean-François Millet (1814–75) fled to the woods to escape the Industrial Revolution and rediscover nature. Rousseau's workshop is now a museum to the Ecole de Barbizon (open daily; closed Tues and 12.30–2pm weekdays; entrance fee; tel: 01 60 66 22 38).

Southwest to medieval Chartres

A trip to **Chartres** ❾ – 89 km (55 miles) from Paris – in the Loire Valley can be taken slowly, stopping off at the **Châteaux de Dampierre** and **Rambouillet** (*see below*) on the way, or you can go straight there by train (SNCF from Gare Montparnasse). The two spires of the magnificent Gothic **cathedral** (open daily;

CHÂTEAUX AROUND PARIS

Ile de France is an area rich in châteaux, many built in the wake of the Sun King's extravagant palace at Versailles. The **Château de Sceaux** (tel: 01 46 61 06 71), 7 km (4 miles) south of Paris, was built in 1670 for Fouquet's successor, Colbert, with a beautiful park and gardens designed by Le Nôtre. Rebuilt in Louis XIII style in 1856, the château contains the Musée de l'île de France. More Le Nôtre gardens can be found at the **Château de Dampierre** (tel: 01 30 52 53 24), 35 km (22 miles) southwest of Paris, which has a touch of Versailles. The president's summer residence, **Château de Rambouillet** (tel: 01 34 83 00 25), 15 km (9 miles) further on, was once a feudal castle and is open when the president is away. In the **Château d'Ecouen** (01 34 38 38 50), 19 km (11 miles) north of Paris, is the Musée National de la Renaissance, with the finest tapestries in France and early mathematical instruments on display.

Map, page 250

*Europe's most gut-wrenching roller-coaster ride can be experienced in **Parc Asterix** ⓬ (Apr–Aug: open daily, Sept–mid-Oct: open Wed and weekends; entrance fee), 45 km (28 miles) north of Paris. At Ermenonville, the **Mer de Sable** ⓭ theme park offers acres of sand and Wild West fun (mid-Apr–mid-Oct: open daily; entrance fee).*

BELOW: medieval streets in Rouen.

free) soar above the surrounding fields. Originally Romanesque, the cathedral dedicated to the Virgin Mary (Notre Dame) was destroyed by fire in 1194 but everyone from peasant to lord immediately contributed to the rebuilding, either with labour or finances. The famous rose windows fill the cathedral with changing colours along with 170 more of the finest original stained-glass windows. Behind the cathedral is the **Musée des Beaux-Arts** (open daily; closed Tues and some pub. hols; entrance fee; tel: 02 37 36 41 39) offering Renaissance paintings and fine tapestries. At the recently excavated Gallo-Roman city ruins nearby, a **Maison de l'Archéologie** (14 Rue St-Pierre; Jul–Oct: open afternoons; Oct–May: open Wed and Sun only) has been opened, designed by the British architect Richard Rogers.

Part of a French urban conservation scheme, the town provides an authentic glimpse of life "in the provinces". Along the banks of the Eure, a path passes typical countryside *lavoirs* (wash houses) and steep staircases, and quaint, cobbled streets take you past the medieval Benedictine abbey church of **St-Pierre** to the remains of the old city wall.

Westwards to Monet's Giverny

For a longer break from Paris, head for the industrial city of **Rouen** ⓾ (SNCF from Gare St-Lazare) on the Seine – about 110 km (70 miles) along the N13 from Paris. This road passes through Saint-Germain-en-Laye (*see page 249*) and close to Giverny, home of the Impressionist painter Claude Monet (*see page 123*). Once the capital of Normandy and despite the damage it suffered during World War II, Rouen has a wealth of picturesque houses and narrow streets mostly centred around the impressive Gothic cathedral, much loved by Monet. Joan of Arc was burned at the stake here by a tribunal of clerics in cahoots with the English. They accused her of being a witch and a heretic, although her real "crimes" were courage and patriotism.

Giverny ⓫ (SNCF from Gare St-Lazare to Vernon 6 km/3 miles away) is set on a hillside above the Seine and Monet lived and worked in the small village house for 43 years until his death, in 1926, at the age of 86. Now known as the **Fondation Claude Monet** (Apr–Oct: open daily; closed Mon; entrance fee; tel: 02 32 51 28 21), the house is a museum decorated in the colours that the painter loved. The gardens that the father of Impressionism designed and drew inspiration from are a living work of art – at their colourful best during May, June and July – with the Japanese bridge and the famous waterlilies on the pond. Only copies of his works are on display but, nearby, the modern **Musée d'Art Américain** (Apr–Oct: open daily; closed Mon; entrance fee; tel: 02 32 51 94 65) celebrates the original work of half a dozen American Impressionists, who worked in France during Monet's time, and provides a tea room.

Visitors who want to escape the tourist track should head for the **Forêt de Lyons** (SNCF from Rouen or Gare St-Lazare to Pont de l'Arche). The centennial beech trees, thin and tall, make a walk or cycle ride in this forest a particular pleasure, with fine views over Normandy-style villages full of half-timbered houses set off by potted geraniums in the windows. ❏

THE SPLENDOURS OF VERSAILLES

Paris was not always the capital of France. For a while the country was run from the sumptuous palace at Versailles to the southwest of the city

The Château of Versailles is the ultimate expression of the French monarchy's power and ostentation prior to the Revolution. Built in 1624 as Louis XIII's hunting lodge, the building and surrounding land were developed by Louis XIV, who employed the celebrated creative trio of definite articles – Le Vau, Le Nôtre and Le Brun – and the architect Mansart. Versailles became the capital of France and, by 1774, after alterations by Louis XV and XVI, the palace had 2,143 windows, 67 staircases and was home to 10,000 courtiers and servants. The gardens were designed by Le Nôtre on the same grand scale as the château itself, and adorned with statues and fountains. Their main theme was Louis's emblem of the Sun – he is pictured above dressed as the Sun for a ballet.

THE SOCIAL WORLD OF THE SUN KING

The name Versailles evokes not just a building but also the world of Louis XIV's court and the repetitive rituals that kept it turning around the king. Most famous were his *lever* and *coucher*, a ceremonial rising and going to bed. These normally private routines were performed in public and charged with symbolic meaning. Those present were deemed especially honoured; indeed, every act of the king was designed to establish differences of rank among his courtiers, and to distribute favours and evidence of his displeasure.

▽ **SATURN, OR THE FOUNTAIN OF WINTER**
Designed by Le Brun, this sculpture represents an old man (Saturn) surrounded by playful cupids.

▷ **MARBLE COURTYARD**
This courtyard is enclosed on three sides by the wings of Louis XIII's château. It is overlooked by Louis XIV's bedchamber, a first-floor room located at the exact centre of the palace. Steps leading up to the courtyard prevented anyone in a horse and carriage approaching the royal apartments.

△ **FOUNTAINS**
Bronze statues, some representing the great rivers of France, surround the two large ornamental ponds in the *parterres d'eau* on the main terrace.

▽ **ROYAL CHAPEL**
A Baroque masterpiece, the magnificent two-storey chapel is adorned with carv white marble, gilding and murals. The royal family worshipped from the galler

▽ MARIE-ANTOINETTE
The daughter of the Empress of Austria married the future Louis XVI in the opera house at Versailles in 1770 when she was 14. She wanted to be surrounded by the latest fashions and was responsible for much redecoration. Her frivolity (she was nicknamed "Mme Déficit") contributed to the monarchy's downfall.

UEEN'S BEDCHAMBER
teen royal offspring were n in this sumptuous room; oirths took place in full lic view, so that the timacy of the children d not be disputed.

ALL OF MIRRORS
·run decorated the ceiling is stunning hall in 1686 a gigantic painting, ch depicts the glory of the n of Louis XIV.

PAVILIONS FOR THE MISTRESSES

In 1668, Louis XIV built a pavilion where he could retire with his mistress, Madame de Montespan, and escape the demands of the court. Le Vau designed the charming Trianon de Porcelaine, which was decorated with Delft tiles throughout. It was soon outgrown by Louis and his entourage, and in 1688 it was replaced by the Marble Trianon (Grand Trianon), which had a beautiful white facade decorated with pink marble and balustrades.

Louis XV and XVI took little interest in the residence and during the Revolution furnishings were sold, but the building survived. Napoleon restored and refurnished it, and Louis-Philippe often stayed there with his family. Today, we see it in its 19th-century incarnation.

The Petit Trianon was built almost 100 years later by Jacques-Anges Gabriel for Louis XV and his mistress, Madame de Pompadour. However, this Classical Revival building is best known as the favourite residence of Marie-Antoinette, who transformed the gardens from a French to an English design. She also built the Hameau, a collection of rustic-style houses and the setting for her pretence of living the simple life.

It was in these gardens that, on 5 October 1789, the Queen heard that the mob was marching on Versailles. The days of Versailles as a royal palace were over.

INSIGHT GUIDES

TRAVEL TIPS

New
Insight Maps

Maps in Insight Guides are tailored to complement the text. But when you're on the road you sometimes need the big picture that only a large-scale map can provide. This new range of durable Insight Fleximaps has been designed to meet just that need.

Detailed, clear cartography
makes the comprehensive route and city maps easy to follow, highlights all the major tourist sites and provides valuable motoring information plus a full index.

Informative and easy to use
with additional text and photographs covering a destination's top 10 essential sites, plus useful addresses, facts about the destination and handy tips on getting around.

Laminated finish
allows you to mark your route on the map using a non-permanent marker pen, and wipe it off. It makes the maps more durable and easier to fold than traditional maps.

The first titles
cover many popular destinations. They include Algarve, Amsterdam, Bangkok, California, Cyprus, Dominican Republic, Florence, Hong Kong, Ireland, London, Mallorca, Paris, Prague, Rome, San Francisco, Sydney, Thailand, Tuscany, USA Southwest, Venice, and Vienna.

INSIGHT GUIDES
The world's largest collection of visual travel guides

CONTENTS

Getting Acquainted

The Place

Situation 48°50N, 2°20W, on the same latitude as Mongolia, northern Newfoundland and Montréal city.
Population around 3 million in the city of Paris, 12 million in the whole region of Ile de France.
Area 100sq km (40sq miles).
Language Everyone in France speaks French, but regional languages still exist in Brittany (Breton), Alsace (Alsatian), the western Pyrénées (Basque) and the eastern Pyrénées (Catalan).
Time zone France is one hour ahead of Greenwich Mean Time (GMT) and six hours ahead of Eastern Seaboard Time. Most French people use the 24-hour clock, so 1pm appears as 1300hrs on timetables and is referred to as *treize heures*.
Currency The Euro was introduced as the official French currency in January 1999 but Euro notes and coins will not be used until 2002. The main currency is still the French franc (FF). Approximately 10FF=£1 and 7FF=$1. Prices are quoted in francs and Euros.
Electricity The standard voltage is 220/230 volts, although in a few areas it is only 110 volts. Round-pin plugs are used everywhere, so pack a transformer or adapter.
Weights & Measures Metric for all weights and measures, although old-fashioned terms such as *livre* (about 1lb or 500g) are still used by many. For quick conversion: 2.5cm is about 1in, 1 metre is about a yard, 100g is just over 4oz and 1kg is just over 2lb. Distance is given in kilometres. One kilometre is five-eighths of a mile, so 80km is 50 miles and 80kph is 50mph.

Direct **Dialling** 00 (international code) + 33 (France) + 1 (Paris) + an eight-figure number.

The Climate

The French climate is varied and seasonal. France is the only European country that is both north European and Mediterranean, and it has an Atlantic coastline. In the north the climate is similar to that of southern England, while in the south summer temperatures can frequently rise to over 30°C (86°F). Springtime, when the temperature is ideal for sightseeing, is often suggested as the best time to see Paris, although you should be prepared for showers. In the autumn, mornings can be quite sharp, but by midday the skies are usually clear and bright.

The Economy

France has the fourth largest economy in the OECD (Organisation for Economic Co-operation & Development) and is one of the most visited countries in the world. The Ile de France, which includes Paris, holds about a fifth of the French population and contributes 30 percent of France's gross domestic product. The Paris Stock Exchange is the fifth most active in the world.

Paris is France's largest consumer market and the focal point of all French communication systems. Most of its industry is in the suburbs. Planning restraints downtown (the only building in the central zone over nine floors is the Tour Montparnasse), coupled with increasing demand for quality office space, led to the huge La Défense building project west of Paris.

The Government

France became a Republic in 1792, after the abolition of the monarchy, and constitutional change created the Second, Third and Fourth Republics. The current Fifth Republic was created when General Charles de Gaulle became Prime

Public Holidays

Banks and post offices close on the following dates:
● **1 January** *Jour de l'An*
● **Easter Monday** *Pâques*
● **1 May** *Fête du Travail*
● **8 May** *Victoire 1945*
● **Ascension Day** *Ascension*
● **Pentecost** *Pentecôte*
● **14 July** *Fête Nationale* (Bastille Day)
● **15 August** *Assomption*
● **1 November** *Toussaint*
● **11 November** *Armistice 1918*
● **25 December** *Noël*
For Parisians, days off are an opportunity to escape the city. Banks and most shops close, but the Métro, cinemas, *tabacs* and some museums and restaurants stay open.

Details of public holidays are normally posted outside banks and post offices. A holiday that falls on Thursday or Tuesday is liable to cause a *pont* (bridge), where the day before or after is also taken as leave from work to make a long weekend.

Many small shops and restaurants close in August, when thousands of Parisians leave the city. If you can bear the heat, this is an excellent time to visit the capital as it is much quieter and calmer.

Minister in 1958. The President holds a powerful office, is elected for a term of seven years and appoints the Prime Minister as head of government. Parliament has two houses: the National Assembly and the Senate. The most important political parties are the Partie Communiste Français (PCF) and the Partie Socialiste (PS) on the left, and the Rassemblement pour la République (RPR) and the Union pour la Démocratie Française (UDF) on the right. The Verts (the Greens) are gaining popularity and won several seats in the last election.

Since 1977 Paris has had an elected mayor, based in the Hôtel de Ville. The mayor is seconded by the members of the Conseil

Municipal and the elected mayors of the 20 *arrondissements*. Each *arrondissement* has a town hall (*mairie*) and registers births, deaths and various legal documents; performs marriages (the civil ceremony is required by law, while the religious ceremony is optional); and hears complaints.

The suburban *départements* surrounding Paris each have a *préfecture* responsible for much of the local administration. Every French *département* has a number, which is convenient for administrative purposes: for example, the number forms the first two digits of the postcode in any address (Paris is 75) and the last two digits on vehicle licence plates. The *départements* are numbered alphabetically as follows in the Paris region: Hauts-de-Seine 92, Seine-Saint-Denis 93 and Val-de-Marne 94.

Business Hours

Office workers normally start early (8.30am is not uncommon) and often stay at their desks until 6pm or later. This is partly to make up for the long lunch hours (two hours from around noon) that are traditional in shops and public offices. Many companies are changing to shorter lunchbreaks as employees appreciate the advantages of getting home earlier in the evening. Most banks in Paris open from Monday to Friday from about 9am to 4.30pm, and are closed on Saturday, Sunday and public holidays.

Planning the Trip

Clothing

Paris is a great city to explore on foot, so comfortable walking shoes are essential for visitors. Bring warm clothes if you're coming to Paris in winter, as the weather can be very chilly, and remember your waterproofs (or at least an umbrella) in spring or autumn, as showers are typical. Most Parisians are very style-conscious and won't brave even the corner shop without displaying a fair amount of *élan*. Casual tourists might therefore consider taking a smart change of clothes with them, for example for a night out at one of the city's many upmarket restaurants.

Visas and Passports

All visitors to France require a valid passport. No visa is required by visitors from European Union (EU) member states, the US, Canada or Japan. Nationals of other countries need a visa. If in doubt, check with the French Consulate in your home country. Anyone (including EU nationals) wishing to stay for longer than 90 consecutive days will need a *carte de séjour*, obtainable from their French Consulate or the Préfecture de Police, 9 Boulevard du Palais, 75004 Paris.

Money Matters

The French franc (FF) is divided into 100 centimes (c). Coins come in 5c, 10c, 20c and 50c and 1FF, 2FF, 5FF, 10FF and 20FF denominations. Notes come in 20FF, 50FF, 100FF, 200FF and 500FF denominations.

Credit cards Some credit cards are accepted, especially Visa and

Tourist Information

For brochures on Paris contact the French Government Tourist Office in London, tel: 0891 244123 (calls cost 60p per minute). Operators can also answer most queries, from shop opening hours to details of where to stay and current shows. You can also visit their extremely informative website at: www.franceguide.com.

Carte Bleue (the main card type in France, often known as "CB"). Large shops and restaurants will take American Express (Amex), Diner's Club (DC) or Access/ Mastercard, but check before buying. Many places also now accept Maestro and Cirrus; again, it's advisable to double check before making your purchase.

Eurocheques can be cashed at any bank and are widely accepted by hotels and larger stores and supermarkets.

Bureaux de change Most banks have an exchange counter, or *change*, which is open Monday to Friday from 9am to 4.30pm. A few smaller branches close for lunch.

Airport Orly Sud Exchange, on the departure level at gate H, is open seven days a week until 11pm. Airport Roissy Exchange, at terminals 2A, 2B and 2D, also remains open seven days a week until 11pm.

Bureaux de change at train stations vary their hours according to high or low season but most are open five days a week from 7am to 7pm. Le Change de Paris at 2 Rue de L'Amiral de Coligny, 75001, is open every day from 10am to 7pm. Take your passport to cash travellers' cheques.

Cash machines You can draw cash from bank dispensing machines using a credit card or European bank cashpoint card, with your PIN number. Visa is widely accepted in France but you can withdraw money from most cash machines if your card is: Visa, American Express, Mastercard, Maestro or Cirrus.

Before leaving, check with your bank that your card is valid abroad.

Health

If you are an EU national and you fall ill in France, you are entitled to emergency medical treatment from doctors, dentists and hospitals. You may have to pay part of the cost of this treatment, so you must fill in an E111 form and take this to claim a refund and keep it for any subsequent trips that you take within the EU. The leaflet *Health Advice for Travellers* (available from post offices or by telephoning 0800 555777) outlines the health arrangement that the UK has with France and includes an E111.

As this reciprocal arrangement does not cover all medical expenses, such as the cost of bringing a sick person back to the UK, the Department of Health advises travellers also to take out holiday insurance. If you plan to drive in France, you should check that your motor insurance covers you for accidents abroad.

In North America, contact the International Association for Medical Assistance to Travellers (IAMAT), 40 Regal Road, Guelph, Ontario N1K 1B5, Canada, tel: 519 836 0102. This is a non-profit-making group that offers members fixed rates for medical treatment from participating physicians. Members receive a passport-sized medical record completed by their

doctor and a directory of English-speaking IAMAT doctors in France, who are on call 24 hours a day. Membership is free, but a donation is requested.

Getting There

BY AIR

Most major airlines fly regularly to Paris. Air France is the main agent for flights to France from the US and within Europe (tel: 020-8742 6600). It also handles bookings for smaller operators such as Air Vendée and Brit Air. For British travellers, smaller operators (such as the low-cost airline Ryanair – www.ryanair.com – and British Midland) offer flights from British cities to provincial French airports.

Travellers from the US and Canada can fly direct to Paris and larger cities such as Nice and Lyon on Air France and most US airlines. For long-haul passengers, a charter flight to London then onward to Paris may prove cheaper. In Paris, Nouvelles Frontières and Forum offer competitive fares on scheduled and charter flights.

Students and young people can get discount charter flights through specialist travel agencies. In the UK, try Campus Travel, 52 Grosvenor Gardens, London SW1W OAG, tel: 020-7730 3402. In the US, try USIT, New York Student Centre, 895 Amsterdam Avenue, New York, NY 10025, tel: 212-663 5435.

BY RAIL

Paris has six railway stations with lines radiating across France and Europe. Each connects with at least two Métro or RER lines and has left-luggage facilities (*consignes*) and coin-operated lockers (*consignes automatiques*).

The SNCF's much-publicised *Train à Grande Vitesse* (TGV) offers a rapid and comfortable service from Paris to Bordeaux, Brest, La Rochelle, Lille/Calais, Lyon and Marseille. It is not particularly cheap, so it pays to travel off-peak. You must reserve in advance to travel on a TGV and booking eight to 30 days in advance could get you a reduction of up to 55 percent. Information and reservations are available from Rail Europe, tel: 0990 848 848.

Before boarding an SNCF train you must have your ticket date stamped or *composté*. Failure to do so is an offence and makes your ticket invalid. Simply insert your ticket in the orange *composteur* machine at the platform entrance.

Channel Tunnel The 50km (31-mile) Channel Tunnel enables fast, frequent rail services between London (Waterloo) or Ashford and Paris (Gare du Nord). Tel: 0836 35 35 39 (UK) or 01 43 18 62 22/ 01 41 91 10 15 (France) or visit: www.eurostar.com for details.
Le Shuttle takes cars and passengers from Folkestone to Calais on a

Customs Regulations for EU Nationals

There are no official restrictions on the movement of goods within the European Union, provided that the goods were purchased within the EU. Note that it is no longer necessary for EU nationals to exit Customs through a red or green channel.
Duty-paid goods If you buy goods in France for which you pay tax, there are no longer any restrictions on the amounts you may take home with you. However, EU law has set

"guidance levels" on the following:
• **Tobacco** one of: 800 cigarettes, 400 cigarillos, 200 cigars, or 1kg of tobacco
• **Spirits** 10 litres
• **Fortified wine/wine** 90 litres
• **Beer** 110 litres
If you exceed these amounts you must be able to prove that the goods are for personal use, for example a family wedding.
Duty-free goods If you are from outside the EU and buy goods

duty-free in France, the following restrictions still apply:
• **Tobacco** one of: 200 cigarettes, 100 cigarillos, 50 cigars, or 250g of tobacco.
• **Alcohol** 1 litre of spirits or liqueurs over 22 percent volume, or 2 litres of fortified, sparkling wine or other liqueurs.
• **Perfume** 60cc of perfume, plus 250cc of toilet water.
There are no restrictions on the amount of currency you can take into France.

Travelling with Children

In France, children are generally treated as individuals, not just nuisances, so you can take them into restaurants, even in the evening, without heads turning. French children, however, eat out from an early age and are therefore generally well behaved in restaurants.

Many restaurants offer a children's menu. If not, they may split a *prix-fixe* menu between two children. With very young children, just request an extra plate and give them food from your own. French meals are generous so you won't go hungry yourself and *le patron* (or *la patronne*) won't mind. Alternatively, order a simple dish from the *à la carte* menu, such as an omelette or soup. With the bread that comes automatically to a French table,

and ice-cream or fruit to follow, a small child is sure to be more than satisfied.

Weekly magazines such as *L'Officiel des Spectacles* and *Pariscope* give details of plays, films, puppet shows and circuses and list babysitting services. High-grade hotels may even be able to arrange babysitters for you.

Most hotels have family rooms, so children are not separated from parents. A cot (*lit bébé*) can often be provided for a small supplement, but check if booking in advance.
● **Home Service** (babysitting service), tel: 01 42 82 05 04.
● **Marionettes du Jardin du Luxembourg** tel: 01 43 26 46 47 or 01 43 29 50 97 for a recorded message (in French) about current children's shows.

or Gare Routière Internationale, 2 Avenue Charles de Gaulle, 93541 Bagnolet Cedex, tel: 08 36 69 52 52.

Student Travel

Students and people under the age of 26 can get cut-price travel to Paris (see *Getting There*). For a prolonged stay, it may be worth finding out about an exchange visit or study holiday. The following organisations provide information or arrange visits:

UK services The Central Bureau for Educational Visits & Exchanges, The British Council, 10 Spring Gardens, London SW1A 2BN, tel: 020-7389 4004, produces two books: *Working Holidays* (details on all types of work, from conservation to fruit picking) and *Home from Home* (information on staying with a French family).

Those who can speak French could approach a UK-based camping holiday operator. Many of these, such as Holiday Break, Hartford Manor, Greenbank Lane, Northwich, Cheshire CV8 1HW, tel: 01606 787522, employ students as site attendants in France during the summer months.

US services American Council for International Studies Inc, I9 Bay State Road, Boston, Massachusetts 02215, tel: 617-236 2051.

The Council on International Educational Exchange (CIEE), 205 E. 42nd Street, New York, NY IOOI7, tel: 2I2-822 2600. Offers a wide range of services, including travel.

Youth for Understanding, 3501 Newark Street NW, Washington DC 20016, tel: 202-966 6800.

Study in France Several French tour operators can organise study tours and language courses. The Office National de Garantie des Séjours Linguistiques, 8 Rue César Franck, 75015, tel: 01 47 83 31 65, is a national association that quality-checks the 30 members of the organisation offering language courses. Write for a list of schools, or try the following:

Résidence OTU Bastille, 151 Avenue Ledru Rollin, 75011, tel: 01 43 79 53 86. Offers French study

drive-on, drive-off service taking 35 minutes. Payment is made at toll booths, which accept cash, cheques or credit cards. You can book or simply turn up and take the next available service. Le Shuttle runs 24 hours a day, all year and at least once every hour.

BY SEA

Ferries from the UK, Ireland and the Channel Islands to the northern ports of France have reduced their prices since the Channel Tunnel opened. All ferries carry cars and foot passengers. Hovercraft are faster but make for a bumpy ride in bad weather. The Seacat catamaran is the quickest service but, like the hovercraft, only carries a limited number of cars. Boulogne, Calais and Le Havre all have motorway links to Paris.

Hoverspeed, tel: 08705 240241, runs hovercraft and Seacat services from Dover to Calais or Boulogne.

P&O North Sea Ferries, tel: 01482 795141, runs from Hull to

Zeebrugge, Belgium and Europort, Rotterdam.

P&O Stena Line, tel: 0990 980980, sails from Dover to Calais and Portsmouth to Le Havre and Cherbourg.

Hoverspeed, tel: 08705 240241, sails from Dover to Ostend and Calais and from Newhaven to Dieppe

Irish Ferries, tel: 003531 6610511, runs services from Rosslaire and Cork to both Le Havre and Cherbourg.

BY BUS

Eurolines is a consortium of almost 30 European coach companies. Its services run from London (Victoria) to Paris daily and are one of the cheapest ways to get to the French capital. Discounts are available for young people and senior citizens and the ticket includes the ferry crossing (via Dover). There are National Express coaches from most major UK cities to London.

Eurolines UK, 23 Crawley Road, Luton LU1 1PP, tel: 01582 404511;

programmes, inexpensive accommodation and tours for individuals or groups.

Centre des Echanges Internationaux, 104 Rue de Vaugirard, 75006, fax: 01 45 49 01 70. This is a non-profit-making group offering sporting and cultural holidays and educational tours for 15–30 year-olds.

Students will find a student identity card useful for discounts, including admission to museums, galleries, cinema, theatre, etc. If you don't have your card, your passport may prove your status.

The Centre d'Information et Documentation de Jeunesse (CIDJ), 101 Quai Branly, 75015, tel: 01 44 49 12 00, fax: 01 40 65 02 61, is a national organisation that disseminates information on youth and student activities.

Disabled Travellers

Less-able travellers are well advised to book accommodation in advance. Most official lists of hotels use a symbol to denote wheelchair access, but it is always a good idea to check with the hotel regarding the facilities available.

Budget rooms Hotels in the Campanile chain have at least one

Useful Books

The following guides are useful for the disabled:

● **Access in Paris** A free booklet from the French Government Tourist Office, tel: 0891 244123 (calls 60p per minute).

● **Door-to-Door** is a Department of Transport guide to all types of travel abroad for the disabled, from Stationery Office Bookshops or mail order, tel: 0870 6005522, fax: 020-7873 8200 (orders), fax: 020-7873 8247 (enquiries).

● **Michelin Red Guides** Both *France* and *Camping-Caravanning* note hotels that welcome disabled people.

room for disabled guests and all public areas are accessible. Contact Hotel Campanile, 18 Rue du Pont des Halles, 94656 Rungis Cedex, tel: 01 49 78 01 45, fax: 01 46 86 50 18.

Balladins is a chain of newly built, budget hotels across France, which all have at least one room designed for disabled guests, plus restaurants and public areas that are easily accessible for wheelchair users. For a full list of these hotels, contact: Hotel Balladins, 7 Rue Cap Horn, 91940 Les Ulis, tel: 02 69 29 32 00, fax: 02 69 07 93 89.

Wheelchair users There is a French-language guide, *Paris, Ile de France pour tous*, available from the French Government Tourist Office, that lists accommodation throughout the city that is suitable for wheelchair users. If you have specific needs, double check when booking. The guide is available for FF60 + FF20 post and packing from the Association des Paralysés de France, Service Information, 17 Boulevard August Blanqui, 75013, tel: 01 40 78 69 00. They may also answer specific enquiries and can provide branch addresses.

RADAR The Royal Association for Disability and Rehabilitation (RADAR), 12 City Forum, 250 City Road, London EC1V 8AF (tel: 020-7250 3222 or Minicom: 020-7250 4119), stocks a guide book, *Access In Paris*, which provides information about hotel chains and tour operators.

French organisations France's sister organisation to RADAR is the Comité National Français de Liaison pour la Réadaption des Handicapés (CNFLRH), 263 bis Rue Tolbiac, tel: 01 53 80 66 66; fax: 01 53 80 66 67; e-mail: cnrh@worldnet.net, which offers a useful information service.

The Centre d'Information et de Documentation Jeunesse (CIDJ), 101 Quai Branly, 75740, Cedex 15, has information on services for less-able young travellers. It publishes *Vacances pour Personnes Handicapées* and annual leaflets on activity and sports holidays for young disabled people.

Animals

Animal quarantine has been revised and it is now possible to re-enter Britain with your pet without having to put the animal through quarantine. Conditions are pretty tough, however, with animal subject to stringent health requirements. For further details, contact the Ministry of Agriculture or the French consulate. Note that your pet will need a valid vaccination certificate if you intend to travel between different countries on continental Europe.

Parents may wish to contact the Union Nationale des Associations de Parents d'Enfants Inadaptés (UNAPEI), 15 Rue Coysevox, 75018, tel: 01 44 85 50 50.

The Comité de Liaison pour le Transport des Personnes Handicapées, Conseil National des Transports, 34 Avenue Marceau, 75009, publishes the booklet *Guide des Transports à l'Usage des Personnes à Mobilité Réduite*. This gives brief information on the accessibility and arrangements for less-able passengers on public transport and contacts for special transport schemes in France.

In the US contact the SATH (Society for the Advancement of Travel for the Handicapped), 347 5th Avenue, Suite 610, New York, tel: 212-725 8253, or visit: www.sath.org.

Some concessionary ferry fares are available for members of the following organisations: **The Disabled Drivers' Association**, tel: 01508 489449 **Disabled Drivers' Motor Club**, tel: 01832 734724 **Disabled Motorists' Route Map Service**, tel: 01743 761181.

Practical Tips

Security

If you take sensible precautions with your personal possessions, you should be perfectly safe in Paris. At worst, tourists may be faced with pickpockets, especially in the Métro, but this can easily be avoided by carrying your valuables safely. Obvious centres of prostitution (such as Les Halles and parts of the Bois de Boulogne) are best avoided late at night.

Loss

If your personal documents, cash, belongings or travellers' cheques are lost or stolen, go to the Commissariat de Police nearest to the scene of the crime as soon as possible – even before contacting the travellers' cheque service or your embassy or consulate.

If you lose your passport, report it to your consulate as soon as possible (a full list is in both *Pages Blanches* and *Pages Jaunes* phone books under *Ambassades et Consulats;* www.pagesjaunes.fr).

If your credit card goes missing, numbers to ring are:
● American Express: 01 47 77 72 00
● Diner's Club: 01 49 06 17 50
● Visa or Carte Bleue:
08 36 69 08 80
● Access/Mastercard-Eurocard:
01 45 67 53 53

To reclaim anything else you have lost, you could go (with ID) to the Service des Objets Trouvés, 36 Rue des Morillons, 75732 Cedex 15 (Métro Convention). It is open every weekday from 8.30am to 5pm, and Tuesday and Thursday until 8pm. You need to visit the office in person, as no information is given over the telephone.

Medical Services

In all emergencies **SOS Help** operates an English helpline (tel: 01 47 23 80 80) from 3pm to 11pm daily.

A doctor will pay a house call in an emergency if you dial **SOS Médecins** (tel: 01 47 07 77 77 or 01 43 37 77 77) and explain your situation in French. This is a 24-hour service.

You can reach English-speaking health services at the **American Hospital** (Hôpital Américain de Paris, tel: 01 46 41 25 25) or the **British Hospital** (Hôpital Franco Britannique, tel: 01 46 39 22 22). However, neither of these hospitals has a casualty department.

The **SAMU** 24-hour ambulance service can be contacted by dialling 15. The emergency telephone number for the *pompiers* (or fire brigade, who are trained paramedics) is 18.

For urgent dental treatment contact **SOS Dentaire**, tel: 01 43 37 51 00, which operates a 24-hour emergency service.

If you need to see a doctor, expect to pay at least FF100 per consultation, with prescription charges on top of that. The doctor will provide a statement of treatment (*feuille des soins*). With this, EU citizens can reclaim around 75 percent of the cost of the treatment. Check that the price stamp (*vignette*) from any prescribed medicine has been attached to the *feuille des soins* by the chemist so that you can also reclaim that cost. When complete, the *feuille des soins* should be sent to the local *caisse primaire* (the doctor or chemist will have the address) for your refund, which will be sent on to your home.

If you have any difficulties, contact the **Service Juridique des Relations Internationales**, 173-5 Rue de Bercy, 75586 Cedex 12, tel: 01 53 38 70 00.

Pharmacies

Most pharmacies display flashing green neon crosses and are open from 9am to noon and 2–7pm. At

Hospitals

All state hospitals in Paris have casualty departments. The following are some of the larger ones:
● **Boucicaut**
78 Rue Convention
75015
Tel: 01 53 78 80 00
● **Necker**
(Children's Hospital)
149 Rue de Sèvres
75015
Tel: 01 44 49 40 00
● **Bichat**
46 Rue Henri Huchard
75018
Tel: 01 40 25 80 80
● **Hôtel-Dieu**
1 Place du Parvis-Notre-Dame
75004
Tel: 01 42 34 82 34
● **Saint-Louis**
1 Avenue Claude Vellefaux
75010
Tel: 01 42 49 49 49

night, they all post the address of the nearest open pharmacy in their window or doorway.

Dhéry, 84 Avenue des Champs-Elysées (Métro Georges V), tel: 01 45 62 02 41, is open all hours.

Pharmacie des Halles, 10 Boulevard de Sébastopol, 75004 Paris, tel: 01 42 72 03 23, fax: 01 42 72 52 10, is open 9am–midnight, Monday to Saturday, and noon–midnight on Sunday.

Religious Services

France is predominantly Roman Catholic, and the many churches in Paris, including Notre Dame, are open to the public. For a list of all denominational churches, temples and synagogues, look out for the guide *Plan de Paris par Arrondissement* from a kiosk or bookshop, or contact the Centre d'Information Religieuse, 9–11 Rue Franquet, 75015, tel: 01 56 56 44 00. There are services in English around Paris, notably in the American church, which is situated on Quai d'Orsay.

Media

NEWSPAPERS

The two main national dailies are *Le Monde*, which has a rather dry and leftish slant on politics and economic news, and the more conservative *Le Figaro*; both sell about 400,000 copies. The paper representing the Communist Party is *L'Humanité* and not veering quite so heavily left is Jean-Paul Sartre's brainchild, *Libération*. The major weekly news publications are *Le Point* (right) and *L'Express* (left), which both sell approximately 300,000–500,000 copies. British, American and other European dailies are available at city-centre kiosks and shops showing *journaux* or *presse* signs.

The *International Herald Tribune*, published in Paris, has listings for the city. To find out what is going on in the capital try *l 'Officiel des Spectacles* or *Pariscope* (both out on Wednesday), which give cultural listings (museums, galleries, theatre, concerts, cinema, nightlife etc).

RADIO

France Inter (87.8 MHz) is the main national radio station, offering something to suit all tastes. Radio Classique (101.1 MHz) plays uninterrupted lightweight classical music. If you're looking for something a little less mainstream, try France Musique (91.7 and 92.1 MHz). RTL (104.3 MHz) is the most popular station throughout France, playing music from the charts, interspersed with chat shows etc.

TELEVISION

TF1, France 2, FR3, M6 and Arte are the five main television stations on offer. Most larger hotels receive cable as well. Canal + is a subscription channel, which shows big-name films. CNN is sometimes also available.

Postal Services

The French post office is run by the PTT (Poste et Télécommunications). The main branches are open from 8am to 7pm on weekdays and 8am to noon on Saturday. The central post office at 52 Rue du Louvre, 75001, tel: 01 40 28 20 00, operates a 24-hour, seven-day service for international telegrams and telephone calls. Unless you arrive first thing in the morning or between 2.30pm and 3.30pm, be prepared for a long wait.

To send a telegram in French, telephone 36 55. For telegrams in other languages, call 05 33 44 11.

Stamps (*timbres*) are available at most *tabacs* (tobacconists) and other shops selling postcards or greetings cards. For postcards and letters weighing up to 20g, postage within France and to most of the EU costs FF3. Sending a letter airmail to Ireland, the US and Canada costs FF4.40, and airmail for Australia is FF5.20.

Telephones, telex, Minitel, fax and photocopying facilities are available in larger post offices such as the one at Place de la Bourse, 75001, tel: 01 44 88 23 00, fax: 01 42 33 38 49, open Monday to Friday from 8.15am to 6.30pm, and Saturday 8.15am to noon.

Telecommunications

All telephone numbers in France have 10 digits. Paris and Ile de France numbers begin with 01, while the rest of France is divided into four zones: North West 02; North East 03; South East and Corsica 04; and South West 05. Freephone numbers begin with 08 00; 08 36 numbers are charged at premium rates, and 06 numbers are mobile phones.

There are two kinds of phone box in Paris from which you can make local and international calls: coin-operated phones, which are extremely difficult to find, and the more common card-operated

Useful Addresses and Numbers

● **Air France** 119 Avenue des Champs-Elysées, 75384, Paris Cedex 08, tel: 01 41 56 78 00. For reservations, tel: 08 02 802 802.

● **Automobile Club** 6 Place de la Concorde, 75008, tel: 01 43 12 43 12, fax: 01 43 12 43 43.

● **Customs Information** tel: 01 53 24 68 24.

● **Information Service** For general details about Paris in English, tel: 08 36 68 41 14.

● **Paris Tourist Office** 127 Avenue des Champs-Elysées, 75008, tel: 08 36 68 31 12 (FF2.23 per minute), fax: 01 49

52 53 10. Open 9am–7.30pm daily except 1 January, 1 May and 25 December. The Tourist Office has now put all its information and services on-line, thus paring down services at the main Champs- Elysées office. Visit them at: **www.franceguide.com**. If you don't have access to the web, brochures, guidebooks and maps, plus hotel and train reservation services, theatre and concert ticket sales and a *bureau de change* are available at the office itself; there are also computer terminals to

allow customers access to the website. There are subsidiary tourist offices at the Gare du Nord, the Gare de Lyon and the Eiffel Tower Métro/railway stations, which are open from May to September.

● **RATP information** Métro and bus details in English, tel: 08 36 68 77 14.

● **SNCF information** For information and reservations, tel: 08 36 35 35 35.

● **Traffic information** In English, mainly about *autoroutes*, tel: 01 47 05 90 01.

Operator Services

● **Directory enquiries** 12
● **Operator** 12
● **Reverse charges**
You cannot reverse telephone charges within France but you can to other countries where such calls are accepted. Go through the operator (12) and ask to make a PCV ("pay-say-vay") call.

phones. It may be difficult to find a telephone box that is working. Remember that you get 50 percent more call-time for your money if you ring between 10.30pm and 8am on weekdays, and from 2pm at weekends.

A *télécarte* can be bought from kiosks, *tabacs* and post offices. Insert the card and follow the instructions on the screen: *Décrochez* (pick up the receiver); *Introduire votre carte* (insert your card); *Patientez* (wait); *Numérotez* (dial); *Raccrochez* (hang up). Note that you can only receive telephone calls at telephone boxes displaying a blue bell sign.

You can also dial from all post offices, which have both coin- and card-operated phones. To call long distance, ask at one of the counters and you will be assigned a booth – you pay when your call is over. Cafés and *tabacs* often also have public phones, which usually take either coins or *jetons*, coin-like discs bought at the bar.

To call other countries from France, first dial the international access code (00), then the country code: Australia 61, UK 44, US and Canada 1. If using a US credit phone card, call the company's access number: Sprint, tel: 00 00 87; AT&T, tel: 00 00 11; MCI, tel: 00 00 19.

Doing Business

Business travel accounts for approximately a third of French tourism revenue. This important market has led to the creation of a special Conference and Incentive Department at the French Government Tourist Offices in both London and New York. The Department deals with business-travel enquiries, and will also help organise hotels, conference centres and incentive deals for groups of any size.

Conferences and exhibitions
Paris is a world leader for conferences, exhibitions and trade fairs. The building development at La Défense is the largest business district in Europe. For further information, call Info-Défense, tel: 01 47 74 84 24.

For a list of exhibitions and details about exhibiting, contact Promo Salons, The Colonnades, 82 Bishops Bridge Road, London W2 6BB, tel: 020-7221 3660, fax: 020-7792 3525.

Many *châteaux* offer luxurious accommodation for smaller gatherings, and it's even possible to organise a congress at Disneyland Paris.

Organising a conference
For anyone wishing to put on a major business event in Paris, there are also several tour operators who specialise in conference organisation. Try:

Convergences, 120 Avenue Gambetta, 75020, tel: 01 40 32 47 00, fax: 01 40 31 01 65.

Le Palais des Congrès de Paris, 2 Porte Maillot, 75017, tel: 01 40 68 22 22, fax: 01 40 68 00 05, www.palais-congres-paris.fr.

Chambers of Commerce Another very good source of business information about local companies, assistance with technicalities of export and import, interpretation and translation agencies and conference centres is the Chambres de Commerce et d'Industrie, 45 Avenue léna, 75016, tel: 01 40 69 37 00, fax: 01 47 20 61 28.

Most countries' Chambers of Commerce have conference facilities of some kind. There are French Chambers of Commerce in key cities around the world promoting business with France. In London, the Chambers are situated at 21 Dartmouth Street, London SW1H 9BP, tel: 020-7304 4040, fax: 020-7304 7034.

Embassies

● **Australia**
4 Rue Jean Rey
75015
Tel: 01 40 59 33 00
● **Canada**
35 Avenue Montaigne
75008
Tel: 01 44 43 29 00
● **Ireland**
4 Rue Rude
75016
Tel: 01 44 17 67 00
● **New Zealand**
7 Rue Léonard de Vinci
75016
Tel: 01 45 01 43 43
● **United Kingdom**
35 Rue du Faubourg
St Honoré
75008
Tel: 01 44 51 31 00
www.amb-grandebretagne.fr
● **United States**
2 Rue St-Florentin
75001
Tel: 01 43 12 22 22

Getting Around

From the Airports

FROM ROISSY/CHARLES DE GAULLE

Train

The quickest and most reliable way to get to central Paris, RER trains go direct from terminal 2 (Air France flights), or you can take the shuttle bus (*navette*) from terminal 1. Trains run every 15 minutes from 5am to 11.45pm to métros at Gare du Nord or Châtelet. The average journey time is about 45 minutes.

Bus

The Roissy bus runs between the airport and Rue Scribe, near the Place de l'Opéra from terminals 1 gate 30, 2A gate 10 and 2D gate 12. It runs every 15 minutes from 6am to 11pm and takes between 45 and 60 minutes.

Alternatively, the Air France bus (to Métro Porte de Maillot or Charles-de-Gaulle Etoile) leaves from terminals 2A and 2B or terminal 1 arrival level gate 34. The bus runs every 12 minutes from 5.40am to 11pm.

Taxi

This is by far the most expensive but unquestionably the easiest way to get to Paris from the airport. It can take 30 minutes to over an hour, depending on traffic. The cost appears on the meter, but a supplement is charged for each

Between Airports

An Air France bus links Roissy/ Charles de Gaulle and Orly every 20 minutes from 6am to 11pm.

large piece of luggage, pushchair or animal.

FROM ORLY

Train

Take the shuttle from gate H at Orly Sud or arrivals gate F at Orly Ouest to the Orly train station. The RER stops at Austerlitz, Pont St-Michel and the Quai d'Orsay. It runs every 15 minutes from 5.50am to 10.50pm and takes approximately 30 minutes to Austerlitz.

The Orlybus (to Place Denfert-Rochereau) leaves from Orly Sud gate F or Orly Ouest arrivals gate D. It runs every 10–12 minutes from 6am to 11.30pm.

The Orlyval automatic train is a shuttle to Antony (the nearest RER to Orly). It runs every 5–8 minutes from 6.30am to 9.15pm Monday to Saturday and 7am–10.55pm on Sunday, and takes 30 minutes.

Air France buses (to Invalides and Gare Montparnasse) leave from Orly Sud, gate J or Orly Ouest arrivals gate E. They run every 20 minutes from 6am to 11pm and take 30 minutes. Tickets are available from the Air France terminus.

Taxi

The journey from Orly to the centre of Paris takes between 20 and 40 minutes, depending on the time of day and the traffic.

Public Transport

MÉTRO AND RER

Run by the Régie Autonome des Transports Parisiens (RATP), the Paris Métro is one of the world's oldest subway systems, and some of its stations are almost historic monuments. It is used by approximately 9 million people every day. Despite that, it is quick and efficient.

The Métro operates from 5.30am, with the last train leaving end stations at 12.30am. Its comprehensive map (free at any Métro station) and signposting make it virtually impossible to get

lost. The lines are identified by numbers, colours and the names of their terminals, so Line 4 running north is shown as Porte de Clignancourt, while going south it is Porte d'Orléans. Follow the orange *correspondance* signs to change Métro lines.

The Métro runs in conjunction with the RER (suburban regional express trains), which operates five main lines, identified as A, B, C, D and E. RER trains run daily every 12 minutes from 5.30am to midnight.

The Métro and the bus system use the same tickets (FF8 for a single fare). A book or *carnet* of 10 tickets, which is available from bus or Métro stations and some *tabacs* (tobacconists), offers a considerable saving at just FF55.

Another option is the *Paris Visite* card, valid for three or five consecutive days on the Métro, bus and railway in the Paris/Ile de France region. The card entitles you to a discount at several tourist sites and can be bought from main Métro, RER and SNCF stations. It is only available to tourists. Fares start at FF105 for three zones over three days.

For shorter stays, you can buy the *Mobilis* card, which allows an unlimited number of trips for a day on the Métro, bus, suburban SNCF, RER and the night buses, extending as far as Disneyland Paris. It can be bought in all Métro stations. Fares range from FF30 for 1–2 zones up to FF70 for 1–5 zones.

A *Carte Orange* allows unlimited travel on the number of zones of your choice on any public transport system for a month. A *Carte Jaune* gives you unlimited travel from Monday to Monday. To buy either of these you need to take along a passport photograph to any Métro or SNCF station. Sign your card and copy its number onto your ticket – you will be fined by ticket inspectors if you fail to do this.

For further information on the Paris Métro and RER network, contact RATP (see *Useful Addresses box on page 264, tel: 08 36 68 41 14 for 24-hour information in English, or visit: www.ratp.fr*).

BUSES

Taking the bus is a pleasant way to see the city but can be much slower than the Métro because of traffic. Tickets can be bought from the driver or from Métro stations, as buses accept the same tickets as the Métro. Remember to punch your ticket, and not your travel card, in the *compositeur*.

Buses don't automatically stop, so when you want to get off push one of the request buttons and the *arrêt demandé* ("bus stopping") sign will light up. Each bus has a map of its route posted at the front and back and at every bus stop. Most buses run from 6.30am to 8.30pm, although some routes continue until 12.30am.

A night service – the Noctambus – leaves Place de Châtelet (Avenue Victoria or Rue St-Martin) at 1.30, 2.30, 3.30, 4.30 and 5.30am on 10 routes. Travel passes are valid on the bus and stops are marked by a special black-and-yellow owl logo.

Look out for the Balabus service at certain stops. It visits the main tourist sites every Sunday and on public holidays between 11 April and 26 September, 12.30–8pm. The tour lasts about 50 minutes.

Private Transport

Driving in Paris requires equal measures of insanity and desperation and acceptance of other drivers' madness.

Seat belts are obligatory in both the front and back of the car, and the speed limit in town is 50kph (30mph). Do not drive in bus lanes at any time and give priority to vehicles approaching from the right. This applies to some roundabouts, where cars on the roundabout stop for those coming on to it. If in doubt, be cautious. Helmets are compulsory for motorbike riders and passengers. Street parking is usually metered and the maximum stay is two hours. Most car parks are of the underground variety.

Petrol can be difficult to find in the city centre, so if your tank is

Taxis

Taxis are readily available at the airports and railway stations. In the city itself there are almost 500 taxi ranks, but be careful to hail only a genuine taxi – one with a light on the roof – as other operators may charge exorbitant fares. The white light will be on if a cab is free, while a glowing orange light means that the taxi is engaged.

Taxi drivers in Paris operate on three rates:
● **Tariff A** 7am-7pm Monday to Saturday
● **Tariff B** 7pm-7am Monday to Saturday and all day Sunday
● **Tariff C** at night in the suburbs and during the day in the outlying districts of Hauts-de-Seine, Seine St-Denis and Val-de-Marne, when the taxi has no client for the return journey.

The following taxi companies take phone bookings 24 hours a day:
Alpha 01 45 85 85 85
Artaxi 01 42 03 50 50
G7 01 47 39 47 39
Taxis Bleus 01 49 36 10 10.

If you have a complaint about Paris taxis, it should be addressed to: Services des Taxis, Préfecture de Police, 36 Rue des Morillons, 75015, tel: 01 55 76 20 00.

almost empty you should head for a *porte* (exit) on the Périphérique (the multi-lane ring road). They have petrol stations that are open 24 hours a day all year round.

Drivers are liable to heavy on-the-spot fines for speeding and drunk driving. The drink limit in France is 50mg/litre of alcohol in the blood (equivalent to about two glasses of wine) and is strictly enforced.

CAR HIRE

Hiring a car is expensive, partly because it incurs the highest rate of

TVA tax at 33 percent. Some fly/ drive packages are good value, if you are on a short visit. The SNCF offers a good deal on its combined train/car hire bookings (train + auto). Weekly rates often work out better than a daily rate, and it may be cheaper to hire a vehicle from the UK or the US before leaving. The minimum age to hire a car is 23, or 21 if paying by credit card. The hirer must have held a full licence for at least a year.

Central reservation offices of the major car hire firms are:
Avis, tel: 01 43 25 55 32, fax: 01 47 78 98 98.
Budget/Milleville, tel: 01 40 35 33 33.
Europcar/National/InterRent, tel: 08 03 35 23 52 (calls charged at around FF1 per minute).
Hertz, tel: 01 39 38 38 38 (www.hertz.com).

BICYCLES

If you know Paris well and have nerves of steel, a bicycle is an excellent way to explore the quieter areas. You can rent a bicycle from:
Paris-Vélo, 2 Rue du Fer à Moulin, 75005, tel: 01 43 37 59 22, fax: 01 47 07 67 45.
Paris à Vélo C'est Sympa, 37 Boulevard Bourdon, tel: 01 48 87 60 01.

Hitchhiking

With sensible precautions, hitchhiking can be an interesting and inexpensive way to get around France. Would-be hitchhikers may be discouraged by the difficulty of getting a lift out of the channel ports, so take a bus or train for the first leg of your journey. Hitching is forbidden on the *autoroutes* (motorways), but waiting on slip roads or at toll booths is allowed.

Allostop is a nationwide organisation that aims to connect hitchhikers with drivers. You simply pay a registration fee and a contribution towards the total petrol cost. For further information, tel: 01 53 20 42 42.

Where to Stay

Paris is renowned for the diversity of its hotels, from the small, simple family-run guesthouse to the palatial four-star de-luxe hotel. It is advisable to reserve accommodation in advance, either with the hotel or via the Paris Tourist Office (see *Useful Addresses and Numbers, page 264*) or one of its subsidiary offices, which will book your first night's accommodation if you apply in person. The tourist offices supply a free booklet listing all hotels (pensions and similar establishments) in Paris and its neighbouring suburbs that have been awarded a classification by the Direction de l'Industrie Touristique.

The following organisations also offer reservation services:

Paris Séjour Réservations, 90 Avenue des Champs-Elysées, tel: 01 53 89 10 50, fax: 01 53 89 10 59.

Prestotel, 1 Rue Condorcet, 75009, tel: 01 45 26 22 55, fax: 01 45 26 05 14.

Hotel Listings

BUDGET

Albouy
4 Rue Lucien Sampaix
75010
Tel: 01 42 08 20 09
Fax: 01 42 08 76 60.
The 34 rooms in the Albouy are well equipped, but the hotel's location close to Canal St-Martin is not the most central. Credit cards: Amex, DC, V. **

Allies
20 Rue Berthollet
75005
Tel: 01 43 31 47 52
Fax: 01 45 35 13 92

Few rooms in this simple yet well-maintained hotel in the middle of the Latin Quarter have a bath or shower. Credit cards: V. *

Andrea
3 Rue St-Bon
75004
Tel: 01 42 78 43 93
Fax: 01 44 61 28 36
This modest hotel with 26 rooms is handily situated just off the Rue de Rivoli. Credit cards: V. **

Castex
5 Rue Castex
75004
Tel: 01 42 72 31 52
Fax: 01 42 72 57 91
Small well-run family hotel with 29 rooms close to Bastille and the Place des Vosges. Popular, so book in advance. Credit cards: V. **

Price Guide

Price ranges, per double room, are as follows:
- **Budget** FF200–350
- **Inexpensive** FF350–550
- **Moderate** FF550–1,200
- **Expensive** FF1,200–2,500
- **Deluxe** FF2,500+

The official star rating is also quoted (*, ** etc).

Credit cards:
Amex = American Express
DC = Diner's Club
MC = Mastercard
V = Visa
Most hotels accepting credit cards also take Carte Bleue.

Chat Noir
68 Boulevard de Clichy
75018
Tel: 01 46 06 22 91
Fax: 01 46 06 35 03
All 48 rooms in this relaxed hotel near to the Sacré Coeur have their own WC. Pets are welcome. Credit cards: Amex, MC, V. **

Des Argonautes
12 Rue de la Huchette
75005
Tel: 01 43 26 79 86
Fax: 01 44 07 18 84
Hotel in a bustling part of town by the Théâtre de la Huchette. Credit cards: Amex, DC, V. **

Marignan
13 Rue du Sommerard
75005
Tel: 01 43 25 31 03
Elegant-fronted hotel in the lively Latin Quarter. Offers 30 rooms and free kitchen and laundry facilities. No credit cards. *

Pacific
77 Rue du Ruisseau
75018
Tel: 01 42 62 53 00
Fax: 01 46 06 09 82
Situated just a couple of streets away from the Périphérique. The Pacific has 44 rooms – all have microwaves, some have full kitchen facilities. Credit cards: V. *

Palais Bourbon
49 Rue Bourgogne
75007
Tel: 01 44 11 30 70
This is a modern hotel with 33 rooms in a smart quiet area. It's popular, so you're advised to book ahead, especially for the cheaper rooms. Credit cards: V. **

Régence
3 Rue Laferrière
75009
Tel/fax: 01 48 78 29 96
Small comfortable hotel with 18 rooms near the Place St-Georges. Accepts dogs. Credit cards: V. **

Rouen
42 Rue Croix-des-Petits-Champs
75001
Tel/fax: 01 42 61 38 21
A small, cosy hotel with 22 rooms in an excellent location by the Louvre. Credit cards: V. *

Tiquetonne
6 Rue Tiquetonne
75002
Tel: 01 42 36 94 58
Fax: 01 42 36 02 94
In an old part of Paris close to Les Halles, the Tiquetonne is well maintained with 47 sizeable rooms – all doubles with en-suite bathrooms. Closed: August. Credit cards: DC, MC, V. *

INEXPENSIVE

Ibis Montparnasse
71 Boulevard de Vaugirard
75015

Tel: 01 43 20 89 12
Fax: 01 43 22 77 71
Handy for antique shops in the
area; 31 rooms. Credit cards:
Amex, V. **

Glasgow
3 Rue de la Félicité
75017
Tel: 01 42 27 93 95
Fax: 01 40 53 92 52
The Glasgow has good facilities for
the disabled, parking and 38 rooms.
Credit cards: Amex, DC, V. ***

Abbatial St Germain
46 Boulevard St-Germain
75005
Tel: 01 46 34 02 12
Fax: 01 43 25 47 73
E-mail: abbatial@hotellerie.net
Situated 200m (660 ft) away from
Notre Dame, at the quieter end of
St-Germain; 43 rooms. Credit
cards: Amex, V. **

Place des Vosges
12 rue Birague
75004
Tel: 01 42 72 60 46
Fax: 01 42 72 02 64
A charming former stables that has
been carefully renovated. There are
only 16 rooms, all with bath or
shower, making the hotel intimate
but comfortable. Popular, so book
ahead. Note that the lift only goes
as far as the fourth floor. Credit
cards: Amex, DC, MC, V. ***

Saint-Thomas-d'Aquin
3 Rue du Pré-aux-Clercs
75007
Tel: 01 42 61 01 22
Fax: 01 42 61 41 43
Close to the Eiffel Tower and the
Musée D'Orsay, this hotel offers 21

rooms, each with TV and telephone.
Good for those holidaying with pets
– animals are allowed. Credit cards:
Amex, DC, V. **

Timhôtel
A reliable chain with several hotels
around the capital, including ones
at the Place d'Italie, Montmartre,
St Lazare, the Louvre and on the
Boulevard Clichy. All hotels are fairly
modern, well equipped and
individually decorated. The one at
Montmartre is in an attractive,
tree-lined square with a fountain.
Central reservations, tel: 01 53 38
37 36, fax: 01 53 38 40 60. Credit
cards: Amex, DC, V. **/***

Victoria Chatelet
17 Avenue Victoria
75001
Tel: 01 40 26 90 17
Fax: 01 40 26 35 61
A small hotel in a bustling part of
town with 24 rooms. Credit cards:
Amex, V. ***

Vivienne
40 Rue Vivienne
75002
Tel: 01 42 33 13 26
Fax: 01 40 41 98 19
E-mail: paris@vivienne.com
The Hotel Vivienne is situated close
to the Bourse and has 44 rooms.
Credit cards: V. **

MODERATE

Angleterre
44 Rue Jacob
75006
Tel: 01 42 60 34 72
Fax: 01 42 60 16 93

Booking Hotels

Hotel prices in Paris are not
subject to restrictions and can
be changed without notice, so
check before booking. The
majority of hotels vary prices
by season. State your arrival
time if you book by phone or
the hotelier will not keep your
room after 7pm.

This was once the home of the
British Ambassador and the site on
which the treaty of US
independence was drawn up in
1783. Elegant yet relaxed and very
comfortable, it is located in a smart
corner of the Left Bank. With 27
good-sized rooms, all en suite.
Credit cards: Amex, DC, V. ***

Aramis
124 Rue de Rennes
75006
Tel: 01 45 48 03 75
Fax: 01 45 44 99 29
One of the Best Western Group,
Aramis offers 42 attractive and
comfortable rooms, with well-
equipped bathrooms and TV. Some
rooms have air-conditioning. Not far
from the Jardin du Luxembourg.
Credit cards: Amex, DC, V. ***

Bac Saint-Germain
66 Rue du Bac
75007
Tel: 01 42 22 20 03
Fax: 01 45 48 52 30
This is a very pleasant hotel with
21 rooms and a glassed-in terrace
on 7th floor. Credit cards: Amex,
DC, V. ***

Hotel Star Ratings

* Hotels offer rooms with a bed, a minimum of furniture and (for at least 80 percent of the rooms) a shared
bathroom. Many of these hotels are in the Marais or the Quartier Latin, and they can be pleasant if well run
and kept clean. They are generally run by families, so there is often a curfew after which the front door is
locked.
** Hotels have to equip 40 percent of their rooms with private bathrooms (shower or bath) and provide
breakfast and telephones.
*** Eighty percent of the rooms must have private bathrooms and all rooms must have a telephone and
television. Breakfast must be offered to all guests.
**** (standard/de luxe) Hotels must have reception staff who speak several languages. All rooms should be
equipped with private bathrooms, a telephone and a TV. Breakfast may be taken in the dining room or the
bedroom and restaurant service must be available morning and evening. Four-star deluxe hotels have all
conceivable amenities, top-quality service and very spacious rooms and bathrooms.

Price Guide

Price ranges, per double room, are as follows:
- **Budget** FF200–350
- **Inexpensive** FF350–550
- **Moderate** FF550–1,200
- **Expensive** FF1,200–2,500
- **Deluxe** FF2,500+

The official star rating is also quoted (*, ** etc).

Credit cards:
Amex = American Express
DC = Diner's Club
MC = Mastercard
V = Visa
Most hotels accepting credit cards also take Carte Bleue.

Berne
37 Rue de Berne
75008
Tel: 01 43 87 08 92
Fax: 01 43 87 08 93
A comfortable hotel with 36 rooms in a quiet street. Welcoming to young families. Credit cards: Amex, DC, V. ***

Banville
166 Boulevard Berthier
75017
Tel: 01 42 67 70 16
Fax: 01 44 40 42 77
www.hotelbanville.fr
Located near to L'Etoile and the Porte Maillot, this family-run hotel is clean and cosy. There are 38 well-appointed rooms, with chic marble bathrooms. Some rooms have terraces looking out towards the Eiffel Tower. Credit cards: Amex, DC, MC, V. ***

Britannique
20 Avenue Victoria
75001
Tel: 01 42 33 74 59
Fax: 01 42 33 82 65
This comfortable hotel near the Ile de la Cité is furnished in a typically British style with some inviting leather sofas in the sitting room. Service is courteous. 40 rooms. Credit cards: Amex, DC, V. ***

Deux-Iles
59 Rue St-Louis-en-l'Ile
75004
Tel: 01 43 26 13 35
Fax: 01 43 29 60 25

A lovely peaceful and charming hotel in a 17th-century mansion house in the heart of the Ile-St-Louis. There are 17 rooms, some with views over a pretty courtyard. Credit cards: V. ***

Hôtel Lenox
9 Rue de l'Université
75007
Tel: 01 42 96 10 95
Fax: 01 42 61 52 63
Trendy hotel decorated in the Art Deco style and very popular among creative types such as dress designers, photographers and artists. The rooms are spotless. Reserve well ahead. Bar. Credit cards: Amex, DC, MC, V. ***

Louisiane
60 Rue de Seine
75006
Tel: 01 43 29 59 30
Fax: 01 46 34 23 87
The Louisiane has 80 rooms and overlooks the bustling Buci market in St-Germain. Credit cards: Amex, DC, V. **

Saint-Germain
50 Rue du Four
75006
Tel: 01 45 48 91 64
Fax: 01 45 48 46 22
In an excellent location on the Left Bank, with 30 comfortable rooms. Credit cards: Amex, DC, V. **

Saint-Louis-Marais
1 Rue Charles V
75004
Tel: 01 48 87 87 04
Fax: 01 48 87 33 26
Comfortable but small with an impressive reception area. Offers 16 rooms with 17th-century beams. TV in rooms. Credit cards: MC, V. **

EXPENSIVE

Ambassador
16 Boulevard Haussmann
75009
Tel: 01 44 83 40 40
Fax: 01 40 22 08 74
Pleasant, tranquil 1920s' hotel situated in the heart of the business area. Very handy for the Opéra and the Grands Boulevards. 286 rooms and a trendy brasserie. Credit cards: Amex, MC, V.****

Bradford Elysées
10 Rue St-Philippe-du-Roule
75008
Tel: 01 45 63 20 20
Fax: 01 45 63 20 07
Large, light rooms by the Champs-Elysées in this elegantly furnished, intimate 1900s' hotel. 50 rooms, 2 non-smoking floors, air conditioning and a bar. Good facilities for children. Credit cards: Amex, DC, MC, V. ****

Buci Latin
34 Rue de Buci
75006
Tel: 01 43 29 07 20
Fax: 01 43 29 67 44
www.bucilatin.com
The Buci Latin, in the fashionable St-Germain area overlooking the lively Buci antiques market, is trendily furnished in the style of cult designer Philippe Starck. The theme in each of the 27 rooms is inspired by the work of a different artist. Credit cards: Amex, DC, V. ***

Château Frontenac
54 Rue Pierre Charron
75008
Tel: 01 53 23 13 13
Fax: 01 53 23 13 01
Modern, stylish and intimate, in a great location between the Champs-Elysées and the Avenue George V. Offers 106 well-equipped rooms plus a restaurant and cocktail lounge. Credit cards: Amex, V. ****

InterContinental Paris
3 Rue de Castiglione
75001
Tel: 01 44 77 11 11
Fax: 01 44 77 14 60
www.interconti.com

Bed and Breakfast

The following organisations offer bed and breakfast and sometimes an evening meal in individual homes around Paris:
- **France Lodge**, 41 Rue La Fayette, 75009, tel: 01 53 20 09 09, fax: 01 53 20 01 25.
- **Alcôve & Agapes**, 8 bis Rue Coysevox, 75018, tel: 01 44 85 06 05, fax: 01 44 85 06 14, e-mail: info@paris-bedandbreakfast.com.

Hotel Star Ratings

* Hotels offer rooms with a bed, a minimum of furniture and (for at least 80 percent of the rooms) a shared bathroom. Many of these hotels are in the Marais or the Quartier Latin, and they can be pleasant if well run and kept clean. They are generally run by families, so there is often a curfew after which the front door is locked.

** Hotels have to equip 40 percent of their rooms with private bathrooms (shower or bath) and provide breakfast and telephones.

*** Eighty percent of the rooms must have private bathrooms and all rooms must have a telephone and television. Breakfast must be offered to all guests.

**** (standard/de luxe) Hotels must have reception staff who speak several languages. All rooms should be equipped with private bathrooms, a telephone and a TV. Breakfast may be taken in the dining room or the bedroom and restaurant service must be available morning and evening. Four-star deluxe hotels have all conceivable amenities, top-quality service and very spacious rooms and bathrooms.

This lavish 19th-century hotel was designed by Charles Garnier, of Palais-Garnier opera-house fame. Some of the elegantly decorated *salons* here are listed. Top-class service and all modern conveniences. Credit cards: Amex, DC, MC, V. ****

Lutetia
45 Boulevard Raspail
75006
Tel: 01 49 54 46 46
Fax: 01 49 54 46 00
www.lutetia-paris.com
An early Art Deco palace conveniently situated in the heart of the bustling St-Germain-des-Prés and once frequented by such literary lights as Parker, Hemingway and Fitzgerald. Catherine Deneuve is a regular visitor nowadays. Credit cards: Amex, DC, V. ****

La Montalembert
3 Rue de Montalembert
75007
Tel: 01 45 49 68 68
Fax: 01 45 49 69 49
Ornate Beaux-Arts-style exterior and stylish rooms furnished with antiques. The attic suite is Sir Terence Conran's *pied à terre*. Credit cards: Amex, DC, MC, V. ****

Normandy
7 Rue de l'Echelle
75001
Tel: 01 42 60 61 08
Fax: 01 42 60 45 81
Between the Louvre and the Opera, the Normandy offers traditional comfort. With 115 well-appointed rooms, all en suite, plus a bar and restaurant. Credit cards: Amex, MC, DC, V. ****

Pavillon de la Reine
28 Place des Vosges
75003
Tel: 01 40 29 19 19
Fax: 01 40 29 19 20
Arguably the smartest hotel in the Marais, housed in an imposing mansion. Has 55 rooms furnished with Louis XIII-style antiques, some of which overlook the lovely Pavillon de la Reine courtyards. Credit cards: Amex, MC, V. ****

DE LUXE

Bristol
112 Rue du Faubourg St-Honoré
75008
Tel: 01 53 43 43 00
Fax: 01 53 43 43 01
This is a discreetly upmarket 1920s' hotel with period furniture in all 195 rooms. Lovely gardens. Credit cards: Amex, DC, V. ****

Costes
239 Rue St-Honoré
75001
Tel: 01 42 44 50 01
Fax: 01 4 44 50 01
Opened in 1995, this fashionable hotel is located near the Tuileries in the chic Rue St-Honoré. High points include a gorgeous terrace, where guests can dine in the summer, a fitness centre and a pool. Credit cards: Amex, DC, V. ****

Crillon
10 Place de la Concorde
75008
Tel: 01 44 71 15 00
Fax: 01 44 71 15 02
www.crillon.com

The Crillon is perhaps the grandest hotel in the capital, set in a truly stunning location fronting the Place de la Concorde. Frequented by film stars, heads of state and the very, very rich, the grand building – Marie Antoinette used to have singing lessons here – is also home to the Michelin-starred Ambassadeurs restaurant. Credit cards: Amex, DC, V. ****

George V
31 Avenue George V
75008
Tel: 01 53 53 28 00
Fax: 01 53 53 28 10
www.fourseasons.com
Now owned by the Four Seasons group, this spectacular hotel was fully refurbished for the millennium. Rooms have lavish marble bathrooms, and the hotel offers a restaurant, a top-class wine cellar and a health club among its many facilities. George V is supremely elegant, stylish and extremely exclusive. Credit cards: Amex, DC, V. ****

Hilton International
18 Avenue de Suffren
75015
Tel: 01 44 38 56 25
Fax: 01 44 38 56 10
In a good quiet location on the Left Bank, the Hilton offers impressive views of the Eiffel Tower. Credit cards: Amex, DC, V. ****

Meurice
228 Rue de Rivoli
75001
Tel: 01 44 58 10 10
Fax: 01 44 58 10 15
www.meuricehotel.com

Price Guide

Price ranges, per double room, are as follows:
- **Budget** FF200–350
- **Inexpensive** FF350–550
- **Moderate** FF550–1,200
- **Expensive** FF1,200–2,500
- **Deluxe** FF2,500+

The official star rating is also quoted (*, ** etc.).
Credit cards:
Amex = American Express
DC = Diner's Club
MC = Mastercard
V = Visa
Most hotels accepting credit cards also take Carte Bleue.

The hotel's elegant 18th-century-style *salons* and Michelin-starred restaurant, Le Meurice, have been restored, as has the hotel's decorative Art Nouveau roof. The hotel is extremely expensive but offers 152 soundproofed, air-conditioned rooms, 28 suites, 7 private rooms (*salons*), all under the arcades of the Rue de Rivoli, with views over the Tuileries. Credit cards: Amex, DC, V. ★★★★

Plaza-Athénée
25 Avenue Montaigne
75008
Tel: 01 53 67 66 65
Fax: 01 53 67 66 66
This palatial, top-notch hotel, featuring lavish Versace décor, is situated near the Champs-Elysées and offers 190 soundproofed rooms, a disco, a restaurant and suites furnished in Louis XVI or Regency style. Credit cards: Amex, DC, V. ★★★★

Ritz
15 Place Vendôme
75001
Tel: 01 43 16 30 30
Fax: 01 43 16 36 68/69
The Ritz offers pure, unashamed luxury in one of the finest squares in the capital. The hotel even offers a cookery school. Now infamous as the setting for the last supper between Princess Diana and Dodi Al Fayed (son of the owner, Mohammed Al Fayed). Credit cards: Amex, DC, MC, V. ★★★★

Royal Monceau
37 Avenue Hoche
75008
www.royalmonceau.com
Tel: 01 42 99 88 00
Fax: 01 42 99 89 90
The Royal Monceau offers grand, marble-floored public areas, lavish antique furnishings and a central location near the Champs-Elysées and the Arc de Triomphe. Caters mainly for business clientele. 220 rooms and 40 suites. Credit cards: Amex, DC, MC, V. ★★★★

Holiday Flats

The following companies let apartments to tourists. These range from bedsits to five-bedroom flats.
France-Ermitage, 5 Rue Berryer, 75008, tel: 01 42 56 23 42, fax: 01 42 56 08 99.
Flatotel Expo, 52 Rue d'Oradour-sur-Glane, 75015, tel: 01 45 54 93 45, fax: 01 45 54 93 07.
ABM Rent-a-flat, 12 Rue Valentin Haüy, 75015, tel: 01 45 67 04 04, fax: 01 45 67 90 15.
At Home in Paris, 16 Rue Médéric, 75017, tel: 01 42 12 40 40, fax: 01 42 12 40 48.

Camping

The only campsite in central Paris is a four-star site at the Bois de Boulogne, to the west of the city: Allée du Bord de l'Eau, tel: 01 45 24 30 00, fax: 01 42 24 42 95. Head for Métro Porte Maillot, then take the 244 bus.

However, there are plenty of other campsites within reach of Paris. Lists are available from the following organisations:
- **The Caravan and Camping Service**
69 Westbourne Grove
London W2 4UJ
Tel: 020-7792 1944
Fax: 020-7792 1956
- **Fédération Française de Camping Caravanning**
78 Rue de Rivoli
75004
Tel: 01 42 72 84 08
Fax: 01 42 72 70 21

Youth Hostels

Holders of accredited Youth Hostel Association cards may stay in Paris hostels for about FF115 per night. These are run by two organisations:
Fédération Unie des Auberges de Jeunesse (FUAJ), 27 Rue Pajol, 75018, tel: 01 44 89 87 27, fax: 01 44 89 87 10 (www.fuaj.fr), is affiliated to the International Youth Hostel Federation.
Ligue Française pour les Auberges de Jeunesse (LFAJ), 67 Rue Vergniaud, 750013, tel: 01 44 16 78 78, fax: 01 44 16 78 80, website: auberges-de-jeunesse. com, e-mail: lfaj@club-internet.fr.

The British YHA publishes the *International Youth Hostel Handbook Vol I* (revised at the end of each year), which includes all the hostels in the Paris region. It is available by post from the Youth Hostel Association, 8 St Stephen's Hill, St Albans AL1 2DY, tel: 01727 845047, fax: 01727 844126.

In the US, apply to American Youth Hostels Inc, PO Box 37613, Dept USA, Washington DC 20013/7613, tel: 202 783 6161.

The Office de Tourisme Universitaire (OTU) will also help find hostel accommodation, tel: 01 40 29 12 12, fax: 01 40 27 08 71.

Some of the main youth hostels are as follows:
Auberge Jules Ferry
8 Boulevard Jules-Ferry
75011
Tel: 01 43 57 55 60
Fax: 01 43 14 82 09
Located near the Bastille.
Auberge Internationale des Jeunes
10 Rue Trousseau
75011
Tel: 01 47 00 62 00
Fax: 01 7 00 33 16
Also near the Bastille.
Centre Internationale de Paris/Louvre
20 Rue Jean-Jacques Rousseau
75001
Tel: 01 53 00 90 90
A large hostel near the Louvre.
Le Fauconnier
11 Rue du Fauconnier
75004

Disneyland Paris

If you're planning to visit Disneyland Paris, you might like to try your local travel agents first – they may offer better deals than Disney, especially for two or three-day stays. Reservations from Paris, tel: 01 60 30 60 30; from the UK, tel: 0990 0303 03.

Disneyland Hotel
Luxury class; 500 rooms; expensive.****

Hotel New York
Luxury convention-class; 574 rooms; expensive.****

Newport Bay Club
First class; 1,098 rooms; moderately expensive.****

Sequoia Lodge
First class; 1,011 rooms; moderately expensive.****

Hotel Cheyenne
Moderate class; 1,000 rooms; moderately expensive.***

Hotel Santa Fe
Moderate class; 1,000 rooms, inexpensive.**

Davy Crockett Campsite
3 miles from the resort and difficult to reach without your own car; 181 pitches; 414 cabins for 4–6 people; inexpensive.

Tel: 01 42 74 23 45
A renovated 17th-century building near the Marais (Métro St-Paul/Pont-Marie).

Le Fourcy
6 Rue de Fourcy
75004
Tel: 01 42 74 23 45
Fax: 01 40 27 81 64
In the Marais.

Maubuisson
12 Rue des Barres
75004
Tel: 01 42 74 23 45
Impressive medieval building near to the Hôtel de Ville.

Where to Eat

The restaurants below cover every level of dining in Paris. Fixed-price menus generally do not include wine: they are indicated by the word *menu* in this listing. *A la carte* estimates are for a full meal with a reasonably priced bottle of wine. For a fuller restaurant list, try the red *Michelin Guide to France* or *Time Out Paris Eating & Drinking Guide*.

It's a good idea to reserve tables in most of the restaurants listed below in advance. At those restaurants listed under the heading *The Chefs*, reservations should be made up to several months in advance. Most restaurants in Paris close in August, and some are closed on both Saturday and Sunday night.

Restaurant Listings

BRASSERIES, BISTROS, CAFÉS & WINE BARS

Allard
41 Rue St-André-des-Arts
75006
Tel: 01 43 26 48 23
Haute cuisine served in a traditional bistro atmosphere near the Place St-Michel. Credit cards: Amex, DC, MC, V. £££

L'Ange Vin
168 Rue Montmartre
75002
Tel: 01 42 36 20 20
The cooking is tasty, the cheeses superb and the wine list impressive. Usually filled with a noisy young crowd. Reservations advisable. Closed Sunday, Monday. Credit cards: DC, MC, V. ££

L'Apparement Café
18 Rue des Coutures-St-Gervais
75003
Tel: 01 48 87 12 22

Price Guide

£ Under FF150
££ FF150–200
£££ FF250–350
££££ Over FF350
Prices are per head for a three-course meal with half a bottle of wine.
Credit cards:
Amex = American Express
DC = Diner's Card
MC = Mastercard
Most restaurants accepting credit cards also take Carte Bleue.

A cross between a café and your own home, this cosy place in a very handy spot near the Musée Picasso is equipped with comfortable sofas, books and board games. Ideal for solo travellers wanting a quiet coffee. Credit cards: MC, V. £/££

Astier
44 Rue Jean-Pierre Timbaud
75011
Tel: 01 43 57 16 35
A modern bistro in the north of Paris. Home cooking with an inventive touch and a few classics, all for a modest price. Good wine list. Advisable to reserve. Closed weekends and public holidays, 10 days at Easter, end July/August and 1 week at Christmas. Credit cards: MC, V. £ (*menu* only)

Aux Crus de Bourgogne
3 Rue Bachaumont
75002
Tel: 01 42 33 48 24
Popular with tourists and locals alike, this quirky 1900s' bistro has

Café Prices

All cafés, bistros and restaurants in Paris must display their prices (including service charges) outside. However, in cafés, bars and bistros, prices vary according to whether you eat or drink standing at the counter or sitting down; prices may also increase after 10pm. If in doubt, ask before you order.

Dogs in Restaurants

Dogs are so loved in France that few restaurants refuse them entry. Don't be surprised, even in the finest establishments, to see them under tables or in laps sharing meals with their owners. However, "doggy bags" are virtually unknown (there is no French term for them).

tables spilling out onto the pedestrianised Rue Montorgueil market area in the summer. The house specialities include lobster and Burgundian dishes. Closed at weekends. Credit cards: Amex, MC, V. **£–££**

Aux Fins Gourmets
213 Boulevard St-Germain
75007
Tel: 01 42 22 06 57
Classic French cuisine, with *cassoulet* (white bean and meat stew) a house speciality. Great bistro atmosphere and a mature crowd. Good wine list. No credit cards. **££**

Benoît
20 Rue St-Martin
75004
Tel: 01 42 72 25 76
One of the most expensive bistros in Paris, but arguably the best, with a chic clientele. The excellent *boeuf à la mode* (braised beef) merits every bit of applause and the wine list, although pricey, rivals those of restaurants in much more prestigious surroundings. Closed August and 1 week in winter. Credit cards: Amex. **££££**

Bofinger
5 Rue Bastille
75004
Tel: 01 42 72 87 82
A classic brasserie that claims to be the oldest in the city, with a stunning Art Nouveau interior. It serves excellent *fruits de mer* and one of the best Alsatian *choucroute* (sauerkraut) in Paris. However, the more creative dishes can sometimes be disappointing. Open daily. Credit cards: Amex, DC, MC, V. **££** (*menu*), **£££** (*à la carte*)

Brasserie de l'Isle St-Louis
55 Quai de Bourbon
75004
Tel: 01 43 54 02 59
Lively Alsatian brasserie with charming, typically French décor. Good prices. Closed Wednesday and Thursday lunchtimes and the month of August. Credit cards: MC, V. **££**

La Buddha Bar
8 Rue Boissy d'Anglas
75008
Tel: 01 53 05 90 00
A mecca for anyone who is anyone, including Isabelle Adjani and Naomi Campbell. Pacific Rim dishes overlooked by a giant buddha. Open Monday to Friday noon–3pm, and 6pm–2am. Closed Saturday and Sunday lunch. Credit cards: Amex, DC, MC, V. **£££**

Café Beaubourg
43 Rue St-Merri
75004
Tel: 01 48 87 63 96
Fashionably designed café in a superb location opposite the Pompidou Centre. Ideal for a light bite to eat and a spot of people-watching. Credit cards: Amex, DC, MC, V. **££**

Tearooms

Angelina's
226 Rue de Rivoli
75001
Tel: 01 42 60 82 00

Les Enfants Gatés
43 Rue des Francs Bourgeois
75004
Tel: 01 42 77 07 63

Mariage Frères
30–32 Rue du Bourg-Tibourg
75004
Tel: 01 42 72 28 11 or 13 Rue des Grands-Augustins
75006
Tel: 01 40 51 82 50

Café de la Mairie
8 Place St-Sulpice
75006
Tel: 01 43 26 67 82
A typical Left Bank eaterie, undiscovered by most tourists. The décor leaves something to be desired, but this place is authentic enough for it not to matter. Open 7am–2am Monday to Saturday. No credit cards. **£**

Chez Paul
13 Rue de Charonne
75011
Tel: 01 47 00 34 57
A neighbourhood restaurant serving traditional French cuisine at the corner of the popular Rue de Lappe. Informal atmosphere. Popular, so reservation recommended. Credit cards: Amex, MC, V. **££**

Chez Henri
20 Rue des Fosses St-Bernard
75005
Tel: 01 43 54 99 37
Moderately priced, family-style French cooking and a good wine list. Closed Sunday, Monday, and August. Credit cards: MC, V. **££**

Chez Ribe
15 Avenue Suffren
75007
Tel: 01 45 66 53 79
Chez Ribe is located just near the Eiffel Tower and is very good value. It offers traditional bistro fare with a sprinkling of southern dishes (fish soup, salt cod, etc). Closed Saturday lunch and Sunday and August. Credit cards: Amex, DC, V. **££** (*menu* only).

La Coupole
102 Boulevard du Montparnasse
750014
Tel: 01 43 20 14 20
Classic 1920s' French brasserie – a Paris institution in the heart of Montparnasse. Waiters offer elegant service in a vast dining hall. The seafood platters and the desserts are delicious. Credit cards: Amex, DC, MC, V. **££/£££**

La Closerie des Lilas
171 Boulevard du Montparnasse
75006
Tel: 01 40 51 34 50
The classy place has been the watering hole of numerous rich and famous, including Picasso and Hemingway. A pianist plays in the evening. Open daily 11.30am–1am. Credit cards: Amex, DC, MC, V. **£££**

L'Ecluse
15 Quai des Grands-Augustins
75006
Tel: 01 46 33 58 74

Open daily, 11.30am–1.30am. The choicest of wine bars, serving Bordeaux only, L'Ecluse is a mini-chain offering famous growths by the glass and a small collection of elegant dishes: smoked salmon and green bean salad, beef in red wine, *foie gras* and much more. Very busy at lunch. Other branches in Paris include: 64 Rue François 1er, 15 Place de la Madeleine and 13 Rue de la Roquette. Credit cards: V and Amex. **££**

Price Guide

£ Under FF150
££ FF150–200
£££ FF250–350
££££ Over FF350
Prices are per head for a three-course meal with half a bottle of wine.
Credit cards:
Amex = American Express
DC = Diner's Card
MC = Mastercard
Most restaurants accepting credit cards also take Carte Bleue.

La Gare
19 Chaussée de la Muette
75016 (Métro: La Muette)
Tel: 01 42 15 15 31
This restaurant in a converted railway station is the height of style. There's a good, varied menu, including fish, seafood and roast meat dishes. Open daily until midnight. Credit cards: Amex, DC, MC, V. **££/£££**

Ma Bourgogne
19 Place des Vosges
75004
Tel: 01 42 78 44 64
Busy but worth a visit if only for the wonderful setting under the arcades of the Place des Vosges. Vibrant atmosphere, Burgundian dishes. No credit cards. **££/£££**

La Palette
43 Rue de Seine
75006
Tel:01 43 26 68 15
A favourite haunt for artists, art students and St-Germain art dealers. Closed 3 weeks in August.

Open Monday to Saturday 8am–2am. Credit cards: V, MC and DC. **£**

Le Pause Café
41 Rue de Charonne
75011
Tel: 01 48 06 80 33
One of the many hip café/brasseries in the increasingly trendy East End, around the Bastille. Service is slow at peak times, but the food is tasty and the heated terrace out front makes for a stylish place to sit and chat. Credit cards: Amex, MC, V. **£/££**

Le Petit Marcel
65 Rue Rambuteau
75004
Tel: 01 48 87 10 20
In a great location, only paces away from the Pompidou Centre, this gorgeous little café/bar is a real find. With just eight tables plus a few more on the pavement outside when the weather's fine, the atmosphere is cosy and typically French. Art Nouveau tiles decorate the interior. Good drinks selection, tasty affordable food and very friendly service. Recommended. No credit cards. **£**

La Régalade
49 Avenue Jean-Moulin
75014
Tel: 01 45 45 68 58
Classic bistro fare re-interpreted by a former chef of Le Crillon, one of the city's palatial hotel kitchens. Much praised and very popular, so reservations are a must (at least 2 weeks in advance for one of the three dinner settings). Closed Saturday lunch, Sunday, Monday and from mid-July to mid-August. Credit cards: V and MC. **££** (*menu*).

Le Rubis
10 Rue du Marché St-Honoré
75001
Tel: 01 42 61 03 34
This wine bar/bistro is a favourite spot for a glass of Beaujolais and a slice of pâté. Several *plats du jour* are served, ranging from *boeuf bourguignon* to *petit salé aux lentilles* (lentils with salt pork). It's very informal, crowded and extremely good. Closed Saturday dinner, Sunday, public holidays and two weeks in August. No credit cards. **££**

René
14 Boulevard St-Germain
75005
Tel: 01 43 54 30 23
Classic French bistro with elegant décor and service and an excellent wine list. The speciality is *trompette de la mort* mushrooms, when they are in season. Credit cards: V. **£££**

Le Temps des Cerises
31 Rue de la Cerisaie
75004
Tel: 01 42 72 08 63
Modest family restaurant in the Marais by the Bastille. Simple working-man's food that is extremely good value. Lunch only. Closed Saturday, Sunday, public holidays and August. **£**

REGIONAL SPECIALITIES

Campagne et Provence
25 Quai de la Tournelle
75005
Tel: 01 43 54 05 17
This place gives a contemporary view of Provençal cooking. Especially notable is the excellent *salade niçoise*. Reservations are a must. Closed Saturday lunch, Monday lunch and all day Sunday. Credit cards: V. **££**

L'Oulette
15 Place Lachambeaudie
75012
Tel: 01 40 02 02 12

Tipping

● **Restaurants** Most restaurant bills include a service charge. If in doubt ask, "*Le service, est-il compris*?" Even when this charge is included, it is common to leave a small additional tip for the waiter if the service has been very good. Remember to address waiters as *Monsieur* (never *Garçon*) and waitresses as *Mademoiselle*, if they are young, or *Madame*, if older.
● **Taxis** A FF3–5 tip is regarded as polite.

Marcel Baudis's restaurant is difficult to class. It could have been listed with *The Chefs,* as he is equally at home with creative dishes and traditional fare. Dishes from Baudis's native Quercy in the southwest are exceptionally well done, the fixed-price menu (lunch and dinner) is particularly good value, and during the winter months the *grand menu* provides the best glimpse of Gascony cooking in the city today. Closed Saturday lunch and all day Sunday. Credit cards: Amex, DC, MC, V. **£** (*menu*), **££** (*menu*), **£££** (*à la carte*).

Moissonnier
28 Rue Fossés St-Bernard
75005
Tel: 01 43 29 87 65
A Parisian institution serving a mix of specialities from the Jura and the Rhône. Tempting dishes include a *saladier lyonnais* (a trolley full of salads to sample) and *quenelles de brochet* (poached-pike dumplings). Closed Sunday evening, Monday and August. Credit cards: MC, V. **££**

THE CHEFS

Alain Ducasse
59 Avenue Raymond Poincaré
75016
Tel: 01 47 27 12 27

Ducasse is one of the most admired chefs in France. He delights in juxtaposing ingredients to create unexpected and revealing taste combinations (such as cauliflower and caviar) and turning humble dishes into culinary masterpieces – his mashed potatoes are as talked about as any *foie gras* dish. Closed weekends and from July to mid-August. Reserve months in advance. Credit cards: V. **££££**

Les Amongnes
243 Rue Faubourg St-Antoine
75011 (Métro Faidherbe-Chaligny)
Tel: 01 43 72 73 05
Once second to Alain Senderens (see *Lucas Carton* below), Thierry Coué is slowly making a name for himself. His fixed-price menu is exceptionally good value. Closed Monday lunch, Sunday and the first 2 weeks of August. Credit cards: V. **££** (*menu*), **£££** (*à la carte*).

Arpège
84 Rue Varenne
75007
Tel: 01 45 51 47 33
Fax: 01 47 05 09 06
Alain Passard is one of the rising stars of French cuisine. His small restaurant is generally crowded, and yet he still offers a fixed-price lunch menu that is one of the best in town. A rare chance to taste

haute cuisine at a *bonne cuisine* price. Closed Saturday and Sunday. Credit cards: Amex, DC, MC, V. **£££** (*menu*, lunch only), **££££** (*à la carte*).

Le Bistro de L'Etoile
19 Rue Lauriston
75016 (Métro Etoile)
Tel: 01 40 67 11 16
This is not really a bistro but a fully fledged restaurant run by another of Paris's innovative chefs, Guy Savoy. The vegetables and fish are particularly good. Wines are reasonably priced. Closed Saturday lunch and Sunday. Credit cards: Amex. **£££**

La Cagouille
10 Place Constantin Brancusi
75014
Tel: 01 43 22 09 01
Gérard Allemandou learned to love seafood on the Atlantic coast where he grew up. His restaurant could easily be transported to California, and his cooking has much in common with that of chefs in West-Coast USA. "The less you do to fish the better," is his minimalist creed. Grilled, roasted or fried, his seafood has an exquisite taste. Don't leave without trying one of the superb Cognacs culled from cellars in his native Charente. Credit cards: Amex, MC, V. **££** (*menu*), **£££** (*menu*, wine included), **££££** (*à la carte*).

Lucas Carton
9 Place de la Madeleine
75008 (Métro Madeleine)
Tel: 42 65 22 90
Alain Senderens is one of the most exciting chefs in France and gastronomic sparks fly here amid the magnificent Art Nouveau décor. A jolting culinary experience and a bill to match. Closed Saturday lunch and Sunday, the first 3 weeks of August and the last 2 weeks of December. Credit cards: Amex, DC, MC, V. **£££** (*menu*, lunch only), **££££** (*menu*) and **££££** (*à la carte*).

La Timonerie
35 Quai de la Tournelle
75005
Tel: 01 43 25 44 42
Chef De Givenchy is from Brittany and it shows. He loves fish but also serves an extraordinary variety of meat dishes. Despite his rising popularity, he still offers a good-

Cyber Cafés

Enjoy a drink or light meal and surf the Net at:
Café Orbital
13 Rue de Médicis
75006
Tel: 01 43 25 76 77
www.cafeorbital.com
Cyber Cube
12 Rue Daval
75011
Tel: 01 49 29 67 67
Cyber Restaurant
42 Avenue des Champs-Elysées
75008
Tel: 01 53 83 94 50
Net Coffee
27 Rue Lacépéde
75005
Tel: 01 43 36 70 46

Le Shop
3 Rue d'Argout
75002
Virgin Cafe
Virgin Megastore
52 Avenue des Champs-Elysées
75008
Tel: 01 49 53 50 00
www.virgin.fr
Web Bar
32 Rue de Picardie
75003
Tel: 01 42 72 66 55
www.webbar.fr
Zowezo
37 Rue Fontaine
75018
Tel: 01 40 23 00 71
www.zowezo.fr

WHERE TO EAT ♦ 277

Price Guide

£ Under FF150
££ FF150–200
£££ FF250–350
££££ Over FF350
Prices are per head for a three-course meal with half a bottle of wine.
Credit cards:
Amex = American Express
DC = Diner's Card
MC = Mastercard
Most restaurants accepting credit cards also take Carte Bleue.

value fixed-price *menu* at lunch. Closed Sunday, Monday pm, and 22–28 February. Credit cards: V. **££** (*menu*, lunch only), **£££** (*à la carte*).

INTERNATIONAL

Au Pays du Sourire
32 Rue de Bièvre
75005 (Métro Maubert-Mutualité)
Tel: 01 43 26 15 69
Not the best-known Chinese restaurant in town but on Sunday and Thursday the chef makes pork dumplings (*raviolis pékinois*) just as they are served in Beijing. An excellent and inexpensive meal. Closed Monday and August. Credit cards: Amex, MC, V. **£**

Da Graziano
83 Rue Lepic
75018 (Métro Abesses/Blanche)
Tel: 01 46 06 84 77
In a location just below the old Moulin de la Galette in Montmartre, this Italian restaurant combines kitsch and charm. The food is great, the service attentive and the ambience relaxed. Past customers include the artist Toulouse-Lautrec. Open daily till 11pm. Credit cards: MC, V. **£££**

Davé
39 Rue St-Roch
75001
Tel: 01 42 61 49 48
This excellent Chinese is especially popular with the fashion world. Closed Saturday and Sunday lunch. Credit cards: Amex, DC, MC, V. **££**

Diep
22 Rue de Ponthieu
75008
Tel: 01 42 56 23 96
Chinese cuisine, featuring *nem* (spring rolls). A small, quiet restaurant just off the Champs-Elysées. Closed Sundays. Credit cards: Amex, V. **££**

Esther Street
6 Rue de Jarente
75004 (Métro St-Paul)
Tel: 01 40 29 03 03
The young chef prides herself on serving lightened versions of traditional Jewish fare. Delicious gefilte fish and a variety of starters that can be turned into a main meal (chopped liver, marinated herring and so on). Closed Friday, Saturday lunch and August. Credit cards: V. **££**

Fellini
47 Rue de L'Arbre Sec
75001
Tel: 01 42 60 90 66
Fellini is an upmarket Italian restaurant, offering an excellent wine list and great service. Elegant, dedicated clientele. Credit cards: Amex, MC, V. **£££**

Hawai
87 Avenue d'Ivry
75013 (Métro Tolbiac)
Tel: 01 45 86 91 90
A Vietnamese soup kitchen on the edge of what Parisians call Chinatown. Inexpensive, authentic and popular. Credit cards: V. **£**

Hôtel Costes
239 Rue St-Honoré
75001 (Métro Concorde)
Tel: 01 42 44 50 25
The ultra-hip restaurant of the Hôtel Costes is the place to see and be seen, making booking essential. Stars and VIPs come to enjoy fine *nouvelle cuisine*. A down side is that portions can be minimalist and may not satisify the heartiest appetites. Open till 1am. Credits cards: Amex, DC, MC, V. **££££**

Isami
4 Quai d'Orléans
75004
Tel: 01 40 46 06 97
To its credit, this Japanese restaurant is very popular with Japanese diners. The sushi is a work of art and the surroundings

are unpretentious. Closed Monday and two weeks in August. Credit cards: MC, V. **£££**

Juvenile's
47 Rue de Richelieu
75001 (Métro Palais Royal)
Tel: 01 42 97 46 49
Juvenile's offers the unusual combination of British owners, French wines and Spanish *tapas*. Tim Johnston knows his wines (his selection of Rhône wines is exceptional) and the cooking can be fairly decent, which all makes for a perfect post-cinema rendezvous. Closed Sunday. Credit cards: DC, MC, V. **££** (*menu*), **££** (*à la carte*).

Le Mansouria
11 Rue Faidherbe
75011 (Métro Faidherbe-Chaligny)
Tel: 01 43 71 00 16
Considered the best Moroccan restaurant in Paris, Mansouria serves excellent couscous and a collection of *tajines* (stews baked in a special utensil of the same name). Relaxed atmosphere. Closed Monday lunchtime and Sunday. Credit cards: MC, V. **££** (*menu*); **£££** (*à la carte*).

Mitsuko
8 Rue du Sabot
75006
Tel: 01 42 22 17 74
Mitsuko is a bustling Japanese that becomes particularly popular at lunchtime. Quick, friendly service. Credit cards: V, DC and Amex. **££**

Noura
21 Avenue Marceau
75016 (Métro Alma-Marceau)
Tel: 01 47 23 02 20
The finest Lebanese *mezze* in town and reasonably priced at that. If you're in a rush, a take-away shop run by the same owner faces the restaurant. Open daily. Credit cards: Amex, DC, V. **£££** (*mezze* for four people); **££** (*à la carte* each)

La Ville de Jagannath
101 rue St Maur
75011
Tel: 01 43 55 80 81
This Indian restaurant offers fresh Thali food made with delicately fragranced herbs and spices. The fabulous colourful décor makes dining here a real treat. Credit cards: Amex, MC, V. **££**

Attractions

BY BOAT

Cruises on the Seine last an hour with commentaries in several languages. In the high season, boats leave every half hour from 10am to 10pm.

Bâteaux Mouches depart Pont de l'Alma, tel: 01 42 25 96 10. **Bâteaux Parisiens** depart Quai Montebello, evening cruises from the Eiffel Tower, tel: 01 44 11 33 55. **Vedettes Paris Ile de France** depart Port de Suffren, tel: 01 47 05 71 29. **Vedettes du Pont Neuf** depart Pont Neuf, tel: 01 46 33 98 38.

There are several interesting boat trips along the Canal St-Martin, starting at the Port de l'Arsenal (Bastille) and continuing almost to the Périphérique at the northeast of the city. Lasting three hours they are well worth the money, but take warm clothes as you spend a lot of time in shaded locks and under bridges. **Canauxrama**, 13 Quai de la Loire, 75019, tel:01 42 39 15 00. **Paris Canal**, 19–21 Quai de la Loire, 75019, tel: 01 42 40 96 97.

BY COACH

Coach trips let you see Paris with minimum effort. Most companies provide a cassette commentary in several languages and will pass the major sights such as the Eiffel Tower and Notre Dame, but do not stop along the way. **Cityrama** leaves from 4 Place des Pyramides, 75001, tel: 01 44 55 61 00 (www.cityrama.com). **Paris Vision** leaves from 214 Rue de Rivoli, 75001, tel: 01 42 60 30 25.

Parisbus runs double-decker buses that stop at Trocadéro, the Eiffel Tower, the Louvre, Notre Dame, the Musée D'Orsay, the Opéra, the Arc de Triomphe and the Grand Palais. You can hop off, sightsee, then catch a later bus. A commentary runs in English and French. Tel: 01 43 65 55 55.

Paris L'Open Tour runs a similar service, also with open-topped double-decker buses.

Most state-owned museums charge a modest entrance fee. Entrance is often cheaper on Sunday, and reductions are usually given for children, senior citizens and students with a valid student card.

If you plan to visit several museums during your stay, buying a *Carte Musées* means you queue only once to visit 70 museums or monuments in Paris and the Ile de France region and you also save money on entrance prices. Tickets are available for one, three or five days and can be purchased from tourist offices, Métro stations or from museum ticket offices.

Paristoric screens an excellent audiovisual history of Paris and its monuments over the past 2,000 years. Translated into around 11 languages, performances are on the hour every hour, 9am–8pm 1 April to 30 October, and 9am-6pm 1 November–31 March. Details from Paristoric, 11 Bis Rue Scribe, 75009, tel: 01 42 66 62 06.

Most museums are open daily, though times vary on public holidays. As a general rule, national museums are closed on Tuesday and municipal museums close on Monday. Major museums stay open through lunch, especially in summer, but smaller ones usually shut for a long lunch from noon or 12.30pm to about 2.30pm.

Culture

The listings magazines *L'Officiel des Spectacles* and *Pariscope* (which includes a very useful section in English by Time Out) appear every Wednesday with full details of cultural events and venues in and around the city.

The tourist office publishes a monthly listing, *Paris Selection*, and its information service is updated weekly, tel: 08 36 68 31 12 (about FF3 per minute). Details are also available on their website: www.franceguide.com.

Ticket agencies include: **Agence Spectaplus**, Salle Pleyel, 252 Rue du Faubourg St-Honoré and 26 Avenue des Lernes, 75017 and other branches.

FNAC Billeterie, at the FNAC stores, 136 Rue de Rennes, 75006, and 26 Avenue des Ternes, 75017. Accept: Amex, MC and Visa. Bookings can also be made online at: www.fnac.fr.

Virgin Megastore, 52 Avenue des Champs-Elysées, 75008, tel: 01 49 53 50 00. Ticket bookings can be made by phone, tel: 01 44 68 44 08, and in person, Monday to Saturday 10am–12am, and 12pm–12am on Sunday. Accept: Amex, DC, MC and Visa.

Kiosque, 15 Place de la Madeleine, 75008, sells tickets on the day at half price. Open Tuesday to Friday 12.30–8pm; on Saturday from 12.30pm for matinées and from 2pm for evening shows; on Sunday 12.30am–4pm.

CROUS (Centre Régional des Oeuvres Universitaires et Scolaires), 39 Avenue Georges-Bernanos, 75005, tel: 01 40 51 36 00. Offers reduced-price seats for students.

Paris Calendar

A listing of the major events in Paris is available from the tourist office (see *Useful Addresses and Numbers, page 264*). Ask for the *Saisons de Paris* brochure. Alternatively, visit the tourist office's website at: www.francetourism.com. The following is a list of the main shows and festivals that run regularly every year:

- **January** Fashion shows
- **April** *Foire de Paris*
- **June** (first week) French Tennis open
- **June** Air Show
- **21 June** Paris celebrates the longest day of the year with a huge musical festival (*Fête de la Musique*). Enjoy just about every type of music, from chamber to karaoke, in the streets. Everything is free.
- **Bastille Day** on 14 July celebrates the fall of the monarchy and the rise of the modern constitution. Celebrations begin the evening before. Only the brave and the particularly foolhardy take their cars into Paris on 13 or 14 July. A military parade starts at 10am on the Avenue des Champs-Elysées. Get there early if you want a good vantage point.
- **September** The Autumn Festival, which runs right through to December, starts in September.
- **October** is wine month as the Beaujolais Nouveau arrives. It also heralds the Montmartre Wine Harvest, Jazz Festival and Contemporary Art Fair.
- **December** Boat Show

Theatre, Opera and Ballet

There is a wonderful choice of theatre, concerts, ballet and opera in Paris, to suit all tastes. Some of the main venues for these arts are listed below:

Cité de la Musique, 223 Avenue Jean-Jaurès, 75019, tel: 01 44 84 45 00, fax: 01 44 84 45 01. Opened in 1995, this complex at La Villette includes a concert hall, information service, museum and bookshop dedicated to music.

Comédie Française, 2 Rue Richelieu, 75001, tel: 01 44 58 15 15, fax: 01 44 58 15 00. Principal National Theatre, where work by such greats as Molière and Racine are performed. More recent plays including those by Genet and Anouilh are also shown here. Excellent productions.

Opéra Bastille, 130 Rue de Lyon, 75012, tel: 08 36 69 78 68. The 20th-century addition to Paris's operatic/ballet scene, where both opera and ballet are performed. Booking tickets can be a lengthy process, so allow plenty of time.

Opéra National du Palais Garnier, Place de l'Opéra, 75009, 08 36 69 78 68. The 19th-century Paris opera house. Opera and ballet in grandiose surroundings.

Théâtre du Châtelet, 2 Rue Edouard Colonne, 75001, tel: 01 40 28 28 40, fax: 01 40 28 29 01. Opera and some modern dance performances; also puts on lunchtime concerts.

Théâtre du Vieux Colombier, 21 Rue du Vieux Colombier, 75006, tel: 01 44 39 87 00, fax: 01 44 39 87 19. Classical and modern drama from the Comédie Française troupe, although on a smaller scale than at the main house.

Cinema

Film programmes change every Wednesday. Films marked "VO" (*version original*) use the original soundtrack. On Wednesday, prices are 30 percent less than the rest of the week. These cinemas frequently show films in English:

Cinéma en Plein Air, Parc de la Villette, tel: 01 40 03 76 92. Sit back on a deckchair as dusk falls for open-air cinema.

Gaumont Champs-Elysées, 66 Avenue des Champs-Elysées, 75008, tel: 01 43 59 04 67.

La Géode, Parc de la Villette, tel: 01 40 05 12 12. An OMNIMAX cinema housed inside a huge glittering dome. Mainly natural-themed films. Accept: MC and Visa.

Le Grand Rex, 1 Boulevard Poissonnière, 75002, tel: 01 42 36 83 93. One screen only but it is the biggest in Paris.

La Pagode, 57 bis Rue de Babylone, 75007, tel: 01 45 55 48 48. The latest films in a Japanese setting. Good tea.

Useful Websites

There is an enormous wealth of tourist information available over the web, from pages on how to get to your destination to how to speak the local language when you get there. The following sites are only the tip of the iceberg:

- www.paris-touristoffice.com (official site of the French tourist office, with information on hotels, sites, events, exhibitions etc)
- www.paris.org (general information on Paris)
- www.magicparis.com (travel, shops, hotels etc)
- www.pariscope.com (*Pariscope* on-line)
- www.ratp.fr (the official Paris transport system site)
- www.musexpo.com (guide to museums and exhibitions)
- www.centrepompidou.fr (Pompidou Centre)
- www.louvre.fr (Louvre)
- www.tour-eiffel.fr (Eiffel Tower)
- www.musee-orsay.fr (Musée d'Orsay)
- www.oda/fr/aa/musee-picasso (Musée Picasso)
- www.musee-rodin.fr (Musée Rodin)
- www.invalides.com (Les Invalides)
- www.chateauversailles.fr (Château de Versailles)
- www.france.com (general information on France)
- www.meteo.fr (the weather on-line)
- www.pagesjaune.com (the French Yellow Pages)

Nightlife

Cabaret

Chez Michou
80 Rue des Martyrs, 75018, tel: 01 46 06 16 04, fax: 01 42 64 50 50. Drag shows every night.

The Crazy Horse
12 Avenue George V, 75008, tel: 01 47 23 32 32, fax: 01 47 23 48 26. Two or three shows every night.

Aux Folies-Bergère
32 Rue Richer, 75009, tel: 01 44 79 98 98, fax: 01 47 70 98 28. You can hardly get near for the tour buses and it's pricey. Dine at 7pm for a 9.30pm show. Closed Monday.

Au Lapin Agile
22 Rue des Saules, 75018, tel: 01 46 06 85 87, fax: 01 42 54 63 04. Old-fashioned mayhem in Picasso's old haunt. Arrive early for a seat. It helps if you understand French.

Le Lido
116 bis Avenue des Champs-Elysées, 75008, tel: 01 40 76 56 10, fax: 01 45 61 19 41. Three shows daily. The slickest of Parisian cabarets and home to the Bluebell Girls.

Moulin Rouge
82 Boulevard de Clichy, 75018, tel: 01 53 09 82 82, fax: 01 42 23 02 00. Two shows a night. Tourist prices and a host of tour buses.

Paradis Latin
28 Rue Cardinal-Lemoine, 75005, tel: 01 43 25 28 28, fax: 01 43 29 63 63. One show every week night.

Nightclubs and Discos

Le Balajo
9 Rue de Lappe, 75011, tel: 01 47 00 07 87. Popular club with a chic crowd; Latin and rock-and-roll music. Open Thursday and Sunday pm, and Thursday to Sunday evening.

Les Bains
7 Rue du Bourg-l'Abbé, 75003, tel: 01 48 87 01 80, fax: 01 48 87 13 70. Former Turkish baths frequented by the smart set, who are there more for rubber necking than dancing. Open daily 11.30pm–5am.

Elysée Montmartre
72 Boulevard Rochechouart, 75018, tel: 01 44 92 45 38. Fun for all ages, with theme evenings from rock 'n' roll to salsa (check listings magazines for details). Open most Saturdays 11pm–5am.

Les Etoiles
61 Rue du Château d'Eau, 75010, tel: 01 47 70 60 56. This is a stylish Latino club in an old cinema. Attracts top-quality musicians and a hip crowd.

Folies Pigalle
11 Place Pigalle, 75018, tel: 01 48 78 25 56. Very popular disco in an area that never sleeps. Open Thursday to Saturday midnight–dawn, Sunday 6pm–midnight

La Java
105 Rue du Faubourg-du-Temple, 75010, tel: 01 42 02 20 52. Latin American music in a Belleville dance hall. Open Thursday to Saturday.

La Locomotive
90 Boulevard de Clichy, 75018, tel: 01 53 41 88 88. Rough, ready, mainstream and enormous. Situated right next door to the Moulin Rouge. 11pm–dawn.

Le Moloko
26 Rue Fontaine, 75009, tel: 01 48 74 50 26. Chic, sharp and bedraggled – they're all here for cocktails, wine or a boogie.

Régine's
49 Rue de Ponthieu, 75008, tel: 01 43 59 21 13, fax: 01 42 49 35 06.

Club Prices

Entrance to a club usually includes one drink, but take plenty of cash with you as food and drink are expensive. Most clubs accept credit cards for drinks only, not entry, and close in August.

One of the most famous Parisian clubs, frequented by the rich and famous, and hard to get into unless you are a member. Open 11.00pm–dawn. The restaurant is open from 9pm.

Sherezade
3 Rue de Liège, 75009, tel: 01 40 16 17 18. Spectacular Middle-Eastern décor and good dance music. Open Friday and Saturday, midnight–5am.

Jazz Clubs

Caveau de la Huchette
5 Rue de la Huchette, 75006, tel: 01 43 26 65 05. Young clientele for cellar jazz. Open Monday to Friday from 9.30pm to 2.30am, and weekends 9.30pm–3.30am.

La Chapelle des Lombards
19 Rue de Lappe, 75011, tel: 01 43 57 24 24. Lively music in a popular club. Open Thursday, Friday and Saturday 10.30pm–dawn.

La Cigale
120 Boulevard de Rochechouart, 75018, tel: 01 49 25 81 75, fax: 01 42 23 67 04. Popular club. Telephone beforehand for specific details of concerts.

New Morning
7–9 Rue des Petites-Ecuries, 75010, tel: 01 45 23 51 41. For aficionados. Concerts usually start at 9pm.

Le Sunset
60 Rue des Lombards, 75001, tel: 01 40 26 46 60. There's a restaurant on the ground floor and jazz in the basement at 10pm (9pm on Sundays).

Shopping

Food shops, especially bakers, tend to open early. Most boutiques and department stores open about 9am, although some do not open until 10am. Traditionally in France, most shops close noon and around 2.30pm, but in Paris, many shops remain open until 7pm.

In the suburbs, hypermarkets usually stay open until 8–9pm. Most shops are closed on Monday morning, some all day Monday. If you want to buy a picnic lunch, get everything you need before midday.

To complain about a purchase, return it to the shop as soon as possible. In a serious dispute, contact the local Direction Départementale de la Concurrence et de la Consommation et de la Répression des Fraudes (consult the telephone directory for details).

Department Stores

Le Bon Marché Rive Gauche
22 Rue de Sèvres, 75007, tel: 01 44 39 80 00. One of Paris's most stylish *grands magasins*, in a building designed by the architect Gustave Eiffel. Sells *haute couture* fashions and make-up.
Le Bon Marché
38 Rue de Sèvres, 75007, tel: 01 44 39 80 00. The Grande Epicurie at this branch sells every delicacy under the sun.
BHV (Bazar de l'Hôtel de Ville)
52–64 Rue de Rivoli, 75004, tel: 01 42 74 90 00. All you ever wanted for DIY to your house, and more. Great art department.
Galeries Lafayette
40 Boulevard Haussmann, 75009, tel: 01 42 82 34 56. An entire floor devoted to lingerie and the

largest perfume department in the world beneath a breathtakingly beautiful domed roof – just some of the delights of this massive department store.
Printemps
64 Boulevard Haussmann, 75009, tel: 01 42 82 50 00. Good selection of new designer collections, plus large china, kitchen and stationery departments.
La Samaritaine
19 Rue de la Monnaie, 75001, tel: 01 40 41 20 20. An Art Nouveau building just by the Pont Neuf, with fantastic views over the Seine from the rooftop bistro.

Clothes

Paris is the designer city of the world. Alongside France's chains such as Naf Naf and Kookaï, all the top-name couturiers have boutiques. As Calvin Klein said when he opened his Avenue Montaigne store, "It's the most important city in Europe to show the world what you do." The top couture houses are in the Avenue Montaigne area and around the Faubourg St-Honoré, with more individual boutiques clustering around the Marais and St-Germain-des-Prés.

Other main shopping areas include the Rue de Rivoli, which runs from the Marais to the Louvre, the streets around the Opéra, the *grands magasins* and the Boulevard Haussmann. For smaller boutiques and more individual designs you're best advised to visit the charming narrow alleys of the Marais.

Export Procedures

Most prices include TVA (value-added tax, or VAT). The base rate in France is currently around 20 percent but it can be as high as around 35 percent on some luxury items.

Foreign visitors can claim back TVA, and this is worth doing if you spend over around FF4,200 (FF2,000 for non-EU residents) in one place. Ask the

store for a *bordereau* (export sales invoice). This must be completed and presented with the goods to customs officers on leaving France. Pack items separately for ease of access. The form is mailed back to the retailer, which refunds the TVA in a month or two. Certain goods (such as antiques) may need special clearance.

DESIGNER NAMES

Agnès B
2–19 Rue du Jour, 75001, tel: 01 45 08 56 56 (women's clothes), tel: 01 42 33 04 13 (men's). The quintessential French designer.
Georgio Armani, 25 Place Vendôme, 75001, tel: 01 42 61 02 34. Classic chic Italian design.
Azzedine Alaïa
Silhouette-hugging dresses from around FF4,000 at 7 Rue de Moussy, 75004, tel: 01 42 72 19 19. Open 10am–7pm. Or last season's designs at a fraction of the price at 18 Rue de la Verrerie, tel: 01 42 72 19 19. Open 10am–1pm, 2pm–7pm.
Calvin Klein
56 Avenue Montaigne, 75008, tel: 01 56 89 07 92. Cool minimalism from the New York designer.
Christian Lacroix
2–4 Place Saint-Sulpice, 75006, tel: 01 46 33 48 95; 73 Faubourg St-Honoré 75008.
Comme des Garçons
42 Rue Etienne Marcel, 75002, tel: 01 42 33 05 21 (women), 40 Rue Etienne Marcel, tel: 01 42 36 91 54 (men).
Givenchy, 3 Avenue George V, 75001, tel: 01 44 31 50 23. French couture by British *enfant terrible* Alexander MacQueen.
Gucci
23 Rue Royale, 75008, tel: 01 40 06 90 12. Italian style house headed by fashion guru Tom Ford.
Jil Sander
52 Avenue Montaigne, 75008, tel: 01 44 95 06 70. Trend-setting German fashion.

English Shops

- **Virgin Megastore**
52 Avenue des Champs-Elysées, 75008, tel: 01 49 53 50 00. Open until midnight.
- **Village Voice**
6 Rue Princesse, 75006, tel: 01 46 33 36 47. English books and films.
- **W.H. Smith**
248 Rue de Rivoli, tel: 01 44 77 88 99. Superior version of the British chain.
- **Marks & Spencer**
Branches are dotted round the city. The main two are at 88 Rue de Rivoli, 75004, tel: 01 44 61 08 00, and 35 Boulevard Haussmann, 75009, tel: 01 47 42 42 91.

Kenzo
3 Place des Victoires, 75001, tel: 01 40 39 72 03. Flamboyant colours from the celebrated Japanese designer.
Patrick Cox
62 Rue Tiquetonne, 75002, tel: 01 40 26 66 55. The shoes to be seen in from the British designer.
Plein Sud
21 Rue des Francs-Bourgeois, 75004, tel: 01 42 72 10 60.
Prada
10 Avenue Montaigne, 75008, tel: 01 53 23 99 40.
Sonia Rykiel
175 Boulevard Saint-Germain, 75006, tel: 01 49 54 60 60. Menswear is across the road. Also at 70 Rue du Faubourg St-Honoré.
Studio Lolita
2 bis Rue des Rosiers, 75004, tel: 01 48 87 09 67. Half-price items from Lolita Lempicka's previous seasons' collections.
Thierry Mugler
45 Rue du Bac, 75007, tel: 01 45 44 44 44. Innovative clothing from the Strasbourg-born designer.

BOUTIQUES

Abou Dhabi
10 Rue des Francs-Bourgeois, 75003, tel: 01 42 77 96 98.

This stylish shop sells a range of imaginatively designed, pretty womenswear. Clothes are arranged according to their colour and come in a range of styles by up-and-coming young designers including Tara Jarmon, Paul et Joe, and Les Petites.
La Boutique de Floriane
17 Rue Tronchet, 75008, tel: 01 42 65 25 95. Top-quality children's clothes – plus Barbar.
L'Habilleur
44 Rue de Poitou, 75003, tel: 01 48 87 77 12. End-of-line and ex-catwalk clothes from some of the top designers.
Loft Design By
12 Rue du Faubourg St-Honoré, tel: 01 42 65 59 65. Gap French-style.
Tara Jarmon
18 Rue du Four, 75006, tel: 01 46 33 26 60. Elegant, pretty fashions from this Canadian designer.
Ursule Beaugeste
15 Rue Oberkampf, 75011, tel: 01 49 23 02 48. Selling dinky, handmade bags, this cute shop is one of a growing number of lovely Bohemian boutiques around the trendy Rue Oberkampf.

HIGH-STREET FASHIONS

There is a growing number of high-street chains in France, many of which have branches across the capital – only one branch of each is listed for most of the following. This selection should start you off.
Cacharel
34 Rue Tronchet, 75009, tel: 01 47 42 11 46. Delicate, feminine designer lingerie.
Etam
57 Rue de Rivoli, 75001, tel: 01 45 08 13 45. Pretty, affordable lingerie, aimed primarily at the younger market.
Gap
102 Rue de Rivoli, 75001, tel: 01 44 88 28 28. The popular US chain has gone down a storm in the French capital and there seem to be branches of Gap everywhere. Practical urbanwear at good prices. Womenswear, menswear and some very lovely childrenswear.

Kookaï
2 Rue Gustave-Courbet, 75016, tel: 01 47 55 18 00. Inexpensive fashion for the young. Other branches are at: Forum des Halles, Place St-Eustache, 75001, and 155 Rue de Rennes, 75006.
Morgan
165 Rue Rennes, 75006, tel: 01 45 48 96 77. Familiar to the young UK market, this French chain offers groovy styles, which are strongly influenced by catwalk trends.
Promod
60 Rue Caumartin, 75009, tel: 01 45 26 01 11. French fashions at very reasonable prices. Good for jumpers, jewellery and coats.
Zara
128 Rue de Rivoli, 75001, tel: 01 44 82 64 00. Growing Spanish chain offering funky designs for men, women and children at high-street prices.

Sales

Traditionally the sales *(soldes)* have been held in July and just after Christmas but, with France struggling through a recession, many shops are offering mid-season reductions, so you may pick up bargains all year round.

SHOES

The main shoe chains across Paris include the following, both offering this-season's styles at very affordable prices. Branches across the city.
André
106 and 138 Rue de Rivoli, 75001, tel: 01 42 33 81 13
France Arno
98 Rue de Rivoli, 75001, tel: 01 40 28 00 10.

Gifts

Androuet
6 Rue Arsène Houssaye, 75008, tel: 01 42 89 95 00. This is an excellent cheese shop connected to the Androuet restaurant. Branches at 83 Rue St-Dominique, 75007, tel:

01 45 50 45 75, and at 19 Rue
Daguerre, 75014, tel: 01 43 21
19 09.

Bains Plus
51 Rue des Francs-Bourgeois,
75004, tel: 01 48 87 83 07.
Everything you could possibly
imagine for the bathroom.

Beauvais
14 Rue du Bac, 75007, tel: 01 42
61 27 61. Designer stationery.

Conceptua
9 Rue de la Roquette, 75011, tel:
01 43 38 68 87. Candlesticks,
glassware and gifts.

The Conran Shop
117 Rue du Bac, 75007, tel: 01 42
84 10 01. Sir Terence Conran's
emporium in a former Bon Marché
warehouse designed by the
architect Eiffel. All manner of
designer gifts.

Debauve et Gallais
30 Rue des Saints-Pères, 75007,
tel: 01 45 48 54 67. Chocolates.

Fromagerie Barthélémy
51 Rue de Grenelle, 75007, tel: 01
42 22 82 24. Cheeses.

Fauchon
26–8 Place de la Madeleine,
75008, tel: 01 47 42 60 11.
Enormous luxury foodstore, much-
celebrated for its gourmet buffets,
excellent in-house brasserie and
Italian trattoria.

FNAC
74 Avenue des Champs-Elysées,
75008, tel: 01 53 53 64 64.
Books, music, hi-fi and videos are
all sold in this giant, long-
established French chain. Concert
tickets can also be purchased here.
Branches across the city. Very late
opening most nights.

Guerlain
68 Avenue des Champs-Elysées,
75008, tel: 01 45 62 52 57. The
French perfumer in a breathtakingly
beautiful flagship store.

Il Etait une Fois
1 Rue Cassette, 75006, tel: 01 45
48 21 10. Children's toys.

La Maison du Chocolat
8 Boulevard de la Madeleine,
75009, tel: 01 47 42 86 52.
Chocolate emporium.

Pétrossian
18 Boulevard La Tour-Maubourg,
75007, tel: 01 44 11 32 22. Caviar

Coiffure

If you need a haircut while in
Paris, you could head for the
ubiquitous Toni and Guy salon
at 248 Rue St-Honoré, 75001,
tel: 01 40 20 98 20.

specialists. Also delicious smoked
salmon and foie gras.

Séphora
70 Avenue des Champs-Elysées,
75008, tel: 01 53 93 22 50.
Perfume chain with branches
across the capital. This branch is
huge – a perfume-lover's heaven.
Also at: 50 Rue Passy, 75016 and
28 bis Rue Faubourg, 75012.

Markets

Ile de la Cité
Place Louis-Lépine, 75004.
Flowers. Open daily 8am–7pm.
Birds. Open Sun 9am–7pm.

Place de la Madeleine
Coté est de l'Eglise, 75008.
Flowers. Open daily except Mon
8am–7.30pm.

Quai de la Mégisserie
75001. Birds, dogs, cats and fish.
Open daily 10am–7pm.

Marché d'Aligre
Rue and Place d'Aligre. General.
Open daily, mornings only.

Les Puces de St-Ouen
Between the Portes de St-Ouen and
de Clignancourt, 75018. Flea
market. Open Sat–Mon,
7.30am–7pm.

Les Puces de Vanves
Porte de Vanves–Porte Didot,
Avenue Georges Lafenestre, Rue
Marc Sangnier, 75014. Flea
market. Open Sat–Sun,
7am–7.30pm.

Rue Mouffetard
75005. Produce (mainly food and
flowers). Open Tues, Thurs, Sat.
9am–1pm, 4–7pm. The nearby
market at **Place Monge** offers a
variety of homemade produce,
flowers, cheese and other
comestibles on Wed, Fri and Sat.

Rue de Buci and Rue de Seine
75006. Off Boulevard St-Germain.
Food – fruit and cheese – wine and
flowers. Open Tues–Sun, 8am–1pm.

Sport

Participant

Parisians expend a lot of energy on
lively exchanges of views,
stereotypically from behind the
wheel of a car or the butt of a
cigarette. Nevertheless, Paris
caters fairly well for the sports
enthusiast. You can find information
on sporting events in *Le Figaro*
each Wednesday or by phoning
Allo-Sports, tel: 01 42 76 54 54.
The latter can give you information
about sporting facilities in Paris.

FITNESS CENTRES

Club Quartier Latin
19 Rue Pontoise, 75005, tel: 01
55 42 77 88. Health club with
squash courts and pool.

Gymnase Club
17 Rue du Débarcadère, 75017,
tel: 01 45 74 14 04. One of a chain
of health clubs that offer step
classes, weights, sauna and pool.
Telephone 01 44 37 24 24 for a list
of clubs.

HORSE RIDING

Societé d'Equitation de Paris
Rue de la Muette, Bois de Boulogne,
75116, tel: 01 45 01 20 06.

**Ligue de Paris de la Féderation
Française d'Equitation**
69 Rue Laugier, 75017, tel: 01 42
12 03 43.

SWIMMING

Piscine des Halles
Centre Suzanne-Berlioux, 10 Place
de la Rotonde, 75001, tel: 01 42
36 98 44. This is part of the Forum

des Halles. Equipped with a 50-metre (55-yd) pool.

Piscine Georges Vallery
148 Avenue Gambetta, 75020, tel: 01 40 31 15 20. This swimming pool was built for the 1924 Olympic Games, when Johnny Weissmuller (aka Tarzan) won the gold medal.

Aquaboulevard
4–6 Rue Louis Armand, 75015, tel: 01 40 60 10 00. This is a massive waterworld offering the athletic an exciting choice of waves, flumes and both indoor and outdoor pools.

TENNIS

Centre Sportif d'Orléans
7 Avenue Paul Appell, 75014, tel: 45 40 55 88.

Courcelles
149 bis Rue Blomet, 75015, tel: 01 45 30 07 00.

Spectator

Football fans should pay homage at the massive **Stade de France** stadium, designed by architects Zubléna, Macary, Regembal and Constantini and built in 1997 for the 1998 World Cup. The stadium is also used for rock concerts, seating around 100,000 spectators. (Rue Francis de Pressensé, 93200 St-Denis, Métro Porte de Paris/RER B or La Plaine-Stade de France/RER D-Stade de France/St-Denis. Open: 10am–5.30pm daily, except when events are taking place. Entrance fee. Guided tours available. Credit cards: MC and Visa.)

The huge Bercy sports stadium, built in 1984, offers a vast range of events including football, ice sports, motor sports and horse riding: Palais Omnisports de Bercy, 8 Boulevard de Bercy, 75012, tel: 01 44 68 44 68, fax: 01 40 02 61 15.

Major sporting events include the Marathon in April, the French Tennis Open in June and the Paris Triathlon in September. For racing buffs, the Grand Prix de l'Arc de Triomphe takes place at Hippodrome de Longchamp in October.

Courses

Paris hosts many schools and courses, ranging from language study breaks and cookery courses to much more in-depth education at the celebrated Grandes Ecoles created by Napoleon.

Information sheets on education in France can be bought for a nominal sum from Le Centre d'Information et de Documentation Jeunesse (CIDJ), 101 Quai Branly, 75015 Paris, tel: 01 44 49 12 00.

Language and cookery schools will be able to send you detailed information about the course plus information on Paris, and they may also be able help you with your travel and accommodation arrangements.

French Language

Alliance Française
101 Boulevard Raspail, 75006, tel: 01 45 44 38 28, www.alliancefrancaise.fr

Ecole de Langue Française pour Etrangers (ELFE)
8 Villa Ballu, 75009, tel: 01 48 78 73 00. All levels of language courses in small classes of between four and six students.

Eurocentre
13 Passage Dauphine, 75006, tel: 01 40 46 72 00. Organises language and civilisation courses held at Paris, Amboise and La Rochelle.

France Langues
2 Rue de Sfax, 75116, tel: 01 45 00 40 15. Various levels of French-language courses.

Cookery

Le Cordon Bleu
8 Rue Léon Delhomme, 75015, tel:

01 53 68 22 50, fax: 01 48 56 03 96. Courses are taught in French, English and Japanese.

Ritz Escoffier
15 Place Vendôme, 75001, tel: 01 43 16 31 43, fax: 01 43 16 31 50, www.ritzparis.com

History and Culture

Cours de Civilisation Française à la Sorbonne
47 Rue des Ecoles, 75005, tel: 01 40 46 22 11. Run at several levels throughout the year.

Institut Parisien de Langue et de Civilisation Française
87 Boulevard de Grenelle, 75015, tel: 01 40 56 09 53, fax: 01 43 06 46 30. Language and culture combined at the Parisian Institute.

Language

French is the native language of more than 90 million people and the acquired language of 180 million. It is a Romance language descended from the Vulgar Latin spoken by the Roman conquerors of Gaul. It still carries the reputation of being the most cultured language in the world and, for what it's worth, the most beautiful. People often tell stories about the impatience of the French towards foreigners not blessed with fluency in their language. In general, however, if you attempt to communicate with them in French, they will be helpful.

Since much of the English vocabulary is related to French, thanks to the Norman Conquest of 1066, travellers will often recognise many helpful cognates: words such as *hôtel, café* and *bagages* hardly need to be translated.

You should be aware, however, of some misleading "false friends" (see panel on page 289).

Words & Phrases

How much is it? *C'est combien?*
What is your name? *Comment vous appelez-vous?*
My name is... *Je m'appelle...*
Do you speak English? *Parlez-vous anglais?*
I am English/American *Je suis anglais/américain*
I don't understand *Je ne comprends pas*
Please speak more slowly? *Parlez plus lentement, s'il vous plaît?*
Can you help me? *Voulez-vous m'aider?*
I'm looking for... *Je cherche*
Where is...? *Où est...?*
I'm sorry *Excusez-moi/Pardon*
I don't know *Je ne sais pas*

Basic Rules

Even if you speak no French at all, it is worth trying to master a few simple phrases. The fact that you have made an effort is likely to get you a better response. More and more French people like practising their English on visitors, especially waiters in the cafés and restaurants and the younger generation. Pronunciation is the key; they really will not understand if you get it very wrong. Remember to **emphasise each syllable**, but not to pronounce the last consonant of a word as a rule (this includes the plural "s") and always to drop your "h"s. Whether to use **"vous"** or **"tu"** is a vexed question; increasingly the familiar form of "tu" is used by many people. However it is better to be too formal, and use "vous" if in doubt. It is very important to be polite; always address people as **Madame** or **Monsieur**, and address them by their surnames until you are confident first names are acceptable. When entering a shop always say, "Bonjour Monsieur/Madame," and "Merci, au revoir," when leaving.

No problem *Pas de problème*
Have a good day! *Bonne journée!*
That's it *C'est ça*
Here it is *Voici*
There it is *Voilà*
Let's go *On y va. Allons-y*
See you tomorrow *A demain*
See you soon *A bientôt*
Show me the word in the book *Montrez-moi le mot dans le livre*
At what time? *A quelle heure?*
When? *Quand?*
What time is it? *Quelle heure est-il?*
● *Note. The French generally use the 24-hour clock.*

yes	*oui*
no	*non*
please	*s'il vous plaît*
thank you	*merci*
(very much)	*(beaucoup)*
you're welcome	*de rien*
excuse me	*excusez-moi*
hello	*bonjour*
hi/bye	*salut*

The Alphabet

Learning the pronunciation of the French alphabet is a good idea. In particular, learn how to spell out your name.
a=ah, b=bay, c=say, d=day
e=uh, f=ef, g=zhay, h=ash.
i=ee, j=zhee, k=ka, l=el,
m=em, n =en, o=oh, p=pay,
q=kew, r=ehr, s=ess, t=tay,
u=ew, v=vay, w=dooblah vay,
x-=eex, y=ee grek, z=zed

OK	*d'accord*
goodbye	*au revoir*
good evening	*bonsoir*
here	*ici*
there	*là*
today	*aujourd'hui*
yesterday	*hier*
tomorrow	*demain*
now	*maintenant*
later	*plus tard*
right away	*tout de suite*
this morning	*ce matin*
this afternoon	*cet après-midi*
this evening	*ce soir*

On Arrival

I want to get off at... *Je voudrais descendre à...*
Is there a bus to the Louvre? *Est-ce qu'il y a un bus pour le Louvre?*
What street is this? *A quelle rue sommes-nous?*
Which line do I take for...? *Quelle ligne dois-je prendre pour...?*
How far is...? *A quelle distance se trouve...?*
Validate your ticket *Compostez votre billet*

airport	*l'aéroport*
train station	*la gare*
bus station	*la gare routière*
Métro stop	*la station de Métro*
bus	*l'autobus, le car*
bus stop	*l'arrêt*
platform	*le quai*
ticket	*le billet*
return ticket	*aller-retour*
hitchhiking	*l'autostop*
toilets	*les toilettes*

This is the hotel address *C'est l'adresse de l'hôtel*
I'd like a (single/double) room... *Je voudrais une chambre (pour une/deux personnes) ...*
...with shower *avec douche*
...with bath *avec salle de bain*
...with a view *avec vue*
Does that include breakfast? *Le prix comprend-il le petit déjeuner?*
May I see the room? *Puis-je voir la chambre?*

washbasin	*le lavabo*
bed	*le lit*
key	*la clé*
elevator	*l'ascenseur*
air condition	*climatisé*

On the Road

Where is the spare wheel? *Où est la roue de secours?*
Where is the nearest garage? *Où est le garage le plus proche?*
Our car has broken down *Notre voiture est en panne*
I want to have my car repaired *Je veux faire réparer ma voiture*
It's not your right of way *Vous n'avez pas la priorité*
I think I must have put diesel in the car by mistake *Je crois que j'ai mis le gazole dans la voiture par erreur*

the road to...	*la route pour...*
left	*gauche*
right	*droite*
straight on	*tout droit*
far	*loin*
near	*près d'ici*
opposite	*en face*
beside	*à côté de*
car park	*parking*

On the Telephone

How do I make an outside call? *Comment est-ce que je téléphone à l'exterieur?*
I want to make an international (local) call *Je voudrais une communication pour l'étranger (une communication locale)*
What is the dialling code? *Quel est l'indicatif?*
I'd like an alarm call for 8 tomorrow morning. *Je voudrais être réveillé à huit heures demain matin*
Who's calling? *C'est qui à l'appareil?*
Hold on, please *Ne quittez pas s'il vous plaît*
The line is busy *La ligne est occupée*
I must have dialled the wrong number *J'ai dû faire un faux numéro*

over there	*là-bas*
at the end	*au bout*
on foot	*à pied*
by car	*en voiture*
town map	*le plan*
road map	*la carte*
street	*la rue*
square	*la place*
give way	*céder le passage*
dead end	*impasse*
no parking	*stationnement interdit*
motorway	*l'autoroute*
toll	*le péage*
speed limit	*la limitation de vitesse*
petrol	*l'essence*
unleaded	*sans plomb*
diesel	*le gazole*
water/oil	*l'eau/l'huile*
puncture	*un pneu crevé*
bulb	*l'ampoule*
wipers	*les essuies-glace*

Shopping

Where is the nearest bank (post office)? *Où se trouve la banque (Poste) la plus proche?*
I'd like to buy *Je voudrais acheter*
How much is it? *C'est combien?*
Do you take credit cards? *Est-ce que vous acceptez les cartes de crédit?*
I'm just looking *Je regarde seulement*
Have you got? *Avez-vous...?*
I'll take it *Je le prends*
I'll take this one/that one *Je prends celui-ci/celui-là*
What size is it? *C'est de quelle taille?*
Anything else? *Avec ça?*

size (clothes)	*la taille*

Market Shopping

In a market all goods have to be marked with the price by law. This will be written: 12F50 (centimes). Prices are usually by the kilo or by the *pièce*, that is, each item priced individually. Usually the stall holder (*marchand*) will select the goods for you. Sometimes there is a serve yourself system – observe everyone else! If you are choosing cheese, for example, you may be offered a taste to try first; *un goûter*.

tasting	*la dégustation*
organic	*la biologique*
flavour	*le parfum*
basket	*le panier*
bag	*le sac*

size (shoes)	*la pointure*
cheap	*bon marche*
expensive	*cher*
enough	*assez*
too much	*trop*
a piece of	*un morceau de*
each	*la pièce (eg ananas, 15F la pièce)*
bill	*la note*
chemist	*la pharmacie*
bakery	*la boulangerie*
bookshop	*la librairie*
library	*la bibliothèque*
department store	*le grand magasin*
delicatessen	*la charcuterie/ le traiteur*
fishmonger's	*la poissonerie*
grocery	*l'alimentation/ l'épicerie*
tobacconist	*tabac (also sells stamps and newspapers)*
markets	*le marché*
supermarket	*le supermarché*
junk shop	*la brocante*

Sightseeing

town	*la ville*
old town	*la vieille ville*
abbey	*l'abbaye*
cathedral	*la cathédrale*
church	*l'église*

keep	le donjon
mansion	l'hôtel
hospital	l'hôpital
town hall	l'hôtel de ville/ la mairie
nave	la nef
stained glass	le vitrail
staircase	l'escalier
tower	la tour (La Tour Eiffel)
walk	le tour
country house/ castle	le château
Gothic	gothique
Roman	romain
Romanesque	roman
museum	le musée
art gallery	la galerie
exhibition	l'exposition
tourist information office	l'office du tourisme/ le syndicat d'initiative
free	gratuit
open	ouvert
closed	fermé
every day	tous les jours
all year	toute l'année
all day	toute la journée
swimming pool	la piscine
to book	réserver

Dining Out

Table d'hôte (the "host's table") is one set menu served at a set price. **Prix fixe** is a fixed price menu. **A la carte** means dishes from the menu are charged separately.

breakfast	le petit déjeuner
lunch	le déjeuner
dinner	le dîner
meal	le repas
first course	l'entrée/les hors d'oeuvre
main course	le plat principal
made to order	sur commande
drink included	boisson compris
wine list	la carte des vins
the bill	l'addition
fork	la forchette
knife	le couteau
spoon	la cuillère
plate	l'assiette
glass	le verre
napkin	la serviette
ashtray	le cendrier

Emergencies

Help! *Au secours!* **Stop!** *Arrêtez!*
Call a doctor *Appelez un médecin*
Call an ambulance *Appelez une ambulance*
Call the police *Appelez la police*
Call the fire brigade *Appelez les pompiers*
Where is the nearest telephone? *Où est le téléphone le plus proche?*
Where is the nearest hospital? *Où est l'hôpital le plus proche?*
I am sick *Je suis malade*
I have lost my passport/purse *J'ai perdu mon passeport/porte-monnaie*

BREAKFAST AND SNACKS

baguette	long thin loaf
pain	bread
petits pains	rolls
beurre	butter
poivre	pepper
sel	salt
sucre	sugar
confiture	jam
miel	honey
oeufs	eggs
...à la coque	boiled eggs
...au bacon	bacon and eggs
...au jambon	ham and eggs
...sur le plat	fried eggs
...brouillés	scrambled eggs
tartine	bread with butter
yaourt	yoghurt
crêpe	pancake
croque-monsieur	ham and cheese toasted sandwich
croque-madame	...with a fried egg on top
galette	type of cake
pan bagna	bread roll stuffed with salad Niçoise
quiche	tart of eggs and cream with various fillings
quiche lorraine	quiche with bacon

FIRST COURSE

An *amuse-bouche, amuse-gueule* or appetizer is something to "amuse the mouth", before the first course

anchoïade	sauce of olive oil anchovies and garlic, served with raw vegetables
assiette anglaise	cold meats
potage	soup
rillettes	rich fatty paste of shredded duck rabbit or pork
tapenade	spread of olives and anchovies
pissaladière	Provençal pizza with onions, olives and anchovies

MAIN COURSES

La Viande	Meat
bleu	rare
à point	medium
bien cuit	well done
grillé	grilled
agneau	lamb
andouille/ andouillette	tripe sausage
bifteck	steak
boudin	sausage
boudin noir	black pudding
boudin blanc	white pudding (chicken or veal)
blanquette	stew of veal, lamb or chicken with creamy egg sauce
boeuf à la mode	beef in red wine with carrots, onions, mushroom and onions
à la bordelaise	beef with red wine and shallots
Bourguignon	cooked in red wine, onions, mushrooms
brochette	kebab
caille	quail
canard	duck
carbonnade	casserole of beef, beer and onions

Non, Non, Garçon

Garçon is the word for waiter but is never used directly; say *Monsieur* or *Madame* to attract their attention.

carré d'agneau	rack of lamb
cassoulet	stew of beans, sausages, pork and duck, from southwest France
cervelle	brains (food)
chateaubriand	thick steak
choucroute	Alsace dish of sauerkraut, bacon and sausages
confit	duck or goose preserved in its own fat
contre-filet	cut of sirloin steak
coq au vin	chicken in red wine
côte d'agneau	lamb chop
daube	beef stew with red wine, onions and tomatoes
dinde	turkey
entrecôte	beef rib steak
escargot	snail
faisan	pheasant
farci	stuffed
faux-filet	sirloin
feuilleté	puff pastry
foie	liver
foie de veau	calf's liver
foie gras	goose or duck liver pâté
gardiane	rich beef stew with olives and garlic from the Camargue
cuisses de grenouille	frog's legs
grillade	grilled meat
hachis	minced meat
jambon	ham
langue	tongue
lapin	rabbit
lardons	small pieces of bacon, often added to salads
magret de canard	breast of duck
médaillon	round piece of meat
moelle	beef bone marrow
mouton navarin	stew of lamb with onions, carrots and turnips

oie	goose
perdrix	partridge
petit-gris	small snail
pieds de cochon	pig's trotters
pintade	guinea fowl
Pipérade	Basque dish of eggs, ham, peppers, onion
porc	pork
pot-au-feu	casserole of beef and vegetables
poulet	chicken
poussin	young chicken
rognons	kidneys
rôti	roast
sanglier	wild boar
saucisse	fresh sausage
saucisson	salami
veau	veal

Poissons Fish

Américaine	made with white wine, tomatoes, butter and cognac
anchois	anchovies
anguille	eel
bar (or loup)	sea bass
barbue	brill
belon	Brittany oyster
bigorneau	sea snail
Bercy	sauce of fish stock, butter, white wine and shallots
bouillabaisse	fish soup, served with grated cheese, garlic croutons and spicy *rouille* sauce
brandade	salt cod purée

Slang

métro, boulot, dodo nine-to-five syndrome
McDo McDonald's
branché trendy (literally "connected")
C'est du cinéma It's very unlikely.
une copine/ un copain friend/ chum
un ami friend but **mon ami** (or **mon copain**) boyfriend
un truc thing, "whatsit"
pas mal, not bad, good-looking
fantastique! fantastic! terrible!

cabillaud	cod
calmars	squid
colin	hake
coquillage	shellfish
coquilles Saint-Jacques	scallops
crevette	shrimp
daurade	sea bream
flétan	halibut
fruits de mer	seafood
hareng	herring
homard	lobster
huître	oyster
langoustine	large prawn
limande	lemon sole
lotte	monkfish
morue	salt cod
moule	mussel
moules marinières	mussels in white wine and onions
oursin	sea urchin
raie	skate
saumon	salmon
thon	tuna
truite	trout

Légumes Vegetables

ail	garlic
artichaut	artichoke
aspèrge	asparagus
aubergine	eggplant
avocat	avocado
bolets	boletus mushrooms
céleri rémoulade	grated celery with mayonnaise
champignon	mushroom
cèpes	boletus mushrooms
chanterelle	wild mushroom
cornichon	gherkin
courgette	zucchini, courgette
chips	potato crisps
chou	cabbage
chou-fleur	cauliflower
concombre	cucumber
cru	raw
crudités	raw vegetables
épinard	spinach
frites	chips, French fries
gratin dauphinois	sliced potatoes baked with cream
haricot	dried bean
haricots verts	green beans
lentilles	lentils
maïs	corn
mange-tout	snow pea
mesclun	mixed-leaf salad
navet	turnip

Table Talk

I am a vegetarian *Je suis végétarien(ne)*
I am on a diet *Je suis au régime*
What do you recommend? *Que'est-ce que vous recommandez?*
Do you have local specialities? *Avez-vous des spécialités locales?*
I'd like to order *Je voudrais commander*
That is not what I ordered *Ce n'est pas ce que j'ai commandé*
Is service included? *Est-ce que le service est compris?*
May I have more wine? *Encore du vin, s'il vous plaît?*
Enjoy your meal *Bon appétit!*

noix	nut, walnut
noisette	hazelnut
oignon	onion
panais	parsnip
persil	parsley
pignon	pine nut
poireau	leek
pois	pea
poivron	bell pepper
pomme de terre	potato
pommes frites	chips, French fries
primeurs	early fruit and vegetables
radis	radis
roquette	arugula, rocket
ratatouille	Provençal vegetable stew of aubergines, courgettes, tomatoes, peppers, and olive oil

False Friends

False friends (*faux amis*) are words that look like English words but mean something different.
le car coach, also railway carriage
le conducteur bus driver
la monnaie change
l'argent money/silver
ça marche can sometimes mean walk, but is usually used to mean working (the TV, the car etc.) or going well
actuel "present time" (*la situation actuelle* the present situation)
rester to stay
location hiring/renting
personne person or nobody, depending on the context
le médecin doctor

riz	rice
salade Niçoise	egg, tuna, olives, onions and tomato salad
salade verte	green salad
truffe	truffle

Fruit   Fruit

ananas	pineapple
cavaillon	fragrant sweet melon from Cavaillon, Provence
cerise	cherry
citron	lemon
citron vert	lime
figue	fig
fraise	strawberry
framboise	raspberry
groseille	redcurrant
mangue	mango
mirabelle	yellow plum
pamplemousse	grapefruit
pêche	peach
poire	pear
pomme	apple
raisin	grape
prune	plum
pruneau	prune
reine claude	greengage

Sauces   Sauces

aïoli	garlic mayonnaise
béarnaise	sauce of egg, butter, wine and herbs
forestière	with mushrooms and bacon
hollandaise	egg and butter
lyonnaise	with onions
meunière	fried fish with butter, lemon and parsley sauce
meurette	red wine sauce
Mornay	sauce of cream, egg and cheese

Parmentier	served with potatoes
paysan	rustic style, ingredients depend on the region
pistou	Provençal sauce of basil, garlic and olive oil; vegetable soup with the sauce
provençale	sauce of tomatoes, garlic and olive oil
papillotte	cooked in paper

Pudding   Dessert

Belle Hélène	fruit with ice cream and chocolate sauce
clafoutis	baked pudding of batter and cherries
coulis	purée of fruit or vegetables
gâteau	cake
Ile flottante	whisked eggs whites floating in custard sauce
crème anglaise	custard
pêche melba	peaches with ice cream and raspberry sauce
tarte tatin	upside-down tart of caramelised apples
crème caramel	caramelised egg custard
crème Chantilly	whipped cream
fromage	cheese
chèvre	goat's cheese

In the Café

If you sit at the bar (*le zinc, le comptoir* or *le bar*), drinks will be less expensive than if you sit at a table. It's usual to settle the bill when you leave – the waiter may leave a slip of paper on the table to keep track of the bill or he or she may just bring you the bill at the end before you leave. The French enjoy bittersweet aperitifs, often diluted with ice and fizzy water.

drinks	*les boissons*
coffee	*café*
...with milk or cream	
	au lait or crème

...decaffeinated *déca/décaféiné*
...black espresso *express/noir*
...American filtered coffee *filtre*
tea *thé*
...herb infusion *tisane*
...camomile *verveine*
hot chocolate *chocolat chaud*
milk *lait*
mineral water *eau minérale*
fizzy *gazeux*
non-fizzy *non-gazeux*
fizzy lemonade *limonade*
fresh lemon juice served with
sugar *citron pressé*
fresh squeezed orange juice
 orange pressée
full (eg full cream milk) *entier*
fresh or cold *frais, fraîche*
beer *bière*
...bottled *en bouteille*
...on tap *à la pression*
pre-dinner drink *apéritif*
white wine with cassis, blackcurrant liqueur *kir*
kir with champagne *kir royale*
with ice *avec des glaçons*
neat *sec*
red *rouge*
white *blanc*
rose *rosé*
dry *brut*
sweet *doux*
sparkling wine *crémant*
house wine *vin de maison*
local wine *vin de pays*
Where is this *De quelle région*
wine from? *vient ce vin?*
pitcher *carafe/pichet*
...of water/wine *d'eau/de vin*
half litre *demi-carafe*
quarter litre *quart*
mixed *panaché*
after-dinner drink *digestif*
brandy from Armagnac region of
France *Armagnac*
Normandy apple brandy
 calvados
cheers! *santé!*
hangover *gueule de bois*

Standard Fare

AOC, *Appellation d'Origine
Contrôlée*, is a legal regulation
for cheeses and poultry as
well as wines, and it ensures
the products conform to
a particular standard.

Days of the Week

Days of the week, seasons and
months are not capitalised in French.

Monday *lundi*
Tuesday *mardi*
Wednesday *mercredi*
Thursday *jeudi*
Friday *vendredi*
Saturday *samedi*
Sunday *dimanche*

Seasons

spring *le printemps*
summer *l'été*
autumn *l'automne*
winter *l'hiver*

Months

January *janvier*
February *février*
March *mars*
April *avril*
May *mai*
June *juin*
July *juillet*
August *août*
September *septembre*
October *octobre*
November *novembre*
December *décembre*

● Saying the date
20th October 2000, *le vingt
octobre, deux mille*

Numbers

0	zéro
1	un, une
2	deux
3	trois
4	quatre
5	cinq
6	six
7	sept
8	huit
9	neuf
10	dix
11	onze
12	douze
13	treize
14	quatorze
15	quinze
16	seize
17	dix-sept
18	dix-huit
19	dix-neuf
20	vingt
21	vingt-et-un
30	trente
40	quarante
50	cinquante
60	soixante
70	soixante-dix
80	quatre-vingt
90	quatre-vingt-dix
100	cent
1000	mille
1,000,000	un million

● *Note that the number 1 is often
written like an upside down V, and
the number 7 is always crossed.*

Further Reading

The Arts and Architecture

A Propos de Paris, by Henri Cartier-Bresson. Bulfinch Press, 1998. More than 130 stunning black-and-white photographs of the French capital, taken by Cartier-Bresson over a period of more than 50 years.
Brassai: The Eye of Paris, by Richard Howard. Abrams, 1999. Part biography, part catalogue of a photography exhibition of Brassai's pictures of Paris organised by Houston Fine Arts Museum.
Change, New Haven: Yale University Press, 1979. An illustrated architectural history of Paris.
The Cathedral Builders, by Jean Gimpel. New York: Harper & Row, 1984. First published in French. The story of the hands and minds behind the cathedrals of France.
Paris: An Architectural History, by Anthony Sutcliffe. Yale University Press. A great book on the architecture of the capital across the ages.
Three Seconds of Eternity, by Robert Doisneau. Neues Publishing Company, 1997. A collection of gorgeous photographs of 1940s and 1950s Paris, chosen by the champion of black-and-white photography himself.

History and Society

A Concise History of France, by Roger Price. Cambridge University Press, 1993. Excellent overview of French history.
The Eiffel Tower: And Other Mythologies, by Roland Barthes. University of California Press, 1997. A collection of essays by this influential French social and literary critic, in which he considers Paris's most famous landmark.
France Today, by John Ardagh. London: Secker and Warburg. Up-to-date, hefty tome.

France Today, J.E. Flower (ed). New York: Methuen & Co., Ltd, 1983. Essays on contemporary France.
Foreign Correspondents: Paris in the Sixties, by Peter Lennon. Picador/McClelland & Stewart) An Irish journalist, Lennon spent the turbulent swinging decade in Paris where he witnessed such events as the 1968 student riots.
The Illustrated History of Paris and the Parisians, by Robert Laffont. New York: Doubleday & Co., 1958.
A Woman's Life in the Court of the Sun King, by Duchesse d'Orléans. Introduction and translation by Elborg Forster. Baltimore: Johns Hopkins University Press, 1984. The letters of the Duchesse d'Orléans reveal the court-life of the 17th century.

Literature

The Oxford Companion to French Literature, by Sir Paul Harvey and J.E. Heseltine. Oxford: Oxford University Press, 1959.

Classics by Date/Author

Various editions of each title are available.
La Chanson de Roland (circa 1100)
Prévost, Abbé, Manon Lescaut (1728–31)
Hugo, Victor, The Hunchback of Nôtre-Dame (1831). Les Misérables (1862)
Balzac, Honoré de, Eugénie Grandet (1833). Old Goriot (1834)
Dumas, Alexandre, The Count of Monte Cristo (1844)
Zola, Emile, Thérèse Raquin (1867). L'Assomoir (1877)
Flaubert, Gustave, Sentimental Education (1869)
Maupassant, Guy de, Bel-Ami (1885)
Proust, Marcel, Remembrance of Things Past (1913–32)
Breton, André, Nadja (1928)
De Beauvoir, Simone, The Second Sex (1949)

Other Literature

The Maigret series, by Georges Simenon. Popular detective stories, some of which are set in Paris. Maigret and the Tavern by the Seine. Harcourt Brace, 1990.

Down and Out in London and Paris, by George Orwell. Various editions.
A Moveable Feast, by Ernest Hemingway. New York: Scribner, 1964. The life of the artist in Paris.
Perfume, by Patrick Süskind. Penguin, 1989
Pig Tales (Truisms), by Marie Darrieussecq. Distribooks Int., 1999. Bizarre contemporary feminist literature. Woman turns into a pig.
Satori in Paris, by Jack Kerouac. New York: Grove Press, 1966. Satori is the Japanese word for sudden illumination. These are 10 days of travel à la Kerouac as he searches for Jean Louis Lebris de Kérouac in France.
A Tale of Two Cities. Various Editions, by Charles Dickens. Various editions.
Time Out Book of Paris Short Stories, ed. Nicholas Royle. Penguin, 1999
Tropic of Cancer, by Henry Miller. Various editions.
Zazie in the Métro, by Raymond Queneau. Various editions. Racy, comic cult novel.

Food and Wine

The Food Lover's Guide to Paris, by Patricia Wells. Workman Publishing, 1991. The best restaurants, food shops and markets in Paris, plus 50 recipes.
Gourmet Paris, by Emmanuel Rubin. Flammarion, 2000. Good advice on where to go to eat what in Paris by one of the city's restaurant critics. Very handy, portable pocket-sized guide.
Paris Bistro Cooking, by Linda Dannenberg. Clarkson Potter, 1991. Tasty dishes from a wealth of Paris brasseries.
The Paris Café Cookbook, by Daniel Young. William Morrow & Co, 1998. Recipes and excerpts on recommended cafés in the capital.
Wine Atlas of France, by Hugh Johnson and Hubrecht Duijker. London: Mitchell Beazley. Well-illustrated atlas, concentrating on wine and vineyards, but also supplementary information on history, architecture and culture.

Other Insight Guides

Apa Publications has more travel guide titles in print than any other guide book publisher, with over 200 *Insight Guides*, more than 100 *Pocket Guides* and over 200 *Compact Guides*.

Insight Guides

Insight Guide: France is the major book in the French series covering the whole country, with features on food and drink, culture and the arts as well as a broad picture of the nation. Other Insight Guide titles cover **Alsace**, **Brittany**, **Burgundy**, **Corsica**, the **Côte d'Azur**, the **Loire Valley**, **Normandy** and **Provence**.

Pocket Guides

Insight Pocket Guides are written by host authors who show you the best of the places they know well. The books are designed in a series of day trips and excursions, and are particularly useful for people with only a short time to make the most of their visit. Titles include **Alsace**, **Brittany**, **Corsica**, the **Côte d'Azur**, the **Loire Valley**, **Paris** and **Provence**. Complete with pull-out map.

Compact Guides

Compact Guides are the handiest guide books around. These inexpensive, full-colour mini-encyclopaedias give you the best routes of the region with a star-rated system of all the sites worth seeing, plus all the practical information you will need for your stay. Titles include **Brittany**, **Burgundy**, **French Riviera**, **Normandy**, **Paris** and **Provence**.

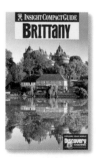

Fleximaps

Insight Fleximaps combine durability and elegance of design with accurate up-to-date information. The foldable maps are easy to use and feature a full index, a list of the top ten sites and handy practical information about your destination. The laminated finish even allows you to use a non-permanent marker pen. Fleximaps in the French series include Paris and Corsica.

ART & PHOTO CREDITS

Ping Amranand 8/9, 10/11, 18/19, 34, 42/43, 52, 65, 70, 72L, 92, 93, 94, 96/97, 102/103, 104/105, 110, 121, 127, 133, 148, 154, 156, 161, 162, 163, 165L, 167, 170, 190, 194, 203, 208, 211, 229, 244/225, 256
Maria Ángeles Sánchez 82
Archiv Für Kunst und Geschicte, Berlin 38
Yann Arthus-Bertrand/Altitude 119
Bodo Bonzio 63
Bridgeman Art Library 32/33
John Brunton 44/45, 46, 48, 49, 53, 61, 76, 116, 157, 160, 178, 180/181, 189, 192
Silvia Cordaiy Photo Library 120, 188, 220
Andrew Eames 84, 164, 197
Annabel Elston 15, 26L, 28L&R, 66, 71, 72R, 74, 77, 83, 85, 87, 90, 95L&R, 111, 117, 118, 119R, 120T, 121T, 124, 126, 126T, 127T, 128R, 129T, 130T, 132T, 138, 139, 142, 142T, 144, 144T, 145, 145T, 147, 147T, 149, 149T, 151, 159, 164T, 166, 171, 172T, 173, 176L&R, 177T, 179, 186, 191, 192T, 193L&R, 205, 205T, 206, 207, 207T, 209, 209T, 210T, 212, 218, 222T, 227, 228T, 230, 230T, 250T
Mary Evans Picture Library 30
Eye Ubiquitous 219, 223, 226
Courtesy of French Embassy 40
Robert Harding Picture Library 6/7, 108/109
Blaine Harrington 56/57, 131
John Heseltine 4/5, 231L, 252
IAURIF, Paris 16/17, 248
Catherine Karnow 14, 50, 51, 88/89, 106/107, 146, 155, 158, 195, 202, 249
Kobal Collection 128T, 190T
Lyle Lawson 29, 148T, 246/247, 253
Grupo Mayher 41
Musées de la Ville de Paris 20/21, 24, 27, 37
Photo Bibliothèque Nationale, Paris 23, 26R, 31, 189T

Maurice Rougemont 58
Tony Stone Worldwide 251
Topham Picturepoint 39, 167T, 194T, 218T, 242T
Steve Van Beek 25, 80/81, 168/169
Bill Wassman 12/13, 60, 62, 64, 67, 68/69, 73, 75, 86, 123, 125, 129, 130, 132, 136/137, 143, 150, 152/153, 165R, 174, 175, 183, 187, 200/201, 210, 213, 214/215, 216, 217, 221, 222, 228, 231R, 232, 233, 234/235, 236, 237, 239, 240
Walt Disney Company 241, 242, 243

Picture Spreads

Pages 54/55: Clockwise from top left: Coco Chanel; Julio Donoso/Sygma; Sygma/Keystone; Mary Pattes/Saba/Katz; Pierre Vauthey/Sygma, Pierre Vauthey/Sygma; Zed Nelson/Katz; Keystone/Sygma; Yves Saint Laurent/Rive Gauche; Katz/Eric Bouvet/Rea
Pages 78/79: Top, left to right: Christine Porter/Impact; Mark Cator/Impact; John Brunton. Middle row, left to right: Mark Cator/Impact; Anthony Blake Photo Library/Nigel Lea-Jones. Bottom, left to right: Mary Evans Picture Library; Blaine Harrington; Blaine Harrington
Pages 134/135: Clockwise from top left: RMN/Hervé Lewandowski; Giraudon; Lauros/Giraudon; Leimdorfer/Rea/Katz; Giraudon; Giraudon; Lauros/Giraudon; Giraudon; Lauros/Giraudon
Pages 198/199: Clockwise from top left: Doisneau/Rapho/Network; Doisneau/Rapho/Network; Magnum Photos Ltd; Topham Picturepoint; Henri Cartier-Bresson/Magnum Photos Ltd; Georges Dudognon; Henri Cartier-Bresson/Magnum Photos Ltd; Doisneau/Rapho/Network

Pages 254/255: Clockwise from top left: Mary Evans Picture Library/Explorer; Tom Craig/Rea/Katz; Giraudon; Gidauron; RMN/Arnaud Février; RMN/J. Derenne; Gidauron/Lauros; RMN; Steven Siewert/Katz

Cover Photography

Front Cover: Pictures Colour Library

All other cover photography by Annabel Elston except:
back flap top: Ping Amranand
back flap bottom: Yves Saint Laurent/Rive Gauche

Maps

Map Production
Polyglott Kartographie
Berndtson & Berndtson
Publications

© 2000 Apa Publications GmbH & Co. Verlag KG (Singapore branch)

Cartographic Editors Zoë Goodwin, Maria Donnelly
Production Mohammed Dar
Design Consultants Klaus Geisler, Graham Mitchener
Picture Research Hilary Genin

Index

Numbers in italics refer to photographs

✵ INSIGHT GUIDES

The world's largest collection of visual travel guides

Insight Guides – the Classic Series
that puts you in the picture

Alaska	China	Hong Kong	Morocco	Singapore
Alsace	Cologne	Hungary	Moscow	South Africa
Amazon Wildlife	Continental Europe		Munich	South America
American Southwest	Corsica	Iceland		South Tyrol
Amsterdam	Costa Rica	India	Namibia	Southeast Asia
Argentina	Crete	India's Western	Native America	Wildlife
Asia, East	Crossing America	Himalayas	Nepal	Spain
Asia, South	Cuba	India, South	Netherlands	Spain, Northern
Asia, Southeast	Cyprus	Indian Wildlife	New England	Spain, Southern
Athens	Czech & Slovak	Indonesia	New Orleans	Sri Lanka
Atlanta	Republic	Ireland	New York City	Sweden
Australia		Israel	New York State	Switzerland
Austria	Delhi, Jaipur & Agra	Istanbul	New Zealand	Sydney
	Denmark	Italy	Nile	Syria & Lebanon
Bahamas	Dominican Republic	Italy, Northern	Normandy	
Bali	Dresden		Norway	Taiwan
Baltic States	Dublin	Jamaica		Tenerife
Bangkok	Düsseldorf	Japan	Old South	Texas
Barbados		Java	Oman & The UAE	Thailand
Barcelona	East African Wildlife	Jerusalem	Oxford	Tokyo
Bay of Naples	Eastern Europe	Jordan		Trinidad & Tobago
Beijing	Ecuador		Pacific Northwest	Tunisia
Belgium	Edinburgh	Kathmandu	Pakistan	Turkey
Belize	Egypt	Kenya	Paris	Turkish Coast
Berlin	England	Korea	Peru	Tuscany
Bermuda			Philadelphia	
Boston	Finland	Laos & Cambodia	Philippines	Umbria
Brazil	Florence	Lisbon	Poland	USA: Eastern States
Brittany	Florida	Loire Valley	Portugal	USA: Western States
Brussels	France	London	Prague	US National Parks:
Budapest	Frankfurt	Los Angeles	Provence	East
Buenos Aires	French Riviera		Puerto Rico	US National Parks:
Burgundy		Madeira		West
Burma (Myanmar)	Gambia & Senegal	Madrid	Rajasthan	
	Germany	Malaysia	Rhine	Vancouver
Cairo	Glasgow	Mallorca & Ibiza	Rio de Janeiro	Venezuela
Calcutta	Gran Canaria	Malta	Rockies	Venice
California	Great Barrier Reef	Marine Life ot the	Rome	Vienna
California, Northern	Great Britain	South China Sea	Russia	Vietnam
California, Southern	Greece	Mauritius &		
Canada	Greek Islands	Seychelles	St. Petersburg	Wales
Caribbean	Guatemala, Belize &	Melbourne	San Francisco	Washington DC
Catalonia	Yucatán	Mexico City	Sardinia	Waterways of Europe
Channel Islands		Mexico	Scotland	Wild West
Chicago	Hamburg	Miami	Seattle	
Chile	Hawaii	Montreal	Sicily	Yemen

Complementing the above titles are 120 easy-to-carry Insight Compact Guides, 120 Insight Pocket
Guides with full-size pull-out maps and more than 60 laminated easy-fold Insight Maps